BEHAVIOR MODIFICATION IN REHABILITATION SETTINGS

Publication No. 949

AMERICAN LECTURE SERIES

A Publication in

The BANNERSTONE DIVISION *of* AMERICAN LECTURES
IN SOCIAL AND REHABILITATION PSYCHOLOGY

Editors of the Series

JOHN G. CULL, Ph.D.

*Director, Regional Counselor Training Program
Department of Rehabilitation Counseling
Virginia Commonwealth University
Fishersville, Virginia*

RICHARD E. HARDY, Ed.D.

*Diplomate in Counseling Psychology
Chairman, Department of Rehabilitation Counseling
Virginia Commonwealth University
Richmond, Virginia*

The American Lecture Series in Social and Rehabilitation Psychology offers books which are concerned with man's role in his milieu. Emphasis is placed on how this role can be made more effective in a time of social conflict and a deteriorating physical environment. The books are oriented toward descriptions of what future roles should be and are not concerned exclusively with the delineation and definition of contemporary behavior. Contributors are concerned to a considerable extent with prediction through the use of a functional view of man as opposed to a descriptive, anatomical point of view.

Books in this series are written mainly for the professional practitioner; however, academicians will find them of considerable value in both undergraduate and graduate courses in the helping services.

BEHAVIOR MODIFICATION IN REHABILITATION SETTINGS

APPLIED PRINCIPLES

JOHN G. CULL

RICHARD E. HARDY

CHARLES C THOMAS · PUBLISHER
Springfield · Illinois · U.S.A.

Published and Distributed Throughout the World by

CHARLES C THOMAS • PUBLISHER

Bannerstone House

301-327 East Lawrence Avenue, Springfield, Illinois, U.S.A.

© 1974, by CHARLES C THOMAS • PUBLISHER

ISBN 0-398-03131-2

Library of Congress Catalog Card Number: 74 1061

Printed in the United States of America

C-1

Library of Congress Cataloging in Publication Data

Cull, John G.
  Behavior modification in rehabilitation settings.

  (American lecture series, publication no. 949. A
publication in the Bannerstone division of American
lectures in social and rehabilitation psychology)
      1. Rehabilitation—Addresses, essays, lectures.
2. Behavior modification—Addresses, essays, lectures.
3. Mentally handicapped—Rehabilitation—Addresses,
essays, lectures. I. Hardy, Richard E., joint author.
II. Title [DNLM: 1. Behavior therapy—Rehabilitation. WM420 B416 1974]
HD7255.C843   362.2   74-1061
ISBN 0-398-03131-2

CONTRIBUTORS

JAMES F. ALEXANDER, Ph.D.: Associate professor at the University of Utah. He is also currently coordinator of community practicum training, consultant to various agencies (Salt Lake Veterans Administration Hospital, Utah State Juvenile Court, and Salt Lake Comprehensive Community Mental Health Center). He has authored numerous journal articles and convention papers on family interaction and family therapy including *Journal of Consulting and Clinical Psychology, Journal of Marriage and the Family*.

K. EILEEN ALLEN, B.S., M.Ed.: Educational Training Coordinator on the Developmental Disabilities Project in the Child Development and Mental Retardation Center at the University of Washington. Formerly, she was coordinator of the Preschool Education for handicapped children in the Experimental Education Unit of the Child Development and Mental Retardation Center. Her professional activities have for more than twenty years been involved with the education of the very young, first as a teacher in the Family Life Parent Cooperative Preschool Program of the Seattle Public Schools during the early 50's and then in the Developmental Psychology Laboratory Preschool at the University of Washington before she came to the Experimental Education Unit in 1968. Her professional activities include the publication of numerous research papers on early childhood education, behavior problems, behavior analysis and behavior modification. Many of these papers were presented at national professional organizations concerned with the education of young children and especially young handicapped children. She is an associate editor for several professional journals. Other media she has used in promoting the aspects of early childhood education include films, television programs and video tape documentaries. Currently, Ms. Allen served as the 1973 National Program Chairman for the Conference for the National Association of the Education of Young Children and she is Vice-President of the Division of Early Childhood in the Council for Exceptional Children.

KENNETH BARKLIND, Ph.D.: Received degrees from Macalester College and the University of Minnesota. He is Associate Professor at the Wisconsin State University, River Falls, Wisconsin and a School Psychologist at the Cooperative School-Rehabilitation Center with the Minnetonka, Minnesota Public School District. Dr. Barklind is licensed as a Psychologist in Minnesota and Wisconsin. Formerly, he was Assistant Professor with the University of Wisconsin in Milwaukee, Vice-President of the Minnesota Montessori Association and a Vocational Rehabilitation Counselor with the Minnesota Department of Education.

WILLIAM C. COE, Ph.D.: Professor of Psychology in the School of Natural Sciences, California State University, Fresno, California. Also, Dr. Coe maintains a private practice in clinical psychology. Formerly, Dr. Coe was a Staff Psychologist and Assistant Clinical Professor of Medical Psychology at the Langley-Porter Neuropsychiatric Institute and the University of California Medical School in San Francisco. Dr. Coe has published extensively in the area of hypnosis, work with the family, and most currently in behavior modification. He has published three texts which are *Challenges of Personal Adjustment, Student Psychologist Handbook,* and *Hypnosis: A Social Psychological Analysis of Influence Communication.*

THOMAS L. CREER, Ph.D.: Received his doctorate from Florida State University specializing in Behavior Modification. He received his BS in Political Science from Brigham Young University and his MA in Psychology at Utah State University. Formerly, he served as a Clinical Psychologist at the Dayton Children's Psychiatric Hospital and Child Guidance Clinic in Ohio. He also was on the staff of the Children's Asthma Research Institute and Hospital as a Clinical-Research Psychologist and later appointed Head of Children's Asthma Research Institute and Hospital's Behavior Science Division. His main research interests are behavior modification and shock elicited aggression. He has authored many papers on these topics in scientific journals and book chapters.

JOHN G. CULL, Ph.D.: Professor and Director, Regional Counselor Training Program, Department of Rehabilitation Counseling, Virginia Commonwealth University, Fishersville, Virginia; Adjunct Professor of Psychology and Education, School of General Studies, University of Virginia, Charlottesville, Virginia; Technical Consultant, Rehabilitation Services Administration, United States Department of Health, Education and Welfare, Washington, D. C.; Editor, American Lecture Series in Social and Rehabilitation Psychology, Charles C Thomas, Publisher; Lecturer, Medical Department, Woodrow Wilson Rehabilitation Center; formerly, Rehabilitation Counselor, Texas State Commission for the Blind; Rehabilitation Counselor, Texas Rehabilitation Commission; Director, Division of Research and Program Development, Virginia State Department of Vocational Rehabilitation. The following are some of the books which Dr. Cull has coauthored and co-edited: *Drug Dependence and Rehabilitation Approaches, Fundamentals of Criminal Behavior and Correctional Systems, Rehabilitation of the Drug Abuser With Delinquent Behavior,* and *Therapeutic Needs of the Family.* Dr. Cull has contributed more than sixty publications to the professional literature in psychology and rehabilitation.

DELOSS D. FRIESEN, Ph.D.: Received degrees from Northwest Nazarene College and the University of Oregon. Dr. Friesen is an Associate Professor in the Department of Educational Psychology and Measurement at the University of Nebraska, Lincoln, Nebraska. He has held positions as Counseling Psychologist at the University Counseling Center and Assistant Professor in the Department of Guidance and Personnel Services at the State University of New York at Albany; Counseling Consultant to Union College, Schenectady, New York; and Instructor at Hudson Valley Community College. Dr. Friesen has particular interest in life planning focusing on career and mate selection.

VICTOR J. GANZER, Ph.D.: Holds degrees from the University of Washington. Dr. Ganzer is licensed to practice psychology in Washington. He is Staff Psychologist with the Child Study and Treatment Center in Fort Steilacoom, Washington. Also, he is consultant with the Echo Glenn School and with the Human Interaction Research Institute. Formerly, Dr. Ganzer was a research Assistant Professor with the University of Washington. He is active in learning and personality theory, group therapy, personality measurement, and hospital care and institutionalization.

ROBERT GOODKIN, Ph.D.: Received his doctorate from Florida State University. He is Senior Research Psychologist (Behavioral Science Department), Institute of Rehabilitation Medicine, New York University Medical Center. Also, Dr. Goodkin is Assistant Professor of Psychology, Montclair State College, Montclair, New Jersey.

RICHARD E. HARDY, Ed.D.: Diplomate in counseling psychology, Professor and Chairman, Department of Rehabilitation Counseling, Virginia Commonwealth University, Richmond, Virginia; Technical Consultant, United States Department of Health, Education and Welfare, Rehabilitation Services Administration, Washington, D. C.; Editor, American Lecture Series in Social and Rehabilitation Counselor in Virginia, Rehabilitation Advisor, Re- Associate Editor, *Journal of Voluntary Action Research,* formerly Rehabilitation Counselor in Virginia, Rehabilitation Advisor, Rehabilitation Services Administration, Unittd States Department of Health, Education and Welfare, Washington, D. C.; former Chief Psychologist and Supervisor of Professional Training, South Carolina Department of Rehabilitation and member of the South Carolina State Board of Examiners in Psychology. The following are some of the books which Dr. Hardy has coauthored and co-edited: *Drug Dependence and Rehabilitation Approaches, Fundamentals of Criminal Behavior and Correctional Systems, Rehabilitation of the Drug Abuser With Delinquent Behavior,* and *Therapeutic Needs of the Family.* Dr. Hardy has contributed more than sixty publications to the professional literature in psychology and rehabilitation.

LAWRENCE C. HARTLAGE, Ph.D.: Associate Professor of Neurology and Psychology and Chief of the Neuropsychology

Section, Department of Neurology, School of Medicine, Medical College of Georgia, Augusta, Georgia. Dr. Hartlage received degrees from the University of Louisville and Ohio State University. Formerly, he was Director of Psychology at the Indiana University affiliated facility for the mentally retarded.

DONALD R. MIKLICH, Ph.D.: Received his Doctorate from Colorado University. He received his BA in History and Political Science at the University of Northern Colorado and his MA degree from Colorado University. Formerly, he was an Assistant Professor of Psychology for two years at the University of Hawaii before joining the staff of the Children's Asthma Research Institute and Hospital as Research Psychologist and Statistician. In 1972, he was appointed Director of Computer Operations at CARIH. His major research interests are psychometrics and psychosomatic aspects of asthma, and he has published a number of papers in various scientific journals.

STEVEN MATHEW ROSS, Ph.D.: Chief, Drug Dependence Treatment Center, VA Hospital, Salt Lake City, Utah; Instructor, Department of Psychiatry, University of Utah Medical Center, Salt Lake City, Utah; Assistant Clinical Professor, Department of Psychology, University of Utah; formerly, Program Supervisor, Behavior Modification Training Center, Salt Lake City, Utah and Staff Psychologist, VA Hospital, East Orange, New Jersey. Dr. Ross is very active in research which has led to a number of publications in psychological and psychologically oriented journals.

This book is dedicated to:
The Royal family of Virginia Beach, Virginia
Nita and Walt
Larry and Martha
Becky and Scott

The following books have appeared thus far in the Social and Rehabilitation Psychology Series:

VOCATIONAL REHABILITATION: PROFESSION AND PROCESS
    John G. Cull and Richard E. Hardy
CONTEMPORARY FIELD WORK PRACTICES IN REHABILITATION
    John G. Cull and Craig R. Colvin
SOCIAL AND REHABILITATION SERVICES FOR THE BLIND
    Richard E. Hardy and John G. Cull
FUNDAMENTALS OF CRIMINAL BEHAVIOR AND
CORRECTIONAL SYSTEMS
    John G. Cull and Richard E. Hardy
MEDICAL AND PSYCHOLOGICAL ASPECTS OF DISABILITY
    A. Beatrix Cobb
DRUG DEPENDENCE AND REHABILITATION APPROACHES
    Richard E. Hardy and John G. Cull
INTRODUCTION TO CORRECTION REHABILITATION
    Richard E. Hardy and John G. Cull
VOCATIONAL EVALUATION FOR REHABILITATION SERVICES
    Richard E. Hardy and John G. Cull
ADJUSTMENT TO WORK: A GOAL OF REHABILITATION
    John G. Cull and Richard E. Hardy
SPECIAL PROBLEMS IN REHABILITATION
    A. Beatrix Cobb
THERAPEUTIC NEEDS OF THE FAMILY: PROBLEMS, DESCRIPTIONS
AND THERAPEUTIC APPROACHES
    John G. Cull and Richard E. Hardy
MARITAL AND FAMILY COUNSELING: TECHNIQUES AND APPROACHES
    John G. Cull and Richard E. Hardy
MODIFICATION OF THE BEHAVIOR OF THE MENTALLY ILL:
REHABILITATION APPROACHES
    Richard E. Hardy and John G. Cull
MODIFICATION OF BEHAVIOR OF THE MENTALLY RETARDED:
APPLIED PRINCIPLES
    Richard E. Hardy and John G. Cull

PREFACE

SOCIAL SERVICE and rehabilitation workers employed in the field of work with the mentally ill have long needed comprehensive materials which would be useful to them as professional persons in self-directed study and as textbooks in college courses. The field of rehabilitation has had a special need for a collection of works such as those which appear in this book.

The ever-increasing complexity of our stress-filled environment causes adjustment difficulties of such magnitude to individuals attempting to "cope" that educational materials of this type must be developed in order for professional persons to improve their helping skills. This book represents an effort to bring together some of the important information which is necessary for effective social and rehabilitation services. It is not all inclusive but is intended to provide a basic pool of information for rehabilitation workers.

Preparation of the papers contained herein was made with careful consideration of the whole field of social and rehabilitation services as these are related to those settings which are most important in terms of the magnitude of work to be done within the field of rehabilitation. The various chapters have been designed to help the newly employed professional person explore the basic concepts concerning behavior modification principles which are applied in rehabilitation work.

Without the support, cooperation, and encouragement of the various contributors, the development of this book would have been impossible. We express our special gratitude to each of them who have taken time from various pursuits to prepare manuscripts. We owe much for the constant support and constructive criticism of Robert A. Lassiter and Keith C. Wright of the Department of Rehabilitation Counseling, Virginia Commonwealth University. Special thanks also go to Joan Tiller for her excellence in secretarial work. JOHN G. CULL
RICHARD E. HARDY

CONTENTS

BEHAVIOR MODIFICATION IN REHABILITATION SETTINGS

CHAPTER I

MODIFYING BEHAVIOR: APPLIED TECHNIQUES

ROBERT GOODKIN

Introduction
Applied Principles
Conclusion
References

INTRODUCTION

B EHAVIOR MODIFICATION has received a great deal of attention in many areas during the past ten years. Methods derived from the behavioral learning laboratory have been applied widely in the fields of education and mental health. One arena which lends itself to behavior modification procedures, but which has received little attention until the past few years, is the field of rehabilitation. Meyerson, *et al.* pointed out the relevance of behavioral learning principles to rehabilitation as early as 1960. The increasingly rich literature on practical means of modifying behavior suggests that the psychologist may have much to offer in the rehabilitation effort in ways which have been relatively unexplored.

One of the major activities in the rehabilitation center, the setting with which I have most familiarity, is increasing certain behaviors and decreasing others. Instances that involve increasing and decreasing behaviors in this setting include teaching ambulation and balance in physical therapy classes; teaching fine perceptual-motor skills such as writing and operating office machines in occupational therapy classes; teaching patients to push their wheelchairs and to transfer from wheelchairs to other furniture in activities of daily living classes; teaching aphasics to increase understandable and appropriate speech and to decrease unintelligible and inappropriate speech in speech therapy classes. In short, any area of rehabilitation that involves the teaching of motor or verbal skills can be broken down into units of behavior to be increased or decreased. Behavior modification principles have relevance to problems in training, motivation and behavior management (Goodkin, 1966).

While the pure psychological researcher is concerned primarily with establishing general principles that operate in all behavior, the applied researcher involves himself with application of these principles to the particular situation. It is essential that the applied researcher have a thorough understanding of the various principles if he is to employ them effectively.

The effective application of behavior modification principles to rehabilitation problems requires several factors including a thorough knowledge of the behaviors to be dealt with, a comfortable working knowledge of the various principles of modifying behavior, the ingenuity to see the relevance of specific procedures to the particular target behaviors under focus, and sufficient sensitivity and clinical judgment to determine how a given ongoing procedure is effecting the individual being treated.

It is often inappropriate to jump in and begin modifying the most obvious problematic behavior. At times one can deal with a complex, molar behavior as a response class to be increased or decreased, but often it is necessary to break the behavior down to smaller units to be modified before focusing on the larger behavior. While in our setting we have worked with some patients on the molar behavior of pushing a wheelchair faster by getting base rates on the speed of pushing a given distance and reinforcing faster total performance, other patients did better when the target behavior was a single element of the larger behavior, such as grabbing hold of the wheel further back or following through more fully. To gain a more thorough knowledge of the given behavior, the therapist in the area is often a valuable source of information and experience. As one works on projects with speech therapists, occupational therapists, or physical therapists, for example, it quickly becomes evident that there are many subtle things to learn in any specific discipline, and to assume that behavior change principles are all that one needs to produce effective treatment changes is not only grandiose, but naive.

Knowing and feeling comfortable with the various behavior change principles offers the psychologist a powerful source of intervention. While most treatment areas in rehabilitation have been built on theoretical and rather subjective clinical methodology, behavior modification principles have come from extensive empirical research. Getting involved in training areas is a new role for psychologists in rehabilitation. In the past, psychologists have been associated primarily with testing and clinical functions and with research focusing primarily on predictive rehabilitation outcomes and acquiring pure science data. Part of the task of the psychologist in this new role is to investigate and demonstrate the practical value or usefulness of behavioral learning principles in the rehabilitation effort.

A knowledge of the various principles of behavior modification aids in understanding why changes in ongoing treatment areas occur or fail to occur and offers many alternative approaches when an ongoing treatment regime is not producing the desired effects. Casually observing most treatment areas shows, for example, that feedback is frequently not given contingently on target behavior. Often patients are told that they are doing very well when in fact they are progressing slowly or are told nothing when they make significant behavioral changes. This lack of honest communication is often quickly recognized by many patients and has the resultant effect that they place little value on the feedback of the therapist. Understanding such concepts as reinforcement, extinction, modeling, punishment, fading, and escape training offer the psychologist or therapist a good basis for accounting for change and the lack of change in ongoing treatment sessions.

While some researchers prefer a particular approach to treatment and attempt to approach most behavior changes with a given theoretical model, the impression is that there is more potential value in being aware of many procedures that have yielded significant behavioral changes and selecting those that seem applicable to the situation. At this early stage of applied research in rehabilitation it would appear most beneficial to be open to many approaches that have been fruitful in other applied areas.

Many contemporary behavioral psychologists are rebelling against many years of psychological theory and writings which were based on little empirical evidence and strongly emphasized untestable and unquantifiable concepts. The extremes of this group are so eager to make psychology into a respectable science that they sometimes seem to lose sight of the fact that in applied, clinical work some concepts may have practical value which has not yet been defined in a rigorous, operational way. I have seen instances in which approaching clinical situations with too much technological rigidity has stood in the way of clinical progress. When I began to study the effects of verbal operant conditioning on the functional speech of aphasics, for example, I had initially functioned in such a machine-like fashion that many patients lost interest in and frequently missed sessions. I was so eager to be rigorous and scientific and paid so much attention to the specific response classes and treatment procedures that I lost some sight of the people with whom I was working. The issue of sensitivity toward the patient's reaction toward the total treatment situation is a real one. It is very important that the experimentor or therapist make every effort to establish himself as a reinforcer. In applied research, while one eye must be on the specific target behavior, the other must be on the person and should not lose sight of the many ongoing relevant behaviors.

Similarly, the ingenuity to see the application of behavioral principles to specific situations involves a kind of conduct (the psychologist's) that is difficult to quantify. It requires a sharp definition of the behavior under focus, a sense for choosing a relevant procedure for the particular behavior and individual, the courage to attempt it, and the flexibility to change procedures if a given method, no matter how comfortable or "right" it feels is not producing changes in the desired direction. The experimentor's ingenuity in seeing potential relevant procedures is, in part, a function of his individual behavioral history, his experience with the given subject matter, and his understanding and feeling for the various behavioral principles.

In our institution, we did a study which investigated whether experienced physical therapists agreed upon major gait deviations in hemiplegic ambulation patients and upon the major treatment approaches to remediate the errors (Goodkin and Diller, 1973). This study indicated considerable differences in both judgments of errors and treatment approaches. In a second study, observers concurrently scored the treatment styles of therapists and the simultaneous changes resulting in the gait deviations being treated. This study revealed considerable differences among senior physical therapists in treatment styles and in the effects of the various approaches on the target behaviors. The differences in therapist approaches were due to such factors as the training of the therapists, the theories held by the therapists, the level of experience, personality characteristics of the therapists, and personality characteristics of the patients. A more empirical basis for evaluating therapeutic changes and for selecting effective treatment procedures suitable to a given situation is clearly needed in many areas of rehabilitation.

Quantification of behavior and rigorous statements of procedures are basic elements of behavior modification research and practice. A functional research design is often employed to assess the effects of various procedures. In this approach, the target behavior (or behaviors) is first counted or timed while no treatment intervention is in effect. Such base rates are carefully taken to obtain a measure of the typical occurrence of the response class under focus. Base rates are generally taken over a comparable period of time for several days, until one is confident that the base rates do, indeed, reflect typical performance. Generally, a criterion level is stated prior to the onset of the base rates to operationalize what will be accepted as stable or typical performance prior to the onset of treatment procedures. Although base rates generally consist of frequency counts or rate of responses, they can also consist of timed behavior. An example of a frequency base rate would be how many errors or desired responses occur during a given period of time (e.g. how many words typed in a minute; how many dysfluencies or perseverations emitted by an aphasic during a five-minute period). A timed base rate would consist of how long it takes for a particular behavioral criterion to be met (e.g. how many seconds it takes an individual to push a wheelchair five feet; how many minutes it takes to eat a given amount of food without assistance).

After base rates are obtained, the next step in a functional design is to carefully state a treatment procedure and to employ it consistently and accurately. The treatment procedure, like the base rate, is in effect for a specified period of time each session until a plateau has been reached for a set number of days. The target behaviors in each response class are carefully recorded each day.

After the behavioral effects of the first treatment procedure have leveled off, a second treatment procedure is stated and employed precisely, and the effects on the target behavior are measured each session. Again, this procedure is continued until the effects on the behavior have stabilized.

In a functional approach, the duration of each treatment is generally determined by its effect on the target behavior rather than predetermined. New base rates can be obtained periodically to reevaluate behavioral performance when treatment procedures are not in effect in order to measure the generalization or carry-over from the treatment. New base rates might also be obtained months after treatment has ended to evaluate long-term effects after given procedures.

APPLIED PRINCIPLES

The principles and procedures to be discussed are derived from extensive basic research in the areas of operant and classical conditioning (Honig, 1966; Krasner and Ullmann, 1965). Basic operant research is generally referred to as the *experimental analysis of behavior,* and application of the principles has come to be called the field of *applied behavior analysis.* Although much of the basic research has been done on lower animals, a rich and sizable body of literature has grown during the past ten years which suggests that the behavioral principles offer a powerful source of leverage in dealing with many problematic clinical behaviors. The basic principles and their application to various clinical areas are discussed in great detail in other sources (Franks, 1969; Ullmann and Krasner, 1965). The intention here is to briefly describe some of the major behavioral learning principles and to give some applied examples relating to the area of rehabilitation.

Reinforcement refers to increasing the frequency or occurrence of a response by controlling the consequences of the response. Reinforcement is defined empirically rather than logically. That is, it is not enough to assume that an intended reinforcer will increase the occurrence of the response—it has to work before the "reinforcer" can be so labeled. This means that while there are some general reinforcers that hold for many people (e.g. money, social approval), the reinforcers for an individual must be tailored to that individual. Primary reinforcement refers to such basic necessities as food and water. Secondary reinforcers are generally thought to acquire their reinforcing qualities by association with primary reinforcers. In physical rehabilitation settings, objective feedback in the form of informing patients of increased frequency or speed of behavior is often an effective reinforcer. Hemiplegics often progress so slowly in their treatment programs that it is difficult for such individuals to see or feel progress from day to day or even from week to week. When specific behaviors are counted or timed on a daily basis and patients are given this information they are often responsive to such feedback. Wilbert Fordyce, at the University of Washington Medical Center, has found graphing such responses on a daily basis to be a valuable motivator and reinforcer for many behaviors. I have found that, while the tangible quality of tokens has been useful in working with low functional level aphasics, high level patients responded much better to verbal reinforcement (Goodkin, Diller, and Shah, 1973). While some general statements can be made about specific reinforcers for a given population, it is important that the reinforcer for each individual be determined on an empirical basis. Some large-scale programmed approaches with aphasics have failed because of the use of inappropriate reinforcers. One program was unsuccessful because the investigator used the correct written answer as reinforcement, an approach which often works well with a "normal" population when presented by means of teaching machines or programmed texts. In this situation, however, many subjects could not process the reinforcer sufficiently to make use of the feedback.

Negative reinforcement refers to increasing a behavior by allowing the occurrence of the response to terminate an aversive or unpleasant stimulus. For example, if an animal receives a continuous shock, and this shock can only be terminated by pressing a lever, the animal quickly learns the lever pressing response. Again, the consequence of the response produces an increase in the target behavior.

Token economies make direct use of reinforcement principles. Such systems are generally set up in group settings to build or decrease specific behaviors in the group members. Token economies basically consist of presenting a group (or an individual) with two lists, one list stating the number of tokens or points which can be earned by making a particular response, and a second list indicating the number of tokens necessary to purchase each of a number of "back-up" reinforcers. Back-up reinforcers generally vary from cigarettes and candy to special out-trips. Token economies have been very effective in patient management as well as in remediating problematic behaviors. Target behaviors have ranged from personal care and cleaning ones room to participating in activities with other people and improving in specific skills. Many listed behaviors can apply to the entire group while others might apply only to specific individuals. Token systems have been employed in mental institutions, special education classes, residential centers for delinquents, and rehabilitation centers.

The concept of *shaping* refers to building a response by reinforcing successive approximations to a desired response. In this procedure, an individual is first reinforced for making any response in the desired direction; then that response is no longer reinforced. The individual must then make a closer approximation to the desired behavior before a reinforcer will be given. This procedure is continued until only the complete response is reinforced. Reinforcement generally consists of something that can be administered immediately and can be consumed or utilized in a short period of time. The reinforcer should not be something that produces rapid satiation if the situation requires many reinforcers during the session. The increased efficiency of immediate reinforcement has been well documented.

I would like to briefly discuss a little boy seen at our center to give an applied example of shaping. Jose was a four-and-a-half-year-old Spanish-speaking boy with cerebral palsy who was making little progress in ambulation classes. Although physicians and physical therapists stated that he had sufficient muscle power and range of motion to walk, he refused to cooperate with therapists in walking activities. When he was referred to us, we spent the first few days in our office playing games he liked, giving him those magical reinforcers—M&M®'s—and doing all we could to establish ourselves as reinforcers. On the fourth day, Jose came in wanting to play and wanting candy, which we refused him. To begin shaping walking behavior, we modeled pulling ourselves from a kneeling position to a standing position using a chair for support. At first he wanted no part of this, but by the middle of the session he made a half-hearted attempt to pull himself up. We immediately placed an M&M in his mouth, applauded and said "Yeah, Jose." He then had to pull himself up a little further before he was given more candy and social reinforcement. Within a few days he had picked himself up all the way to a standing position in order to receive reinforcement. He was then required to take a step or two while holding onto a desk with one hand. Once he walked the length of the desk, we brought him out into the hall where there was a long railing at the proper height. After two weeks he walked the length of the railing—forty to fifty feet—before reinforcement was given. At this point social reinforcement ("Yeah, Jose," smiles, hugs) was sufficient to build the new behavior, although we gave him candy at the end of each session. It is generally advisable to eliminate tangible reinforcers and use social reinforcers when they become effective by themselves. After another week Jose had to walk the length of the railing several times and take a step or two and flop in our arms before he received reinforcement. Once he was able to take five or six steps independently he took off and no longer needed our ambulation sessions. The act of walking received many "natural" and "internal" reinforcers. Natural reinforcers might have consisted of such events as getting where he wanted to go faster, being able to reach things he couldn't reach before, and smiles and compliments from nurses, doctors, and therapists who were aware of his accomplishment. Internal reinforcers might have been feelings and thoughts of being more like other children and feeling proud of accomplishing a difficult new behavior. Although various gimmicks may be necessary to initiate a new behavior, once the behavior has been developed, every effort is made to eliminate them and let natural reinforcers maintain the behavior.

The *Premack principle* is another very useful reinforcement concept (Premack, 1965). This principle essentially states that permitting the occurrence of a high probability behavior can serve as a reinforcer to increase a low probability behavior. While this principle has also been around for many years, its precise statement and application are very useful in many settings. An everyday example is a mother telling a child "After you clean your room (low probability behavior), you may go outside and play" (high probability behavior). The novelty of Premack reinforcement is that a desired response of the individual, rather than a stimulus, serves as the reinforcer. By observing the activities of an individual when left alone, one can easily determine effective reinforcers. If a patient likes occupational therapy classes but dislikes and refuses to attend physical therapy classes, one might make the rule, "If you do not attend and perform such and such in your physical therapy class each day, you will not be permitted to attend your occupational therapy class that day." With a little imagination and consistent application, this simple principle can be applied to motivate patients to do less desired, but necessary, activities within therapy classes or can provide leverage in dealing with many behavioral and training problems.

Extinction refers to the elimination or reduction of a response by withholding reinforcement. This approach differs from other means of decreasing behavior such as punishment, satiation, forgetting, conditioned inhibition, etc. Responses which go by unreinforced or unnoticed often decrease in frequency of occurrence. In studying children who engaged in frequent tantrum behavior, Carl Williams (1959) noticed that two common consequences which tended to maintain tantrum behavior were giving in to the child's demands and attending to the tantrum behavior. If a child gets his way after engaging in tantrum behavior, the parent is in effect reinforcing tantrums. Although a parent may be intending to punish tantrum behavior by scolding the child, often the attention, even negative attention, will serve to reinforce the behavior. In a rehabilitation setting, Fordyce used extinction and reinforcement to eliminate complaints of clinical pain and increase performance in various therapy classes. He noted that complaints of pain often resulted in gaining the attention and sympathy of staff members, permission to not attend or do little work in therapy classes, and acquiring medication to relieve pain. Such consequences served to reinforce complaints of pain. To eliminate such behavior, Fordyce changed the contingencies on pain complaining behavior. He arranged for therapists to pay little attention to such patient behavior, and to give much attention to on-task behaviors. If patients neglected to attend classes, they received minimal attention in their rooms, and received no pain-relieving medication at that time. The physicians spent some time with such patients each morning and evening and prescribed such medication on a noncontingent, time basis depending upon the patient's stated level of discomfort. In this way, complaints of pain were extinguished and increased task-oriented behavior was reinforced by the staff. This plan enhanced motivation and performance in the various therapy classes.

Escape and Avoidance Training—Murray Sidman (1966) did much basic research in the areas of escape and avoidance training. Escape training is similar to negative reinforcement in that the aim is to increase behavior by allowing certain responses to terminate aversive or unpleasant stimuli. In avoidance training, the subject is given a cue (e.g. a light or tone warning) and then allowed a specified time period to emit a given response which delays the aversive consequence. If the behavior is emitted during each response period, the individual never receives the aversive

consequence. Goldiamond did an escape training study to decrease stuttering behavior. As the stutterer's speech became dys-
fluent a constant unpleasant tone was presented and continued
until the speech became fluent. The desired response, fluent
speech, terminated the aversive tone. Although this procedure
initially increased stuttering behavior slightly, in a very short
time stuttering was markedly decreased. In our setting we are
currently working on a device to train wheelchair bound patients
to push up in their chairs periodically. This device makes use of
escape and avoidance training procedures. It is important for
wheelchair bound patients to push up in their chairs frequently
in order to avoid getting decubitus ulcers. In the escape training
phase, this device presents a constant tone every half hour that
the individual is in his wheelchair, and this tone can only be terminated by pushing up in the chair. In the avoidance training
phase, a brief cue tone sounds, signaling that if the patient does
not push up in his chair within the following fifteen seconds a
constant tone will continue sounding until he does push up. The
potential use of mechanical devices which operate on behavioral
learning principles is very great in the areas of assessment and
training in rehabilitation.

Modeling—Bandura (1965) did the initial basic research in
modeling. Modeling refers to an individual increasing or decreasing the frequency of a given target behavior by observing another individual engage in the behavior and seeing the consequences.
In an elementary school classroom, after one child raises his hand
in response to a question and is reinforced handsomely by the
teacher's praise, there is a good chance that many hands will fly
up in response to the next question. Similarly, motorists often
slow down when they reach a stretch of highway where they have
frequently seen speeding tickets being administered. Both are
common examples of modeling. In our work with aphasics, patients observed therapists respond to the same materials that they
were learning, and following each response the therapist stated
whether his utterance was correct or not. After the modeling period, the patients responded to the same tasks. These sessions
were effective in both increasing desired responses and decreasing
errors.

Punishment refers to decreasing the frequency of occurrence of a response by controlling the consequences of the response. As in the case of reinforcement, punishment is also empirically defined. Studies have generally found punishment to be a rather ineffective means of modifying behavior. Punishment generally results in a *temporary* decrement in the target behavior and such side effects as fear of the individual doing the punishing and heightened emotionality in the punishing situation. While strong punishment may result in permanent elimination of a target behavior, extreme emotional side effects are highly probable. Mild punishment of an undesired target behavior coupled with reinforcement of a competing desired behavior can be useful. In such an approach the mild punishment serves to immediately reduce the frequency of an undesired response, thus allowing a greater probability for the desired behavior to occur. When the preferred behavior occurs, reinforcement strengthens the behavior and increases the probability of this behavior occurring again.

Negative Practice is a procedure based on Hull's concept of conditioned inhibition. In this procedure an undesired behavior is overpracticed until it is eliminated. Even the most pleasurable behaviors become increasingly aversive when overdone. Aubrey Yates (1958) employed this procedure with children with multiple tics. After several weeks of sessions of overpracticing the tics, subjects showed a significant reduction in these behaviors. While this behavior was initially reinforcing to the extent that it reduced tension, as the subjects continued the behavior it became increasingly aversive. We have had some success in our center in eliminating hemiplegic gait deviations by having patients overpractice the error each time it occurred.

Systematic Desensitization, developed by Joseph Wolpe (1969), is based upon a classical conditioning paradigm. It is a procedure to condition relaxation to occur in situations that have previously produced fear or anxiety. Basically, it consists of training relaxation by means of progressive muscular relaxation and deep breathing and then associating this relaxation with anxiety-provoking stimuli which the individual imagines. These stimuli are placed in a hierarchy from least to most disturbing situations.

Treatment begins by pairing the least anxiety-provoking stimulus with relaxation until the subject can imagine it without significant anxiety. Then, the second item on the hierarchy is presented. This procedure continues until every item on the subject's hierarchy can be vividly imagined without undue anxiety. Systematic desensitization has been very effective in eliminating a wide variety of fears and anxiety ranging from snake phobias and fear of flying in planes to free floating anxiety. In rehabilitation settings it has been used successfully in eliminating fear of taking needles, reducing the fear of hemiplegics of falling in ambulation classes, and decreasing the anxiety of aphasics of talking in groups.

CONCLUSION

The above principles and applications are by no means a complete listing. Stimulus control, fading, covert sensitization and thought stoppage are just a few other behavior modification procedures that have great potential application in rehabilitation settings.

A major emphasis in behavior modification is to investigate and determine procedures that effect change. The focus is more on what works and how it works than on why it works. The field has not yet reached the point where one can state that a given procedure is most effective to treat a given type of problem. At present, the literature on basic and applied behavioral learning principles is growing rapidly. As suggested above, behavior modification principles provide a great variety of alternative approaches to increase or decrease a wide range of behaviors in rehabilitation and other settings.

REFERENCES

Bandura, A.: Behavior modification through modeling procedures. In Krasner, L., and Ullmann, L. P. (Eds.) *Research in Behavior Modification.* New York, HR&W, 1965, pp. 310-340.

Franks, C. M.: *Behavior Therapy: Appraisal and Status.* New York, McGraw, 1969.

Goodkin, R.: Case studies in behavioral research in rehabilitation. *Percept Mot Skills, 23*:171-182, 1966.

Goodkin, R. and Diller, L.: Reliability among physical therapists in diagnosis and treatment of gait deviations in hemiplegics. *Percept Mot Skills,* 37:727-734, 1973.

Goodkin, R., Diller, L., and Shah, N.: Training spouses to improve the functional speech of aphasics. In Lahey, B. B. (Ed.) *The Modification of Language Behavior.* Springfield, Thomas, 1973.

Honig, W. K. (Ed.) : *Operant Behavior: Areas of Research and Application.* New York, Appleton, 1966.

Krasner, L. and Ullmann, L. P. (Eds.) : *Research in Behavior Modification: New Developments and Implications.* New York, HR&W, 1965.

Meyerson, J., Michael, J., Mowrer, O. H., Osgood, C. E., and Staats, A. W.: Learning, behavior, and rehabilitation. In Logquist, L. H. (Ed.), *Psychological Research and Rehabilitation.* Washington, D.C., *Am Psychol,* pp. 68-111, 1960.

Premack, D.: Reinforcement theory. In Levine, D. (Ed.) *Nebraska Symposium on Motivation: 1965.* Lincoln, U of Nebr Pr, 1965, pp. 123-180.

Sidman, M.: Avoidance behavior. In Honig, W. K. (Ed.) *Operant Behavior: Areas of Research and Application.* New York, Appleton, 1966.

Ullmann, L. P. and Krasner, L. (Eds.) : *Case Studies in Behavior Modification.* New York, HR&W, 1965.

Williams, C. D.: The elimination of tantrum behaviors by extinction procedures. *J Abnorm Psychol, 59:*269, 1959.

Wolpe, J.: *The Practice of Behavior Therapy.* New York, Pergamon, 1969.

Yates, A. J.: The application of learning theory to the treatment of tics. *J Abnorm Psychol, 56:*175-182, 1958.

CHAPTER II

TOKEN ECONOMIES: A DESCRIPTION

WILLIAM C. COE

Introduction
Specific Aspects of the Token Economy
Concluding Remarks
References
Annotated Film Listing

INTRODUCTION

TOKEN ECONOMIES have become fairly common in total and semi-institutional settings like mental hospitals (Ayllon and Azrin, 1968), hospitals for the retarded (Hunt, Fitzhugh and Fitzhugh, 1968), juvenile detention units (Tyler and Brown, 1968), day and night care clinics, sheltered workshops (Zimmerman, Stuckley, Garlick, and Miller, 1969), all sorts of classrooms (O'Leary and Drabman, 1971), foster care homes (Phillips, 1968), and individual families (Christophersen, Arnold, Hill, and Quilitch, 1972; Coe, 1972). In such settings groups of clients are considered to benefit from the same changes in behavior, and the counselor has a relatively high degree of control over their environment. The client populations, of course, are reflected in the nature of these settings and a wide range of rehabilitative problems are encompassed. Probably the most important consideration in deciding whether or not a token economy will be useful is, not so much the behaviors to be changed, but whether or not the counselor is in a position to arrange for the consequences of his clients' behavior.

18

Just what is a token economy? In the most general sense, it is a miniature monetary system in a limited setting. The participants are paid for performing some behaviors and in turn pay for others. In principal it is not different from our usual economic system—you are paid for doing your job, and you pay for your car—but the payoff and the payments are more clearly controlled by the person (s) in charge of the program.

A token, the currency of the economy, is some tangible item, like a poker chip or a check mark on the client's card. Like money, a token has no value of its own, but it may be traded for articles and activities that do. If you were to observe a token economy in action, you would see clients being paid for performing certain behaviors, for example, a mental patient speaks sensibly to a nurse for two minutes, a retarded child completes a simple math assignment, or a truant child goes to school. You would also observe the same persons paying for other behaviors, like entering the dining room at the mental hospital, selecting a small toy in the retarded child's classroom, or watching T.V. in the truant child's home. The number of tokens given to the client, and the number that he pays, are based on a systematic evaluation of all his behaviors. The principles of operant conditioning help to direct the counselor in determining which behaviors receive pay and which are paid for, the planned-for result being an environment that motivates the client to change his behavior in what is considered a positive direction. The primary goal of the economy is to increase those behaviors that are believed to be adaptive and to decrease those that are believed to be deleterious.

A token economy holds some potential advantages over other reinforcement approaches. As was mentioned above, in settings where certain behaviors are considered positive for all of the clients or helpful in managing the institution, they may be incorporated as a stable aspect of the economy. In some token programs many of the behaviors are directly related to the ease of managing the institution. In a mental hospital, for example, patients might receive tokens for getting up in the morning by a certain time, making their beds, and participating in other activities that relieve the staff of custodial duties (Ayllon and Azrin, 1968; Schaefer and Martin, 1969). Other behaviors are considered helpful in overcoming the clients' difficulties, like attending group therapy and academic achievement in a juvenile detention home (e.g. Tyler and Brown, 1968).

Team competition within a client population can be used to include the influence of peers in modifying behavior. A classroom, for example, may be divided into teams and the one that earns the most points during the day may be let out of school early or given some other privilege (Barrish, Saunders, and Wolf, 1969). Of course, the children's individual programs may be continued at the same time.

Vernon (1972, p. 53) lists a number of advantages of the token economy in working with children, most of which are related to using tokens instead of other things, like candy, praise, or trinkets as reinforcers. The child is not likely to become satiated on tokens as he would on food and trinkets or too frequently employed praise. Nor is he distracted with a token as he would be when he eats a piece of candy or plays with a trinket that has been given to him. Tokens are easily administered in a flexible manner, the amount the client receives depending upon his effort and the counselor's judgment of the importance of a particular behavior. In a well-managed program a wide range of items and activities will be available for token purchase; thus, tokens may be exchanged for many potential reinforcers of the child's own choice, and the chances that a reinforcer will not be available for a particular child are reduced. The delay in reinforcement, so characteristic of many commonly used reinforcers, like grades, can be avoided. Tokens can be easily administered very soon after a response occurs. Children who do not respond in the usual way to naturally occurring reinforcers, like praise and attention, may be strongly influenced by tokens. By pairing tokens with natural reinforcers, the child may become sensitive to them, and the chances that he will respond to them in the future and in other settings will increase.

SPECIFIC ASPECTS OF THE TOKEN ECONOMY
Reinforcers: The Key to Positive Motivation and Learning

It is extremely important that a token program provide the clients with items and activities worth purchasing. It is ridiculous, for example, to expect a group of delinquent children to work for tokens when the only thing they may purchase with them is a compliment from their counselor. On the other hand, if they could purchase reduced detention time, stylish clothes, soft drinks, cigarettes, time on pass, or attendance at a dance, we can expect that many of them will be looking for ways to earn tokens.

A POSITIVE CONVENIENCE: TOKENS AS GENERALIZED REINFORCERS. Reinforcers may be *primary*, like food, or they may be *secondary*, like a smile from mother. In the first instance, food is naturally reinforcing and meets a need for survival; in the second case, the value of a smile from mother has been learned because of its association with obtaining other primary reinforcers. When something becomes a means of obtaining a wide variety of primary and secondary reinforcers, it is said to be a *generalized* reinforcer. The best example of a generalized reinforcer in everyday living is money. The primary means of exchange in economic systems is usually a currency of some sort. With it you can purchase goods you need, like food, or activities you prefer, like a vacation. Money may also be used to avoid some of the things you dislike—hiring someone to iron your clothes or paying a fine rather than going to jail. For most of us, money is a generalized reinforcer. We have learned that it can be exchanged for a large variety of things that we prefer. Most of us also recognize that the act of receiving money is reinforcing in itself and that we do things to obtain it, even though it has no direct value to us.

Tokens take the place of money as a generalized reinforcer in a token economy. In most settings it is simply a matter of telling the clients that tokens are to be used for purchasing designated items and activities. The person's acquaintance with money will usually generalize to tokens readily, and no further instructions are needed. However, some clients, like mentally retarded persons or mental patients who have been institutionalized most of their lives, may have to learn the value of tokens. This is typically accomplished by giving the individual tokens immediately before a reinforcing event, then taking them from him before he is allowed to participate. For example, a patient is given several tokens just before meal time and must give them back before he is allowed into the dining area.

As a generalized reinforcer, money is a *tangible* one; that is, it can be seen and felt, carried or stored, and spent or saved. The same is true of tokens in most cases, although their particular form will vary. Specially made chips can be purchased through supply houses, or institutions can design their own and have them manufactured. The common poker chip is often used though it is usually necessary to modify it in some way to prevent counterfeiting. Paper money is also a possibility but its destructibility makes it unfit for some settings. Buttons, toothpicks and an assortment of other small items are also potentially useful though they usually have fewer advantages than chips of some sort.

Besides these tangible, generalized reinforcers there are *intangible* ones. Many intangible reinforcers are related to social approval: a smile, a hug, a nod, attention, verbal approval ("good"), and so on. These are easily administered at the time a behavior occurs and will strengthen the behavior for many clients, but it is difficult to keep track of them and they cannot be passed on from one individual to the next for controlling the behavior of others.

Other examples of intangible, generalized reinforcers are colored stars on gummed labels that can be stuck on children's individual charts or a simple check mark can be made on a client's personal card. These kinds of intangible reinforcers have been used effectively in some programs, especially classrooms. Where the population moves from area to area, however, as in a mental hospital, it is probably more desirable to use something that can be carried and more readily exchanged no matter where the person is.

The employment of generalized reinforcers has a number of advantages over the use of primary reinforcers and secondary reinforcers (Kazdin and Bootzin, 1972, p. 343). They act to bridge the delay between the response desired and obtaining primary or secondary reinforcers later; thus, reinforcement can follow the response very closely at any time, in almost any setting, increasing the chance of strengthening a behavior. Generalized reinforcers also maintain performance over an extended period of time until a back-up reinforcer can be dispensed. Classroom children, for example, can be given points or chips for their work as they do it and then exchange them for trinkets at the end of the day. When tokens are given they do not interrupt ongoing behaviors nearly as much as primary reinforcers because they are not consumable or distracting as are food and desirable items. The client is also less likely to become satiated with generalized reinforcers because they can be used to purchase a wide variety of things, some of which should be reinforcing when others are not.

The use of tangible, generalized reinforcers has some advantages over the intangible types as was mentioned earlier. In programs where mechanical dispensing machines are modified to accept tokens, the tangible variety is a necessity. When having identifiable tokens for each client is helpful (or necessary), specially made or modified, durable tokens are desirable. Usually the most useful token is some form of chip, made of durable mate· rial and capable of being individualized. In classrooms, however, some sort of point reinforcer may be readily adapted.

THE PAYOFFS: BACK-UP REINFORCERS. Token reinforcement will be of little use if the tokens cannot be spent on desirable items or activities. The products that may be purchased are called *back-up reinforcers*. The importance of having a wide variety of desirable back-up reinforcers cannot be overemphasized. A token program is unlikely to get off the ground, or continue to operate effectively without them or if they lose their value. The tokens *must have* some worthwhile redemptive value.

Almost anything is a potential back-up reinforcer. Primary reinforcers, such as food of all sorts (including treats, candy, soda pop, and so on), are obvious examples. In mental institutions it is common for patients to pay tokens for meals, and candy is popular in both child and adult groups. However, secondary reinforcers are usually more readily available and provide a much wider variety of possibilities. They are also less likely to cause negative reactions from outsiders and clients. For example, most people in our culture can more easily accept that a client be deprived of viewing a movie because he cannot afford it than that he be deprived of a meal. If it is possible to set up a token store, all sorts of items, from toothpaste and cosmetics to radio and TV rentals, or the right to go to the store itself, can be made available for purchase. Many kinds of activities and privileges are potential back-up reinforcers: renting a nice bed for the night, playing a radio, being alone, going to a dance, reduced probation time, seeing a therapist, clothing, leadership positions, attending religious activities, an outing, staying up after curfew, smoking, visiting a girlfriend during classtime, or almost anything that is available to the particular setting. It is a challenge to the counselor to discover back-up reinforcers, a challenge that predicts certain failure if not adequately met.

Several techniques have proved helpful in discovering back-up reinforcers. The simplest one is to ask the clients what they would like. You will quickly learn that people have different preferences, though some things will have wide popularity across a given population. It has seemed especially helpful to involve adolescent clients in establishing back-up reinforcers or, for that matter, in establishing the entire program. A primary developmental task for adolescents is to gain independence, and the values of their peers are usually quite important. As they work on determining the particulars of a program, acting as a consultant rather than an authority can be an important step toward success.

Observing what clients do will also provide important information about potential reinforcers. What do they do in their free time? Noting what a particular person chooses to do can direct you to activities that may be especially reinforcing for him. Your observations should lead you to activities and items that are worth trying as back-up reinforcers.

The *Premack principle* is especially useful when things that a person likes are not readily observable. Some people seem not to care about anything; nothing seems to reinforce them. The Premack principle states that any event which is more frequent than another will act as a reinforcer for the less frequent event. As an example, assume that a mental patient sits by himself in a particular chair much of the time but rarely enters into conversations. If increasing social interactions are considered helpful

for him, you could try permitting him to sit in the chair for fifteen minutes at a time, but only after he has engaged in conversation with another patient for at least two minutes. The time
that he must interact before he is allowed to sit in the chair can
gradually be increased. In general, any behaviors you observe that
occur at a high frequency will be potential back-up reinforcers.

Personal ingenuity is very important as well. Take the attitude
that anything is possible even though the resources for reinforcers in your setting seem unlimited. Taking the attitude that
you have complete freedom and unlimited resources, ask yourself what kinds of things would be reinforcing to your clients?
A brainstorming session with the staff and/or the clients is often
enlightening. In a high school classroom, for example, you might
think of things like a new car, not going to school, sexual activities, drugs, smoking, hitting the principal, and other possibilities
that appear impossible to permit. Nevertheless, you are probably
identifying important needs and the closer your reinforcers approach these, the more likely they are to be effective. You may not
be able to furnish a new car, but you may be able to offer the
privilege of special parking permits on campus, using the car
during otherwise restricted times, obtaining donations of car ac-
cessories from local car agencies, a free day's use of a donated
car from a car rental agency, and so on. The sky's the limit if
you let yourself go, forget all the rules, and expend as much effort as possible in coming as close as you can to the ideal.

MANAGING REINFORCERS. Once you have tokens and back-up reinforcers there are several ways to employ them. The most common method is called *positive reinforcement*. In brief, a client
is positively reinforced when he receives a reinforcer after he
makes a response: a child completes an arithmetic problem and
the teacher gives him a token, a mental patient makes his bed and
receives a token, an adolescent brings home a positive report
from his algebra teacher and receives ten points. In theory, the
frequency of a response that is followed by reinforcement
should increase. *Therefore, if it is desirable to build a behavior,
positive reinforcement is the proper method of administration.*
Positive reinforcement has the added advantage that the rein-

forced behavior is associated with a success experience, making it more likely that the client will develop a generally positive attitude toward similar activities. A child who has experienced many failures in the classroom may develop a negative attitude in general toward school, but the chances are that his attitude will change if he is placed in a classroom where the material is presented at a level that he is capable of performing and he is consistently reinforced for doing so. A token program can be set up entirely on a positive reinforcement concept. Behaviors that are desirable are reinforced while undesirable behaviors are ignored and often decrease automatically as their reinforced competitors increase. If a child is reinforced for sitting at his desk, running around the classroom should decrease without any direct attention to it; that is, it is impossible for him to run around if he is sitting at his desk. Desirable behaviors are frequently alternatives to undesirable ones.

Another common way to use reinforcers is to take them away from the client, a procedure that most lay persons would view as punishment. The theoretical differences between punishment (an aversive stimulus following a response) and negative reinforcement (the removal of an aversive stimulus when a response occurs) are often only of academic interest. In fact, it is very difficult to differentiate these concepts at times because people think and anticipate the consequences of their actions, making it difficult to know whether it is the removal of the threat of punishment (negative reinforcement) or the punishing act itself that is effective. At any rate, the common applications of these principles are usually thought of in two ways: paying for a response, *response cost,* or charging for a response, *fining.* Both methods are *employed for reducing behaviors that are considered undesirable.*

Response cost simply means that a person is allowed to pay for doing or not doing something. The child who is being paid for sitting at his desk, for example, would have to pay if he wishes to leave it. Response cost may be employed for positive behaviors that the client does not perform; if a patient is being paid two tokens for sweeping the floor, he would have to pay two tokens if he did not.

Charging tokens as fines is usually reserved for behaviors that are not permitted. Such behaviors are often the same as those that are against the law in our society, for example destroying property, theft, physical abuse, and cursing. Another characteristic of fines is that they are usually (and should be to be effective) severe. Rather than fining a person one or two tokens for destroying property, he should be fined twenty or twenty-five tokens, perhaps as much as he can make in a day or two. Fining is used primarily for suppressing especially undesirable behaviors. A mental patient, who "hallucinates" (says socially inappropriate things), may be fined early in his program in order to suppress that response so that more appropriate ones, like speaking sensibly, can be reinforced. Fining should be used carefully. It can create difficult situations for the staff and cause the client to develop a negative attitude toward the program. It is easy for the staff to become involved in a power struggle with a patient over fines. He may become angry about the fine, find himself deep "in the red" as regards tokens, and refuse to do anything. The staff is then in the bind of fining or punishing him in some way further or backing down and removing the fine. Even though fines have these disadvantages, staff members are often prone to employ them as a major means of control. Punishment is a common method of control in our society and it is also rather easily administered. It "fits" the value systems of many people, including staff, and is reinforcing to a staff member who is angry over a client's negative behavior. Nevertheless, it is not an efficient way to create stable changes and can reduce the effectiveness of a program because of the animosity it causes within the client population. *Use fining sparingly and with careful planning. Always* try more positive alternatives before resorting to heavy fining.

Determining the number of tokens to be given or paid for specific behaviors is nearly always an ongoing process. The overall economic distribution within the system must be frequently monitored to avoid an excess of tokens being earned compared to those being spent. Tokens obviously lose some of their value as motivators if clients have an excess to spend. Why should they work for more when they can go on a paid vacation? Having excess tokens is not necessarily negative, however; in fact, as long as desirable back-up reinforcers are available for a savings account, it can add a positive flavor to the entire program. As examples, delinquents could save excess earnings to purchase fewer days in detention or time on probation, weekly prizes could be set up for the top earners in a classroom, and many other things are possible to make savings accounts worthwhile. On the other hand, a depression in the economy is not desirable. If a client performs at a reasonable rate he should receive reasonable benefits.

The administrator of the program can change the economic balance of the economy by merely raising prices, decreasing incomes, or some combination thereof. But, a word of caution is in order. Arbitrary changes from the top can cause discontent in the population, especially when the changes look more like penalties than adjustments. Ideally, the overall balance should be considered carefully at the start of the program so that only minor adjustments are needed as it progresses.

The amount an individual receives for specific behaviors should be determined in relation to the importance they are believed to hold for him. A child who is often truant should be paid a high percentage of his possible earnings for going to school and much less for things like taking out the garbage. The same is true for response costs: higher charges should be made for behaviors most deleterious to the client's adjustment, lower charges for less deleterious behaviors. More will be said about individualized programs in the next section; but remember, adjusting and deciding prices are important and require a good deal of work on the part of the staff.

Target Behaviors or What to Change

The crux of any token economy is changing behavior in predetermined directions. The behaviors decided upon are called *target behaviors*. You will try to increase the frequency of some, for example the number of days a truant child spends in school; you will try to decrease some, like the amount of crazy talk from a mental patient; and you will try to establish others, such as speech in a mute child. Indeed, if there is no need for changes in behavior, there is no need for the program.

MAKING BEHAVIOR OBSERVABLE. It is this simple. If you cannot define a behavior so that you and others can agree upon when it occurs (or does not occur), it is unlikely that you will be able to change it in any systematic way. It is extremely important that you continuously strive toward a clear understanding of target behaviors.

The *first step* is to define whatever you wish to change in terms of observable behavior. People characteristically speak in trait or dispositional terms, such as, "He's too aggressive, depressed, schizoid, hyperactive, or dependent"; "He has a low self-esteem or low ego strength"; "He's not self-actualized"; "He's hostile"; "He's anxious"; and many others. These terms are too vague to be useful in a token program. It is your job to pin down the specific behaviors that lead someone to attribute these traits and dispositions to a person. If a psychiatrist says John's trouble is low self-esteem, you must clarify what he means in behavior. You ask, "What sorts of things does he *do* that leads you to this conclusion?" He may reply that John does not talk with his peers often enough, and that John says that he has no confidence in himself, does not do his school work, and has no hobbies. It becomes apparent that if John is to be judged as having high self-esteem he must 1) increase the amount of time he talks with his peers, 2) decrease saying that he has no confidence in himself, and/or increase saying he feels confident, 3) do his school work more often, and 4) take up some hobbies. You have the beginnings of a behavioral program for John.

Further specification of a behavior may be necessary before different observers (nurses, teachers' aides, etc.) can agree upon its occurrence. Take the example of a mental hospital patient who "paced." One nurse said he was pacing when he walked past the nurses' office more than three times in an hour, another said he paced when he stayed in the day room area and walked constantly, another said he paced almost anytime he was not sitting or standing still. By defining pacing as walking back and forth more than three times in a twenty-five foot distance, the nurses were able to reach high agreement on the amount of pacing they observed. The important point is that, once they agreed upon what pacing was, contingencies (such as a response cost of two tokens each time observed) could be applied to pacing in a consistent way.

The *next step* in specifying behavior is to evaluate its frequency which means recording it. Recording forms that are easily portable and easily available to all staff members are necessary. The behavior to be observed is clearly described in writing with spaces for check marks next to it (see Schaefer and Martin, 1969, for examples). Some behaviors can be observed every time they occur, like "having bed made before 8:30 A.M." Others, like the "pacing" example above, would require constant surveillance and an impractical amount of staff time to detect every time they occur. A *time-sampling* procedure may be used for these behaviors to bring the staff time within reasonable limits. The person is observed at set time intervals, say once each hour for five minutes, and the behavior is recorded if it occurs. Regardless of the method of observation, the frequency of the behavior over a given time interval is obtained. In the foregoing examples, it might be noted that after a one-week observation period 60 percent of the beds on a ward were made by 8:30 A.M., and that the patient paced during 50 percent of the time-sampled observations. The time-sampling data also has the advantage of discovering at what times during the day the frequency of the patient's pacing is highest, information that may suggest positive changes in his program.

Keeping track of behavior is a *must* if the therapeutic plans are to be evaluated. The only way that you can know for certain whether the methods you are trying are working, is by observing the changes in the frequencies of behavior. If a negative behavior is decreasing, or a positive behavior is increasing, great! Continue your approach. If not, *change it!*

In order to evaluate your effectiveness you must know the frequency of a behavior *before* you started to intervene. The frequency of a behavior before you start to apply tokens is called its *base line*. Base lines should always be collected in a well-managed program. The base lines for many behaviors are obtained before a token economy is started, but when new behaviors are to be incorporated in an ongoing program, base lines should be obtained for them as well.

The span of time over which base lines are taken will vary with the initial frequency of the behavior. Behaviors that occur quite often may be observed for only a few days (talking out in class is an example); less frequent ones, like making the bed, must be followed over a longer period. The main point is to obtain a stable measure of the behavior's frequency. To evaluate the effectiveness of whatever you decide to do, you compare the base line frequency to the frequency of your observations over the same amount of time after you begin.

GROUP AND INDIVIDUAL TARGET BEHAVIORS. As mentioned earlier, a token economy is quite appropriate when the entire client population may benefit from the same behavioral changes or when certain client behaviors are helpful in running the institution. On the other hand, individualized programs may be incorporated readily into a token economy so that each client's needs are more appropriately met.

Group behaviors are nearly always incorporated to some extent in a token system. Quite frequently they benefit the overall goals of the setting by making it more efficient. In an educationally handicapped class, for example, all students may be reinforced for arriving on time. If the children are all ready to begin work each day, the teacher can be more efficient in his job. It is not difficult to think of many other activities that would allow the staff more time at their professional functions. The particular activities will vary, of course, depending on the setting: being on time for meals in a mental hospital, cleaning up materials in a sheltered workshop, handing in homework assignments on time in school, and many others. Another common class of group behaviors are those that disrupt learning or bring harm to others, like throwing articles in class, physical fights or loud yelling, destroying property, and others. These behaviors are usually fined.

There is no good reason that group behaviors cannot be dealt with on an individual basis as well. While all children may be paid for arriving on time, some may have a special problem with it; they can be paid a higher amount than usual to increase its frequency. Once they are arriving on time regularly, their pay can be reduced to the level of the others.

It is possible for a token economy to incorporate nothing but behaviors that are relevant for the entire population, but comprehensive programs nearly always individualize to some extent. *Individual target behaviors* permit the benefits of the program to be maximized for each client. A mental patient may perform all of the group behaviors but still spend much of his time saying strange things and avoiding other people. He is not disrupting the program and he may be little bother to the staff, but it is clear that his behavior will prevent him from functioning outside the institution. Since most patients do not say strange things or necessarily avoid others, it is appropriate to individualize the program for the patient who does. He can be paid for speaking sensibly and interacting with others and pay a response cost for "crazy" talk and being alone. When a specific behavior is deemed very important to the patient who appears very resistant to change, it can be made the only source of the patient's income. If this were the case in the foregoing example, the only way the patient could earn tokens would be by interacting with others and speaking sensibly. Individualization may be much less dramatic in many instances. Children usually require individualized lesson plans depending on their degrees of competence in different subject matters. Complete attention may be given to modifying the classroom behavior of some children before their academic achievement becomes the target for reinforcement.

Individualized programs require a constant evaluation of income and outflow. The amounts charged for back-up reinforcers as well as the token payments can all be varied to keep a person's program at a motivating level. A particular mental patient was highly adept at "conning" the staff and other patients into giving him tokens. Individualizing his tokens reduced this, but he could easily perform whatever general behaviors he wished to obtain enough tokens for his needs. The major reason he remained hospitalized was his "crazy" talk, and this had not reduced in frequency at all. An attempt was made to correct this by allowing him to earn tokens only when he spoke sensibly. This had some effect, but he did not seem to need many back-up reinforcers. He was able to earn enough tokens for his needs with a very low level of performance. The key was finally discovered in a staff conference when it was noted that the one thing he seemed to do with relish was to drink coffee. It was decided to set a high price on each cup of coffee he purchased. The frequency of his sensible talk rose dramatically after that. While a long way from the end of his program, he began steady progress toward discharge.

ESTABLISHING NEW BEHAVIORS. If a person is already able to produce a behavior, positive reinforcement will usually increase its frequency and response cost will usually decrease it. But what about behaviors that the client must learn from scratch? You cannot reinforce a retarded child for undressing himself if he cannot make the response, nor can you charge tokens for playing pool as a back-up reinforcer if a patient will not try it. Several methods are available for dealing with these sorts of difficulties.

For a behavior that is not available, like the retarded child undressing, a *shaping* technique may be employed. Shaping is basically the breaking down of a complex behavior into small incremental acts. Progressive strings of these acts are required before reinforcement is given, until the entire complex behavior can be performed. A number of responses are involved in undressing, for example. The simplest being taking hold of a shirt sleeve to pull it off. Many more small acts follow before a child has completely undressed himself. To teach undressing to a child who cannot do it, you would start by reinforcing his tug on the shirt. After he does that consistently he must not only tug but also pull it down over his shoulder before he is reinforced (food is often used as reinforcement with these children). The process continues with the child learning each step at a time, with the response becoming increasingly complex before he is reinforced. After he has learned the entire act, it may then be reinforced and dealt with like other established behaviors.

Many behaviors may be treated with shaping. Clues that shaping is needed are found in base line data. If the particular behavior has not been observed during base line observations, the chances are that it needs to be shaped. For example, if you decide to reinforce "sitting at the desk for fifteen minutes," but the child is never observed sitting for that long, it is a signal that you must begin at a lower level and build toward the fifteen-minute goal. Depending on the child, you may begin by reinforcing him when he is seated two minutes and gradually increase the time he must sit before he is reinforced.

If the clients understand language, shaping is often much faster when each step is verbally prompted, that is, when the person is told what is expected and then reinforced for each step as it is produced. It is a good idea to try prompting in most cases.

Modeling is another method to teach a new response. The person learns by watching another person perform an act—he learns through imitation. Staff or other clients may serve as models for clients. The client should try the response after it has been demonstrated. Reinforcing the person when he tries to imitate a desired response, even when he approximates it, is often a rapid method of teaching. The teacher should help by correcting inaccurate responses and by demonstrating correct ones.

Priming has been applied in discovering back-up reinforcers or in increasing their consumption. The implicit message is, "Try it. You'll like it!" Some clients are hesitant or indifferent toward items and activities that they might find reinforcing were they to try them. Thus, clients can be taken free of charge or even paid to go on outings, have their hair washed and set, go to religious services, given popcorn, and so on. Whatever reinforcing stimuli are present may be sampled by the individual, and they may then become a source of reinforcement for which he spends tokens. This procedure has worked best with clients who have not engaged in the activity before or for some time, although it tends to increase the consumption in those who have engaged in it rather frequently as well.

GENERAL PRINCIPLES TO FOLLOW. Adherence to the following points will go a long way in avoiding major problems in a token economy (Vernon, 1972):

1. Be certain that the client is capable of performing the behavior you wish to build. This means that it is best to start at a

level at which you are certain he can perform. Too difficult a task causes failure and the development of negative attitudes toward the program in general.

2. Be certain to give tokens only when the desired behavior is produced, and give them immediately after the response if at all possible. Verbal reinforcement and explanation are also helpful at the time of reinforcement. For example, "That's good, John! You've been sitting quietly."

3. You must have back-up reinforcers to value for all of the clients, obtainable only by token purchase. Avoid spontaneous gratuities like bonuses and gifts, but if they are to be implemented, use them in a thoughtful, systematic way.

4. Provide a suitable amount of tokens considering the time and effort involved in the behavior. All clients should receive tokens often, some of course will receive more than others. The idea is to *reinforce,* and that means there must be ample opportunity for earning.

5. Punishment should be minimized, especially in a setting like the classroom where you wish the child to develop a positive attitude toward school in general. In settings where clients tend to "settle in," like mental hospitals, it may be helpful to make it a not very desirable place to reside. Nevertheless, if the client has no reasonable alternative residence or you cannot find one for him, making him uncomfortable is of little value and less than humane.

6. Begin the program with continuous reinforcement and gradually move toward less frequent but larger payoffs. Phasing out tokens for clients as they reach predetermined levels of achieving, a merit system, can be useful for establishing "self-reinforced" behaviors.

STEPS IN SETTING UP A TOKEN ECONOMY. There are no hard and fast rules for establishing a program, but experience has led to some ideas about the most effective steps to follow:

1. Staff training. The way that staff training is handled can be crucial to the success of the program. In most cases the staff has had no formal exposure to behavioral management techniques, and training is necessary for them to do their jobs properly.

Training methods vary, but usually they employ the general run of teaching procedures (lectures, readings, films, demonstrations, etc.). It is highly desirable to provide additional reinforcement for the trainees if possible. The reinforcers, of course, will vary with the setting, like compensation time, bonus pay, and so forth. Teaching by example (modeling) and rehearsals (role playing) are effective methods to incorporate.

It is highly desirable for the staff to demonstrate their understanding of the principles involved and their ability to apply them appropriately *before* actual work with the clients begins. In settings where staff turnover is common, an in-service training program and supervision may be employed to teach them their duties before they begin working with clients. However, initial training is often not sufficient in itself. Ongoing evaluation of the staff member's performance will help them to maintain and improve their skills.

2. Establishing target behaviors. As described earlier, it is important to make the target behaviors as clear as possible before starting in order that reinforcement can be applied appropriately. Of course, a rigid program is not desirable and new target behaviors will arise as the program progresses.

3. Establishing reinforcers. The kind of tokens to be used are determined, and potential back-up reinforcers are decided upon. Again, variations will nearly always be introduced as the program progresses.

4. Beginning. The pay-offs and charges are established initially by the staff or in conjunction with the clients. The clients should be informed about the prices for target behaviors and back-up reinforcers, and a chart of these should be posted for easy reference. The program is then launched with the introduction of tokens. If individual programs are implemented at the outset, each person's program should be discussed with him and clarified. After the program is in operation, variations will be introduced as they become useful or necessary.

Common Problems and Suggestions

STAFF TRAINING. The importance of staff training has already been mentioned. Training can be difficult because attendants and

teachers often maintain maladaptive responses in clients by inadvertently reinforcing them. A child who throws a temper tantrum may be loved and held. Nurses smile at a mental patient
who says absurd things. In both cases, the positive responses to
the maladaptive behaviors maintain or strengthen them. An important aspect of training is to help staff become aware of how
they respond to their clients' actions. Role playing client behavior
and practicing appropriate responses to it are helpful. In many
cases, the therapist's "natural" responses to his client's behavior
will not be the most effective ones.

In hospitals, the usual nursing role of carrying out the doctor's
orders must be changed. In a token system nurses and attendants
are often required to make quick decisions about what to do with
a patient in order to reinforce a desired behavior immediately.
Group discussions about role changes can be helpful to encourage decision making and the feeling of being free to do it.

Many staff people have been trained to administer "tender-
loving-care." While positive attention can be an excellent reinforcer, the indiscriminant application of it can maintain undesired behaviors. Again, examples and discussions are helpful ways
to point up usefulness of positive attention when it is thought-
fully and systematically applied.

Some people may not be able to work in a token economy because of their professional orientation. People who have been
trained in other methods of psychotherapy (psychoanalysis or
client-centered therapy, for example) may find it very difficult to
change their ways of viewing behavior, and they can be very uncomfortable with the planned, active nature of a behavioral approach. It is probably better that these people be assigned elsewhere. Not only is the token program likely to suffer from their
participation, but they will be personally dissatisfied as well.

CLIENT RESISTANCE TO THE PROGRAM. The extent to which
client resistance is encountered is not clear. There is no reason to
believe that resistance will be encountered in all cases, especially
when a program has been planned with an emphasis on positive
reinforcement. However, because many of the back-up reinforcers were freely available before, it is not unusual to encounter
minor resistances at the beginning. Serious resistance is shown by

anger, complaints, disruptive behavior, requests for transfer, rule breaking, and impulsive acts.

The usual cause of resistance is the client's belief that he is being treated unfairly. Thus, one of the most general methods for avoiding resistance is to involve the client in the specifics of the program. The entire client group can be involved in setting up the initial costs and so forth, and complaints can be referred to that group for resolution. Contractual agreements can also be made with individual clients, with the result that he agrees with you about the expectations of his behavior. Employing clients in the routine duties of the system, like checking attendance and banking tokens also helps to involve them in the program. "Emphasis on patient responsibility for his own behavior, lack of coercion, contractual arrangements of programs, and client voice in matters relating to the program, all seem to mitigate against patient rebellion and the possibility of an unjust and oppressive system" (Kazdin and Bootzin, 1972, p. 346).

GENERALIZING BEHAVIOR TO NEW AND DIFFERENT SETTINGS. One of the difficulties encountered with token economies has been developing adaptive behavior that will continue in settings where tokens are not employed. While changing behavior in the token setting has some obvious advantages, long-range goals frequently call for more or less permanent changes in natural settings. Some of the methods that are employed to accomplish these goals will be discussed.

One approach is to teach only those behaviors that will continue to be reinforced in natural settings. Naturally occurring reinforcers, like social approval, praise, or money, take the place of tokens outside the institution in maintaining a response. Job skills are clear examples of naturally reinforced behaviors. Some natural reinforcers may not be reinforcing to some clients; for example, mentally retarded or autistic children may not respond to verbal praise. In such cases the reinforcement value of praise may be increased if it is constantly associated with tangible reinforcers. The child is praised each time he is given tokens, and gradually the tokens are faded out until praise itself is sufficient to maintain the behavior.

Gradual removal of token reinforcement has also been employed. Behaviors are consistently reinforced until they occur regularly, all the time associating other natural reinforcers with tokens (praise, privileges, peer approval, etc.). The frequency of token payment is then gradually reduced while substituting natural reinforcers. Tokens may also be faded by having the client spend increasingly longer periods of time outside the program. This allows him to perform in new stimulus conditions and to be in settings where natural reinforcers are presumably in operation.

It may also be helpful if stimulus conditions can be purposely set up to be as similar as possible to those that will be present in the natural environment. For example, a home-like room could be provided for teaching household skills to retardates. The more similar the training situation is to the client's natural setting, the more likely it is that his training will transfer.

Another possibility is to train relatives or foster parents in behavioral management techniques. In fact, a token system that is very similar to the one in the institution can be set up at home. Daily reports from a child's teacher can be traded for points at home, which in turn are redeemable for home privileges and reinforcing items.

Systematically delaying back-up reinforcement has also been employed to increase generalization. Tokens may be paid at a later time, say once a day or once a week, for certain behaviors, or there can be a delay between the time that tokens are received and the time they may be traded in for back-up reinforcers. Presumably, the delay is similar to many naturally occurring reinforcers, like grades, paychecks and days off, which increases the similarity between the token setting and the natural environment.

The last method to be discussed involves *self-reinforcement*. The client learns to deliver his own reinforcer after he performs adaptively. There is an obvious advantage to this technique because the person is able to monitor and maintain his behavior in many settings. The reader is referred to Watson and Tharp (1972) and Kanfer (1970) for more information on the wide variety of possibilities of self-reinforcement.

COMPLAINTS ABOUT TANGIBLE REINFORCERS. The complaints about tangible reinforcers range from philosophical objections to questioning the desirability of their behavioral effects. I will only summarize the problem here and refer the interested reader to O'Leary, Poulos, and Devine (1972) who have written a comprehensive article dealing with this issue.

A common complaint about tangible reinforcers is that they are bribes, that delivering them amounts to bribery. The term "bribe" carries negative connotations because of its primary dictionary meaning, "A reward that is given or promised for the purpose of perverting the judgment or corrupting the behavior of a person, especially a person of trust, like a public official." Clearly, this definition is not applicable to the use of tangible reinforcers in a token program. However, the secondary definition is relevant, "Something that serves to induce or influence a particular kind of conduct." Hence, in reply to the accusation of bribery, it is appropriate to state that token reinforcement is bribery only in the sense of its secondary meaning, that is for influencing conduct. They are employed in a definite attempt to change maladaptive and adaptive behavior, but not to induce corrupt or immoral behavior. Pointing out the similarity between the procedures of a token economy and the socially acceptable activity of working for pay may also help to reduce the notion of bribery.

O'Leary, *et al.* (1972) respond to eleven kinds of complaints. I have listed them below so that in the event you should encounter them, you will recognize that they have been dealt with in that article:

1. A person should not be reinforced for something that is an established duty or requirement of daily living. This is basically a moral evaluation of the kinds of behaviors that are being reinforced.

2. A person should perform an activity because he wants to (or feels obligated to), not because he is externally rewarded. This is a complaint based on the value of intrinsic vs. extrinsic reward.

3. A reinforcement program teaches greed and avarice.

4. The person receiving tangible reinforcers will learn to use tangibles to control others.

5. Rewarding a child to be good will teach him to be bad. That is, he will do bad things so that he will be given good things when he is good.

6. The person giving tangibles comes to rely almost exclusively on them and loses, or fails to develop, more desirable means of control.

7. There will be adverse effects on other persons, like siblings, classmates, and fellow patients. This complaint is usually aimed at individualized programs or settings where only a few clients are on a token program.

8. The behavior will occur only where reinforcers are given or until they are stopped. This complaint is aimed at the problem with generalizing of behavior that was discussed earlier.

9. The person will come to depend on tangible reinforcers and will not perform any appropriate behaviors without it. This complaint is aimed at the possibility of developing manipulative behavior, "I'll do it if you pay me."

10. "If-then" statements indicate that we doubt the client's ability to perform. "If you talk sensibly, then you will receive five tokens." The complaint also includes the negative aspects of continually prompting a behavior.

11. Tokens and back-up reinforcers interfere with learning, a complaint about the distracting effects of tangible reinforcers.

O'Leary, et al. (1972) recommend that "token programs using tangible, extrinsic reinforcers should be implemented *only after* other procedures of prompting and reinforcing with natural reinforcers have been tried (p. 7)." But, they also state that token programs may prove very helpful where other methods fail.

How Effective Are Token Economies?

Evaluating any form of treatment is no simple matter and it is beyond the scope of this chapter to discuss the many problems encountered in this sort of research. The reader who is interested in a detailed description of this topic is referred to Kazdin and Bootzin (1972) and to Kazdin's (1972) annotated bibliography.

CHANGE IN THE TOKEN ECONOMY SETTING. If your primary goals are to change behavior in a particular setting, like a classroom or workshop, the token economy has shown itself to be quite effective. The emphasis may be on modifying conduct in ways that increase learning efficiency, like changing classroom behavior to facilitate the teaching of academic skills in retarded or educationally handicapped children, learning job skills in a workshop setting, or decreasing disruptive behavior in a mental hospital. If the procedures and precautions that have been presented earlier are followed, you should expect a fairly high percentage of positive gain. Although the data are not precise, you can expect that 80 to 90 percent of the clients will change in the directions you wish, while 10 to 15 percent may not be effected at all.

There appears to be three ways that clients (based on mental hospital patients primarily) typically respond. Some settle right in and make rapid, stable gains. Others will "test" the system before gaining and the level of performance that they reach will not be as high or stable as that of the first type. The last type never responds favorably. Unfortunately, there is no accurate way to predict which clients will respond in which way.

CHANGE OUTSIDE THE TOKEN SETTING. Sometimes the major goals of a program call for generalization of behavior to settings where tokens are not applied. *Stimulus generalization* is the technical term for this phenomenon. For example, a truant child learns to attend class in a juvenile detention facility. Will he attend class when he returns home? Similar goals are desirable in other client populations. In brief, evidence for stimulus generalization is lacking. There are relatively few studies so far that have addressed themselves specifically to this question. (As an exception, see Walker and Buckley, 1972.) Until more information is gathered, the *most reasonable approach is to plan stimulus generalization* by incorporating the methods that were discussed in the section dealing with "common problems and suggestions."

It is sometimes desirable that behaviors which are not directly dealt with will also be strengthened or weakened, *response generalization*. Most of the evidence on this point has been obtained with mental hospital patients, but few studies have made response generalization their primary focus. Patients in token systems, although not directly reinforced for the particular responses, are judged as less "apathetic," interacting more, and so on. In general, you would expect that the more similar the behaviors are to those being worked with, the more likely it is that they will be affected in the same way. If a particular disruptive response is being extinguished, like yelling in class, others similar to it, like talking in class, should weaken as well. However, in most programs the focus is on specific behaviors and response generalization is not hoped for or assumed; indeed, specifying behavioral change is one of the token economy's major advantages. Probably the most realistic position to take is to be pleased when desirable response generalization occurs, but not to depend upon it as long as behavioral specification is possible.

CONCLUDING REMARKS

The token economy is assuming a well-earned place as a rehabilitative and therapeutic modality. Its theoretical simplicity, however, can be misleading in regards to the complexities of practical implementation. An effective token program requires a good deal of preprogram planning and constant monitoring during its operation. It requires *time and effort* on the part of all staff. Embarking upon a token economy should not be taken lightly. Therapeutic decisions will often cause staff inconveniences, and the only reinforcement for the staff will be a client improvement. The effectiveness of methods that employ prompting and natural reinforcers should be evaluated first, but, when these have failed, a well-managed token economy should pay off in positive benefits.

REFERENCES

Ayllon, T., and Azrin, N.: *The Token Economy: A Motivational System for Therapy and Rehabilitation.* New York, Appleton, 1968.

Barrish, H. H., Saunders, M., and Wolf, M. M.: Good behavior game: Effects of individual contingencies for group consequences on disruptive behavior in a classroom. *Journal of Applied Behavior Analysis,* 2:119-124, 1969.

Christopherson, E. R., Arnold, C. M., Hill, D. W., and Quilitch, H. R.: The home point system: Token reinforcement procedures for application by parents of children with behavior problems. *Journal of Applied Behavioral Analysis, 5*:485-497, 1972.

Coe, W. C.: A behavioral approach to disrupted family interactions. *Psychotherapy: Research, Theory and Practice, 9*:80-85, 1972.

Hunt, J. G., Fitzhugh, L. C., and Fitzhugh, K. B.: Teaching "exit-ward" patients appropriate personal appearance by using reinforcement techniques. *Am J Ment Defic, 73*:41-45, 1968.

Kanfer, F. H.: Self-regulation: Research, issues, and speculations. In Neuringer, C., and Michael, J. L. (Eds.) : *Behavior Modification in Clinical Psychology*. New York, Appleton, 1970.

Kazdin, A. E.: The token economy: An annotated bibliography. *JSAS Catalog of Selected Documents in Psychology, 2*:22, 1972.

Kazdin, A. E., and Bootzin, R. R.: The token economy: An evaluative review. *Journal of Applied Behavioral Analysis, 5*:343-372, 1972.

O'Leary, D. K., and Drabman, R.: Token reinforcement programs in the classroom: A review. *Psychol Bull, 75*:379-398, 1971.

O'Leary, D. K., Poulos, R. W., and Devine, V. T.: Tangible reinforcers: Bonuses or bribes? *J Consult Psychol, 38*:1-8, 1972.

Phillips, E. L.: Achievement place: Token reinforcement procedures in a home-style rehabilitation setting for "predelinquent" boys. *Journal of Applied Behavioral Analysis, 1*:213-223, 1968.

Schaefer, H. A., and Martin, P. L.: *Behavioral Therapy*. New York, McGraw, 1969.

Tyler, V. O., and Brown, G. D.: Token reinforcement of academic performance with institutionalized delinquent boys. *J Educ Psychol, 59*:164-168, 1968.

Vernon, W. M.: *Motivating Children: Behavior Modification in the Classroom*. New York, HR&W, 1972.

Walker, H. M., and Buckley, N. K.: Programming generalization and maintenance of treatment effects across time and cross settings. *Journal of Applied Behavioral Analysis, 5*:209-224, 1972.

Watson, D., and Tharp, R.: *Self-directed Behavior: Self-modification for Personal Adjustment*. Monterey, Calif., Brooks-Cole, 1972.

Zimmerman, J., Stuckley, T. E., Garlick, B. J., and Miller, M.: Effects of token reinforcement on productivity in multiply handicapped clients in a sheltered workshop. *Rehabil Lit, 30*:34-41, 1969.

ANNOTATED FILM LISTING

Achievement Place, Kansas University Film Bureau, 1970, 30 min., black and white.

Demonstrates the application of a token system in a foster home for predelinquent boys, ages 11-16. Includes work with the school and family.

An Individual Behavior Modification Program, Dr. Jacqueline Montgomery, Camarillo State Hospital, Camarillo, Calif., 14 min., color.

Used for training hospital technicians. Shows base-lines, charting, etc. for individualizing the token program.

Behavior Analysis Classroom, Kansas University Film Bureau, 1970, 20 min., color.

Shows "Follow Through" classrooms employing token systems and behavioral analysis. Parents are used to supplement the teachers.

Born to Succeed, Appleton-Century-Crofts Films, series of two films, 30 min. each, color.

Demonstrates teaching the concept of numbers (reel 1) and arithmetic (reel 2) using various operant techniques. Not based on a token economy but demonstrates important principles.

Operant Conditioning—Token Economy, Dr. Jacqueline Montgomery, Camarillo State Hospital, Camarillo, Calif., 40 min., color.

Film used for training hospital technicians in applying the token economy.

Operation Behavior Modification, Kansas University Film Bureau, 1967, 40 min., black and white.

A comprehensive behavioral program including a token program for placing institutionalized, trainable retarded girls in the community (Mimosa Cottage).

Reinforcement Therapy, American Medical Association Film Library, Chicago, 35 min., black and white.

Demonstrates token economy in a retarded classroom and a mental hospital. Also includes shaping speech in autistic children.

Teaching With Tokens, Kansas University Film Bureau, 1970, 8 min., color.

Primarily a training film for preschool teachers showing how tokens are used on a one-to-one basis.

Token Economy: Behaviorism Applied, Communications Research Machines (CRM) Films, Del Mar, Calif., 20 min., color.

B. F. Skinner discusses the application of his theories. Demonstrates a token economy with delinquent and retarded populations.

The Undifferentiated Lump, Stanfield House, Santa Monica, Calif., 1972, 10 min., color.

Demonstrates shaping in a natural setting where a professor shapes a student's verbal reports.

Who Did What to Whom? Research Press Co., Champaign, Ill., 17 min., color.

A film with a leader's guide to demonstrate four basic principles: positive reinforcement, negative reinforcement, extinction, punishment. Shows examples of human interactions with leader led discussion throughout.

CHAPTER III

MODELING IN PREVOCATIONAL TRAINING

KENNETH BARKLIND

••

Modeling
Discussion
Summary
References

••

MODELING

T HE MOST DIRECT, common-sense and effective way to teach is to demonstrate, show, or give an example of the skill or item of knowledge that is new or novel to the client. This chapter is written to explore the various aspects of modeling in prevocational training.

Modeling has been referred to as imitation learning, observational learning, vicarious learning, no trial learning, and matched dependent learning, to suggest various aspects of modeling phenomena and attempts to explain its mechanisms. Modeling involves the learner or client observe a model or teacher enact or perform the behavior or skill.

There are three general effects that apparently result from modeling: (A) acquisition of new skills and novel behavior, (B) inhibition or disinhibition of socially prohibitive behavior and (C) elicitation of socially neutral behavior that had been previously acquired.

A. Acquisition of New Behavior (Skill and Social):

It would be difficult to suggest a more effective, concrete method of introducing new skills than by demonstration or modeling of the skill (O'Connor, 1973). This would be especially true in providing prevocational training for clients with inability to follow instructions or difficulty in orientation to learning a skill.

Conventional behavior modification shaping techniques would suggest (a) an initial blind or random trial-and-error learning process, (b) subsequent successive approximation to the execution of the skill, and (c) final criterion achievement after many differentially rewarded (each closer approximation rewarded and lapse in learning nonrewarded) trials. Typically it would be either very expensive or very dangerous to allow random behavior in the use of complex and expensive machinery or in handling sharp, hot, heavy or fast moving materials, tools or implements, circumstances often found in industrial or commercial settings, in industrial arts classrooms, and in sheltered workshops.

It boggles the imagination to think of trying to teach social skills involving subtle and complex series of behavior without demonstration or modeling by the instructor. Role playing gives the client practice in matching or imitating the appropriate social behavior as shown by the instructor. For instance, it would be difficult to teach proper behavior that the client should show during an employment interview without demonstration. It is difficult to give credence to a process of shaping and differential reinforcement in teaching such a skill. On the other hand, talking about the appropriate behavior or giving verbal instructions on how to act would typically be inadequate for many clients needing prevocational training. Modeling or imitation learning provides an effective alternative to behavioral shaping and to verbal instruction.

Modeling can serve to focus the attention of the client on critical cues or aspects of the skill or behavior to be learned. The behavior to be imitated can be presented to the client especially well on video tape or sound film. The camera could focus on critical cues, and the modeling of complex sequences of skilled behavior could be slowed down and/or repeated on video tape or film. Modeling can be utilized in the acquisition of a wide variety of prevocational and technical skills and various complex social skills and can be effective presented either by live actors or by film or video tape.

Modeling techniques are often used for the following operations:

Industrial

Safe operation of machines that cut, shear, grind, burn, stamp or perform other operations

Use of hand tools

Disassembly and assembly procedures

Packaging operation

Food Service

Dishwashing machine operation

Sanitary food handling procedures

Operation of cash register

Cleaning stoves, ovens, food mixers, etc.

Hospital

Bathing patients

Changing beds

Nursing care of bedsores

Taking oral and anal body temperature

Safe operation of wheelchairs and stretchers

Cleaning of hospital rooms with minimal diffusion of dust

Custodial

Use of common hand tools

Procedures in changing fluorescent lighting elements

Proper use of ladders and scaffolds

Use of cleaning equipment (buffers, vacuum cleaners)

Social

Applying for a job—interview behavior

Learning to manage hostility from fellow workers or peers

Learning how to meet new people

Learning to behave appropriately at social functions

Modeling is also a potent mechanism involved in learning social behavior. Behavior modeled by teachers, vocational instructors, and peers has a decisive effect on how students or clients learn new behavior.

Some important factors influencing the efficacy of modeling are:

1. The degree to which the student or client perceives the model as similar to himself.

2. The extent to which the vocational instructor or workshop foreman is perceived as possessing a high degree of competence and status.

3. The degree to which the model controls resources of reward, benefits, or makes important decisions about the client.

4. The degree to which the teacher, or shop supervisor, has been perceived as nutrient or supportive in the past.

5. The use of more than one model exhibiting the appropriate target behavior (Bronfronbrenner, 1970).

6. The specificity and relatedness to training goals of the behavior shown by the model.

7. The degree to which the model's exhibitive has been rewarded.

These factors would suggest that a deliberate effort should be made to have instructors who can gain some identification and respect from the students or clients. Those models who conform in some respects to popular ideals of society (movie stars, rock singers, professional athletes, etc.) would have the most impact on the client's behavior. For instance, a young shop foreman who plays amateur sports might be more effective in modeling appropriate shop behavior than an older, low-status industrial trainer. This would be especially true if the older foreman has little identification with the clients or students. Instructors who show concern for interest in, and support of clients will influence client behavior more through modeling than those who don't.

Modeling can also produce negative effects on training or rehabilitation. Clients who attend rehabilitation facilities where other clients or students model inappropriate behavior will imitate this behavior. Many parents are reluctant to send their sons or daughters to special education or rehabilitation facilities for this reason. Peer modeling and imitation of unconstructive behavior, are among the most difficult management problems in rehabilitation or habilitation.

B. Inhibition or Disinhibition Effects

Modeling not only promotes the growth of new behavior but strengthens or weakens previously learned ways of behavior. Modeling is especially helpful in decreasing the likelihood of immature, destructive, or disruptive social behavior. In other words, modeling can have an inhibitory effect with previously learned, but undesirable, social behavior.

The way that modeling can inhibit behavior is to have the clients observe the model exhibit socially disapproved behavior and be punished or nonrewarded for it. Another method is to have a model, of whom the clients disapprove, exhibit the socially unacceptable behavior. Many studies show that children show less fighting and arguing after witnessing mild punishment of models who exhibit aggressive behavior. Students or clients who are popular, or hold high status among classmates or fellow workers, have the potential of inhibiting or disinhibiting social behavior of the entire class or workshop. If these clients or students exhibit or model undesirable behavior that is either rewarded or not punished, you can expect a ripple effect (Kounin, 1970); other clients or students would certainly be disinhibited from showing undesirable behavior. If, however, this modeling of undesirable behavior is not rewarded or receives a mild punishment or results in "time out" procedures, the ripple effect will reduce the outbreak of undesirable behavior among other students or clients.

Some behaviors to be inhibited are:

Aggressive behavior
   Fighting, fisticuffs, pulling hair
   Arguing
   Defying authority
Cleanliness
   Littering
   Spitting
   Belching and flatulence
   Nose picking
Vocal
   Poorly modulated speaking (loud-soft)
   Whistling during work or eating
   Loud noises
   Too forceful speech
   Irrelevant content of speech during discussions or instruction
Public Sexual Behavior
   Masturbation

Hugging and kissing
Petting

C. Eliciting Effect

There are many behaviors in the student's or client's repertoire that one would wish to elicit or make more predominant in his work behavior. The modeling of these behaviors serves to heighten the frequency of their occurrence. Some of the behaviors that are considered here are:

Seeking help from shop foremen
Showing acts of courtesy
Manifesting altruistic and helpful behavior to peers
Encouragement, friendliness and cheerfulness to others
Putting away tools at completion of the task

Elicitation effects are differentiated from inhibition in that in the latter we are dealing with behavior that has strong social inhibition. In practical terms, inhibition refers to having a model perform inappropriate social behavior and be punished for it (ridiculed, scolded, etc.). Elicitation is modeling to reinforce previously learned pro-social behavior.

Both techniques are seen as being especially important in promoting or discouraging certain social behavior among groups of people. The focus is on classroom or shop management of prevocational trainees, students, or sheltered workshop clients. These techniques of group management become very important in training situations where there is high velocity or turnover. Vocational rehabilitation facilities that serve clients who show socially pathological behavior or have severe emotional or adjustment difficulties would have a special need to self-consciously or explicitly employ these techniques.

Research (Bandura, 1969) indicates that certain client characteristics are important in the use of behavior modification in training and social control. The characteristics that make for greater modeling effects are:

1. Previous history or client experience of being rewarded for imitating the model's behavior. Students would be trained to imitate or match the behavior of the model by standard techniques of behavior modification.

2. Clients, characterized as being dependent or soliciting affection, attention, close physical contact or help in doing tasks, are especially prone to behavior modification through modeling. The student is especially sensitive to the behavior of the shop foreman or instructor. The instructor might also reward the client's peers for modeling appropriate behavior. The dependent client would be especially aware of this contingency and would imitate the behavior of the favored peer. This technique is effective in dealing with the "attention getting" behavior of troublesome clients.

3. The anxious client who may show apprehensiveness upon entering or enrolling in an unfamiliar training program would be especially vulnerable to imitating or matching the behavior of instructor and student peers. The astute rehabilitation professional would be wise to take advantage of this phenomena. He would arrange for the new client to be put into contact with instructors or client peers who model the most adequate and socially appropriate behavior.

4. Clients with high vocational or educational achievement motivation imitate modeled behavior to a higher degree than those with lower achievement aspirations. This phenomena should present a golden opportunity to model appropriate skills and behavior to one's eager clients. Learning should be rapid and progress continuous in the rehabilitation process under these circumstances.

5. Flanders (1968) indicates that there may be some interaction between client or observer characteristics and instructor or model attributes. For instance, angry and authoritarian students imitate aggressive behavior more than less angry or nonauthoritarian clients. This might present an opportunity or make it necessary to assign hostile clients to shop foremen or instructors who do not manifest aggressive behavior. If the instructor or rehabilitation professional is aware of modeling effects, a teacher with an authoritarian personality or teaching style may be effective in modeling appropriate work-oriented or other social behavior to clients with authoritarian or ethnocentric outlooks.

DISCUSSION

What is suggested here is that there are both limitations and opportunities in modeling or imitation learning because of teacher and student characteristics and because of combinations of teacher-student attributes. There is also the prospect that model-observer attributes would also interact with the specific behavior to be learned, inhibited, or elicited to create unexpected results. What begins as a fairly simple, common-sense, and direct matter becomes complicated and abstract. A search through the literature indicates that little has been done to determine the characteristics of modeling, observational learning, or imitation in rehabilitation (or habilitation) settings.

There is plentiful indication in everyday observation and in the research literature (see references for documentation) that some phenomenon such as imitation, identification, modeling, or matched dependent learning, exists, and that it has considerable effect on learning and social behavior among individuals and groups.

Many learning theorists and behavior modification practitioners assert that imitation or observational learning is an epi-phenomenon, or could be experienced by a basic stimulus response paradigm (Baer *et al.*, 1967) but rehabilitation professionals do not have the leisure to wait to decide the true nature of modeling. They must be aware of this phenomenon and attempt to exploit it in their rehabilitation efforts on behalf of their clients.

It would seem natural to consider it as another tool in the armamentarium of learning theory approaches to rehabilitation. It could be used alone and in combination with other techniques such as precision teaching, token economics, extinction procedures, and desensitization.

Some rather amazing results have been demonstrated with combinations of techniques. Morin (1972) showed that video tape presentation of students becoming relaxed (modeling relaxation) accelerated the lowering of test anxiety during desensitization of other groups of students before examinations.

SUMMARY

Modeling or imitation learning provides an efficient means of learning new or novel skills and social behavior, as well as an effective means of regulating previously acquired behaviors. Instructors are live models whose own behaviors set an example of how their clients should act. Influential peer group leaders also exert a great effect on the learning of skills and the performance of previously learned social behavior. Little serious thinking has been done on managing peer modeling influences in rehabilitation facilities. The use of video tape or motion projection presentation of models is just becoming explicitly utilized in educational settings.

Modeling procedures have three basic effects, (1) the acquisition or establishment of new or novel behavior; (2) the inhibition of socially inappropriate existent behaviors or (when modeling effects are ignored or inappropriately applied) the disinhibition or release of socially inappropriate behavior; and (3) the elicitation or facilitation of socially acceptable actions already in the repertoire of the observer or client.

Modeling phenomenon is seen as an important factor in the rehabilitation process. The practitioner ignores it at his own peril. Whether or not modeling or observational learning can be explained or predicted in terms of a S-R paradigm is an important but unanswered question. However, the rehabilitation professional must deal with it as best he can because of its everyday effect on the rehabilitation of his clients. Modeling can be combined with other behavior modification techniques to implement effective rehabilitation programs.

REFERENCES

Baer, D. M., Peterson, R. F. and Sherman, J. A.: The development of limitation by reinforcing behavioral similarity to a model. *J. of Experimental Behavior, 10:*405-416, 1967.

Bandura, A.: *Principles of Behavior Modification.* New York, HR&W, 1969.

Bronfenbrenner, U.: *Two Worlds of Childhood—U.S. and U.S.S.R.* New York. Russell Sage, 1970.

Flanders, J. A.: A review of research on imitative behavior. *Psychol Bull, 69:*316-337, 1968.

Kounin, J.: *Discipline and Group Management in Classrooms.* New York, HR&W, 1970.

O'Connor, Robert: Relative efficacy of modeling, shaping and combined procedures for modification of social withdrawal. In Fank, Cyril and Wilson, G. T., (Eds.) : *Annual Review of Behavior Therapy.* New York: Brunner-Mazel, 1973.

CHAPTER IV

PEER GROUP INFLUENCE IN BEHAVIOR MODIFICATION OF THE MENTALLY RETARDED

LAWRENCE C. HARTLAGE

••

••

INTRODUCTION

IN THE PRECEDING chapters there has been a discussion of modeling and token economy programs used in behavior modification programs with the mentally retarded which are valuable in shaping specific work behaviors.

The involvement of peer influences as an aid in behavior modification programs with the mentally retarded offers an important new dimension in the total rehabilitation of these clients, in that it affords a powerful and effective tool for shaping social and interpersonal behaviors. Although specific job skills are necessary for the gainful employment of a retarded worker, it is his social adjustment, as reflected by his relationships with his co-workers and supervisors, which will likely determine how successful he will be in retaining his employment. Teaching the mentally retarded worker to be both sensitive and responsive to peer influences and reinforcers makes it much more likely that he will develop sufficient social skills to be accepted by his employers, co-workers, and social peers.

A major problem faced by most mentally retarded work trainees or vocational candidates involves their inability to generalize from one skill to another or to apply what they have learned in one setting to another different setting. For specific, fairly circumscribed, and well-defined job skills, this limitation can be overcome or at least minimized by thorough training and careful job placement. Social situations, on the other hand, are rarely well-defined or even similar, and their ambiguity presents the mentally retarded worker with greater difficulty than learning the specific requirements of a given job. The lack of facility in generalizing from one setting to another, common among retarded clients, presents difficulty to the counselor or rehabilitation worker attempting to help develop social skills in retarded workers, since the more traditional counseling approaches depend heavily on the ability of the client to take social skills acquired from his counselor during a circumscribed counseling session and generalize them to a broader social setting. Although traditional didactic counseling can be of some help in imparting specific information or in helping to modify a given behavior, it does not necessarily enable the retarded client to generalize this information or behavior to other social contexts. Similarly, nondirective approaches to counseling depend on the client's being able to make or at least understand generalizations from his own feelings or percepts to other situations; thus, the effectiveness of short-term client-centered approaches to counseling is limited as an aid to preparing the retarded client to function effectively in social situations.

The use of a group counseling approach, on the other hand, allows the mentally retarded client to try out new ideas and behaviors in a social setting and to get feedback from others about how they react to his ideas or behaviors. When we add to this group setting the powerful force of peer influence, we have available a tool for helping the retarded client learn how to cope with real social situations which he is likely to encounter. An illustration of the comparative utility of individual versus group approaches to modifying behavior in mentally retarded workers will probably be of value in helping to reinforce this point.

A COMPARISON OF PEER GROUP INFLUENCES VS. INDIVIDUAL TREATMENT

Although there have not been many attempts to directly compare the relative strengths of the use of peer group influences with individual approaches in behavior modification programs with the mentally retarded, the following project provides a good indication of the comparative strengths of each of the two approaches for modifying several social and behavioral variables.

The project involved twenty-seven adult mildly mentally retarded men and women who were involved in a behavior modification program aimed at preparing them for gainful employment. All of the clients were enrolled in a sheltered workshop work adjustment program. In addition to the traditional rehabilitation programs involved in work adjustment preparation, the clients received a videoplayback of some of their work behaviors to see if actually observing themselves on videotape might help them recognize those behaviors which needed changing. Each worker's workshop behavior was videotaped from a concealed camera room each day, and the next day the worker viewed approximately twenty minutes of playback from his previous day's filming. Measurements were taken each day of the worker's time spent not working, his productivity, his time spent socializing with other workers, and his distractability. To compare the individual versus peer group impact of watching this videoplayback, approximately half of the workers saw their own videoplayback alone, while the others watched their individual videoplayback in a group. The retarded clients who viewed their playback alone, made decided improvements but more in production rate than in social aspects of behavior. Those who watched their videoplayback in a group also improved on production but showed striking improvement on such social variables as socialization, distractability, and time not working, at a level statistically significantly greater than those who viewed alone. Observation of the clients in the group showed the superiority of the group approach, since there was considerable concern expressed by individuals whose inappropriate work behaviors were viewed by their peers. Workers would spontaneously promise other group members "Just you watch me tomorrow. I won't do that again," or exclaim, "There! Ain't that better than yesterday!" Of more importance, however, was the transfer of concern for group acceptance of on-camera behavior to the rest of the working day. Since the videoplayback sessions occupied a comparatively small part of their day but involved their working peer group, the retarded workers began to modify their behavior to seek peer acceptance after the first few days of videoplayback; after about three weeks the use of the playback was not needed. The retarded clients had become sufficiently concerned about peer group acceptance that this factor alone served as a sufficient incentive.

TARGET BEHAVIORS ESPECIALLY RESPONSIVE TO PEER GROUP INFLUENCES

Retarded workers who have acquired a sufficient level of job skills to be placed in competitive employment are often unable to maintain employment due to inadequate social skills, and a number of which are especially suitable for peer group influence prior to job placement. Helping the retarded worker develop these social skills in response to influences of other (retarded peer group) co-workers prior to employment can enhance his likelihood of maintaining these skills in response to influences from his (competitive job) co-workers.

Talkativeness. That retarded workers tend to carry on distracting, job-irrelevant conversations is a complaint often cited by workshop supervisors and competitive labor employers. This tendency can be much more effectively handled in group than in individual settings, since in an individual counseling session the client is commonly encouraged to communicate, while in a group he must learn to let others talk, to wait his turn, and to talk only in terms of what is relevant to the group goals. Although it is possible to help a retarded worker learn to limit his talkativeness by individual conditioning or behavior modification procedures, it is likely that, without some continuing conditioning or behavior modification procedures to inhibit talkativeness, the improvement in this behavior will not spontaneously generalize and continue in a new work setting. With peer influences, however, to help the retarded worker learn to limit his nonjob-relevant conversation, the transition and generalization to other peer groups and other work settings can be much more easily accomplished.

Bothering other workers. A problem closely related to talkativeness and frequently reported by supervisors of retarded workers, is that of bothering other workers with inappropriate comments, questions, demonstrations of friendship, etc. Retarded workers, particularly those who have developed outgoing personalities, want to shake hands, hug others, make comments like "I'm your friend. Am I your friend?," which may bother co-workers. In an individual counseling approach to modifying these behaviors, the risk is run of having the retarded worker feel the counselor rejects or doesn't like him; however, peer group acceptance or rejection can accomplish the modification of these behaviors without overtones of individual acceptance or rejection of the retarded client. Generalization to work settings is much more easily accomplished by the group influences, since bothering behaviors, such as expressions of affection, while inappropriate in a work group, may be quite acceptable in one-to-one settings with counselors or employers.

Modelling of appropriate work behaviors. Retarded workers are especially sensitive to peer group influence in the acquisition of behaviors manifested by other members of his group. Special diligence is required of the counselor, however, to assure that appropriate rather than inappropriate behaviors are selected for modelling. Actions like swearing, for example, will be quickly modelled by a retarded worker unless the counselor quickly mobilizes the peer group to reject them. On the other hand, once a retarded worker has identified with his peer group, he will respond much more quickly to collective behaviors modelled by individual peer group members than to films or demonstrations of how he should act. Although he may often verbalize an identification with a status-irrelevant model, such as the workshop physician or social worker, most of his actual day-to-day, job-related behaviors will reflect modelling of his co-workers or workshop peers. Peer group influence will have a doubly powerful impact in helping the retarded worker identify with and model appropriate behaviors manifested by other members of his peer group, since it provides him with concrete examples of specific behaviors which are appropriate to him and within his range of mastering.

Clowning. Perhaps because it provides the retarded trainee with a good way to get attention, clowning is a very common behavior problem among retarded clients, especially those working in settings with nonretarded co-workers. Clowning behavior, because it is usually met with considerable enthusiasm and reinforcement by co-workers, creates a special kind of problem for the counselor working with retarded clients; he can be fairly certain that clowning behavior, once started in a job setting, will be sufficiently reinforced by co-workers that it will be difficult to eliminate. This is a serious problem because the employers generally will not tolerate clowning behavior and will terminate otherwise qualified retarded workers because of the threat that clowning presents to both group productivity and safety. The peer group represents the primary means for dealing with the problem of clowning since individual responses to it can tend to make it continue. In a group working together, for example, if clowning by any one member is characteristically met by unresponsive silence and withdrawal of attention, there will be both good suppression of the clowning and good generalization to work settings, since the lack of response occurred in the work setting. Through further discrimination by the peer group to accept clowning in informal breaks or nonwork settings, the typical retarded worker can fairly quickly learn that clowning is acceptable only when he is not on the job.

Mothering. Although not so common as clowning or talking, a problem which can be occasionally expected to develop among retarded workers is a sort of mothering hierarchy, in which an older woman becomes a source of support, solace, and arbitration among younger workers. This works to the detriment both of the younger workers, who tend to become somewhat over-dependent and even infantalized in the work setting, and of the older retarded lady who assumes the mother role, since she eventually becomes overburdened with responsibilities and problems beyond her capabilities. Not uncommonly, for example, younger retarded workers may appeal to the older "mother" to intercede for them with the boss, to demand changes in the work situation, to arbitrate grievances with other workers, or to provide personal counseling. When this happens, the total structure of the retarded group suffers, since the disruption of the dependency ties can cause individual crises and regressions to the point of impairing work efficiency. In structuring the peer group influences, the problem can be effectively prevented by making certain that each worker understands that he is an individually responsible person and by mobilizing peer influences to reinforce behaviors that reflect this personal responsibility and that reject any member's efforts to either seek or provide high levels of support with other members.

Buying friendship or acceptance. An occasional token gesture by a retarded worker, sufficiently reinforced, can become a special problem and may result in attempts to buy friendship or acceptance. A retarded worker may bring a peer a token gift like flowers from his garden or a piece of his birthday cake; because of the positive response to this, he may attempt to "buy" everyone's friendship. He can then be easily manipulated to buy cokes, snacks, or even give money, in response to gestures of friendship or acceptance. While this does not typically cause any strong reaction from employees, it can result in the victimization of the retarded worker, who can often be led into giving away personal items that he needs. Another manifestation of this problem is sexual seductiveness in retarded female workers who can manipulate it to gain acceptance. The attempt to buy friendship is difficult to handle on a one-to-one basis, since it may not generalize to a relationship with other individuals. As a behavior to be modified by peer group influence, however, the rejection of this attempt by the group can be handled, not as a personal rejection, but as a means of behavior modification relative to general modes of relating to others. When the group reacts to attempts to buy friendship with responses like "You don't need to give presents for people to like you," the implications are much more easily generalized to future social contacts than would be possible from individual rejections.

PROVIDING THE SETTING

To develop strongest peer group influence, individual members of the group have to feel some identification both with the group and with other members of the group. In institutions where the retarded workers all live in the same ward or in sheltered workshop programs where they all work in the same area in the same job, such identification is very easy to develop. In workshop settings, for example, pushing for increased group productivity, improved punctuality, or reduced number of injuries and giving frequent appropriate recognition to the group and special recognition to individuals WHO HAVE CONTRIBUTED TO THE GROUP EFFORT, a sense of cohesiveness and group identification is fairly quickly developed.

In cases where retarded individuals do not share a common living or working relationship with each other, it is important for the counselor to take a number of specific steps to foster and encourage group identification before attempting to use peer group influences in any behavior modification program. As a general rule, a good beginning is to assume that probably no meaningful peer group exists, since the mere fact that retarded workers may work in the same workshop does not necessarily imply that they feel any sense of group identity. Many job training centers or sheltered workshops for the retarded, for example, have a mixture of a few older, more seriously retarded workers, for whom no competitive employment is realistic, with a number of young, mildly retarded workers, who represent good prospects for vocational placement; although a given worker may have a friend or friends among the group, he does not identify himself with the total group.

One good procedure for helping retarded individuals identify with a group is for the counselor to first identify the group, determine its goals, and its criteria for membership. In sheltered workshops for the retarded, for example, a good basis for forming a group could be that it is composed of the six or eight workers considered most ready for competitive placement. In an institutional setting, a special homebound preparation ward serves a similar purpose. Once such a group has been identified, each individual member should be told that he is being allowed to join that group based on his progress, and he should be personally introduced to each member of the group at a group meeting. If the group is newly formed, the individuals present at the first meeting should receive this same orientation. The group should be told what its goal or goals are to be and how each member must contribute to helping the group accomplish these goals. If the group is composed of submembers of some larger group, such as selected members of a sheltered workshop trainee group, their identification with the group is facilitated if each member has some tangible and visible emblem of membership in that group. A colored armband, a special name badge, or distinctively colored cap will help the retarded worker identify himself as having something special in common with other workers similarly identified. Every attempt should be made to relate an individual client's accomplishment to the group, so that whenever any worker accomplishes all the goals set out for him—typically resulting in his becoming employed—the group identity is strengthened and the motivation of others in the group reinforced.

The placement of a worker from the group into gainful employment can, interestingly enough, serve to weaken the group's influence unless this success is handled properly. When a group of retarded individuals invests something into a group member and he suddenly leaves, there can be a reaction among the group very much like when a member dies. A member is gone, and although the group is told he has gone onto something bigger and better, if he is not physically seen again by the group his success can be seen as their loss. This can and should be prevented by regularly scheduling visits with the group by former members who have "graduated," to give a sort of testimonial, i.e. "Most of you probably remember John. He was one of our group while he was getting ready for a job. Now John has come to visit us and tell us all the interesting things about his new job." Using occasional visits like this can, not only help strengthen the sense of purpose and continuity of the group, but can avoid a sense of institutionalization which occasionally develops among the retarded. Although a sense of togetherness is an important part of the effectiveness of peer group influences, retarded clients tend to attend to the here and now and neglect rather vague, future-oriented goals; this introduction of occasional input concerning the group's direction will help keep peer group acceptance from becoming too static and passive.

A final word about providing the setting in which peer group influences can be used to modify behavior of the retarded deals with the importance of developing support for the group from "significant others" in each retarded individual's own life sphere. Since peer group influences are to be used as a tool in comprehensive rehabilitation planning, it is important to expand the concept of the group to include nonwork settings, as well as workshop supervisors and parents into occasional group activities. An occasional evening coffee and cookies gathering, for example, attended by individuals important to group members, will help enhance the importance of the group and the attendant desirability of acceptance by group peers.

EXAMPLE OF THE USE OF PEER INFLUENCES TO MODIFY BEHAVIOR

Peer influence, as a tool in behavior modifications of the retarded, can be enhanced by gathering together a group of individuals with similar target behaviors to be modified and helping the individual members identify themselves with the group before attempting to focus on peer influences. For example, here is an account of a program developed for use with adult mildly retarded women, who had spent a number of years in a state institution and who were being prepared for vocational placement while still in the institution. All the women had developed sufficient work skills to qualify them for gainful employment but were not placeable due to habits of personal uncleanliness, disregard for personal appearance, and a nearly complete lack of appropriate socialization or interaction skills. Typically, these women were prone to wear untidy and incongruently matched clothing, almost always needed their hair combed and washed, often ate with spoons or fingers, and almost completely ignored the presence of others. Communication with others, when essential, was usually accomplished by monosyllables or gestures. They seldom participated even passively in any recreation or other therapy activities and were generally content to just sit alone.

To provide a basis for measuring changes that might occur during the program, each of the eighteen women was rated by a nurse, an aide, and a psychologist, on such items as appearance, grooming, table manners, sociability, initiative, and friendliness. These behaviors were then used as target behaviors, with the program focused more or less exclusively on using peer influences to modify them.

The program. The program consisted of a series of one-hour meetings, held once a week for six weeks. Each meeting was devoted to the discussion of one of the items on which the women had been initially evaluated. The women were individually invited to attend the meetings and, after urging in some cases, all of them accepted.

The first meeting started with the showing of a ten-minute film on appearance, which a local business college uses in training female applicants for jobs. The film emphasizes the effect of a woman's appearance not only on how others think of her, but on how she thinks about herself. At the end of the film, a discussion about the importance of appearance was started, in which several of the women participated freely with little stimulation from the nurse and aide.

Coffee was served near the end of the hour, at which time the women were encouraged to remember the points made in the film and to discuss the film with each other. After both the nurse and the aide left the group, there was no apparent communication among the members of the group until the time when the group gradually dispersed. During the next week, both the nurse and the aide, in the course of their regular contacts with the women, made casual remarks about the content of the film but did not devote any special time or emphasis to the topic.

At the second meeting, the points made in the previous film were very briefly reiterated, and several of the more outspoken women were asked about the number of other women they had spoken to concerning the film. These questions were asked to let the women know that they were expected to talk with others concerning the topics of the meetings and to give recognition before the group to those who had done so.

The second meeting was intended to cover some aspects of grooming, which were depicted in a dozen color slides. While each slide was being shown, the women were encouraged to discuss its topic with reference to themselves or other people they knew. After the aide had directed questions about the first two slides to specific women, the rest of the group commented fairly spontaneously on the remainder of the slides. Their comments generally concerned persons whom they had known at home. Apparently they saw no connection between good grooming and their current group.

Again, coffee was served near the end of the hour, and the women were encouraged to talk among themselves or with the nurse or the aide about the topics that had been discussed that day. This time when the nurse and the aide left the group, there was an increase in interchange among the women, and several of them remained in conversation well after the hour was ended. During the course of the week, there was a noticeable increase in the spontaneous comments which the women made to both the nurse and the aide; usually these comments dealt with some aspects of the topics covered in the meetings. Several women asked what the topic of the next meeting was going to be.

At the beginning of the third session, each woman was asked how many others she had spoken to in the past week concerning the topics of the meetings. Nearly half of the women volunteered this information, and the majority of the others commented on the matter when the group's attention was directed toward them.

This session dealt with table manners, and the twenty-minute film, "Your Table Manners Reflect You," was shown. The nurse started the discussion with a rather general statement about the topics of all three meetings, and the women spontaneously collaborated on the subject for the remainder of the hour. Partly because of this increased spontaneity, the coffee was not served this time until the end of the hour, and for nearly an hour after the nurse and the aide had gone, the majority of the women stayed in the group, chatting about various topics.

At the noon meals for the next week the aide sat with one or another of the groups of women and complimented them individually for their unusually good application of the table manners movie to their own habits. It was at this point that the women began to relate the topics which had been discussed in the meetings to their own group.

The nurse opened the fourth meeting by asking each lady to tell the group her name and where she was from. This introduction was followed by the showing of an eight-minute film on self-improvement of a type used in courses teaching public confidence. It dealt with the reactions we create in other people by our own appearance, actions, and verbalizations and pointed out ways we can use these reactions to create favorable impressions of ourselves. The film demonstrated instances in which one person could improve the social relations of a whole group of people just by taking the initiative and demonstrating an interest in others.

At the end of the film no comment from the staff was necessary. Participation was so enthusiastic that it slightly exceeded the hour. When the aide got up to bring the coffee, two of the women volunteered to help her. The women did not completely disperse until supper was served. In the following week there was a very big change in the interaction among members of the group; even the more withdrawn occasionally made some comment when approached by others attempting to initiate conversation.

The aide opened the fifth meeting (stressing initiative) by thanking the two women who had offered to help her with the coffee the preceding week and by making a brief statement defining initiative in terms considered familiar to all the women. They were then asked to suggest ways in which they might demonstrate initiative within the group. One of the first suggestions was that some of the women might spend more time with those of the group who were still seclusive and retiring. Other suggestions included trying to decorate their ward more tastefully, to keep their ward more cheerful, and to raise money for this project by sponsoring a coffee hour. Throughout the following week, the atmosphere of the ward was more friendly, the group was more cheerful, and even the physical appearance of the ward reflected attempts at neatness and order.

The final session was a party. Coffee and cake were served, and their was no apparent theme until about midway through the hour. At this time the aide announced her appreciation of the cooperation and help everyone had given her and asked if anyone would further help her by summarizing what the group had learned. An older woman announced that she had been appointed to speak for the group, and outlined with considerable accuracy the information that the sessions had been intended to convey.

Although another short session stressing sociability had been planned for this meeting, it was decided that doing was better than hearing and the party was extended over the full hour. Interaction was very marked during this period; every member of the group contributed to the conversation.

At the end of the six weeks, the women were rated on the standard rating form that had been utilized at the beginning of the program by the nurse, the aide, and the psychologist. The ratings showed a change that was statistically significant beyond the .01 level of confidence, on all the six items.

Many of the changes were obvious to others who were not members of the group. The ladies not only began to take pride in their appearance but initiated requests for trips to the beauty shop, began helping others in their group with hair styles and clothes, and socialized freely and effectively with others who were not members of their original group. Perhaps the greatest changes were noticed by the ward personnel; the whole climate of the interpersonal relationship among the women had become warmer and more socialized, and a genuine concern both for themselves and for others began to become evident in their behavior. The influence of the peer group on the behavior changes becomes apparent when we consider that no professional other than a nurse was involved in the program and that the changes occurred in response to only six hours of actual supervised peer interaction.

INTEGRATING PEER GROUP INFLUENCES WITH OTHER BEHAVIOR MODIFICATION PROCEDURES

Although peer group influences offer a powerful tool in the armamentarium of the counselor working with the vocational preparation of mentally retarded clients, this must be regarded as a tool which can help provide *an* answer to a specific problem rather than *the* answer to vocational habilitation of the mentally retarded. Its main value may lie in modifying social behaviors, or behaviors which occur within a social context, and so can be of maximal utility when integrated into and combined with other behavior modification approaches. Such occasional problem behaviors as rocking or talking to one's self, for example, can probably best be handled by using some combination of operant type conditioning, to decrease the frequency of the behaviors, with augmentation and supplementation by peer group influences to positively reinforce the client when he is not displaying the behaviors in social or group settings. Related behaviors like bizarre, outlandish, or merely inappropriate dress can be similarly handled, perhaps by a combination of didactic, directive individual counseling to let the client know what would be appropriate or acceptable dress standards and of peer influences to reinforce appropriate dress and appearance. In cases where a combination of approaches is to be used, it will be especially important that the counselor predetermine whether the combined behavior modification approaches involving the use of peer group influence and another procedure are to be used concurrently or in some given sequence. In cases where a sequential approach is to be used, it is usually a good idea to prespecify what level of behavior or what criterion ought to be reached by the first treatment approach before the second approach is to be introduced. As a general rule it is best to use peer group influences in a sequence following individual behavior modification procedures, which are used to help the retarded client develop to a level where he possesses a behavior repertoire with enough adaptive behaviors to which the peer group can respond in a positive way.

Although it is probably not fair to generalize about the learning styles of all retarded vocational trainees, as an operational rule, mentally retarded trainees tend to learn at a slower rate than nonretarded trainees. The use of peer group influences enhances the acquisition of modified behaviors in the retarded by providing them with a variety of role models in a diversity of work roles and with a repetition of essentially the same behavioral messages and reinforcers from individual peer group members. This multiplicity and replication of models and reinforcers thus complements the learning style of most retarded workers and can help them more readily generalize their new behavioral skills to the competitive work settings to which their comprehensive vocational preparation efforts have been directed.

SUGGESTED READINGS

Cull, John G. and Hardy, R. E.: *Behavior Modification in Rehabilitation Settings*. Springfield, Thomas, 1974.

Hardy, Richard E. and Cull, J. G.: *Modification of Behavior of the Mentally Ill*. Springfield, Thomas, 1974.

Hardy, Richard E. and Cull, J. G.: *Modification of Behavior of the Mentally Retarded*. Springfield, Thomas, 1974.

CHAPTER V

DEVELOPING PSYCHOLOGICAL SERVICES IN VOCATIONAL REHABILITATION WORK

RICHARD E. HARDY and JOHN G. CULL

••

Developing and Using Psychological and Related Services with the Mentally Ill and Others
Referral for Psychological Services
Developing Models of Psychological Services for State Rehabilitation Agencies
State Rehabilitation Administrators' Views on Psychological Evaluation
Summary
References

••

DEVELOPING AND USING PSYCHOLOGICAL AND RELATED SERVICES WITH THE MENTALLY ILL AND OTHERS

THIS CHAPTER will purposely broaden from mental illness to include various concepts concerning the development of psychological services in state vocational rehabilitation settings. The number of mentally ill persons being rehabilitated at present through state vocational rehabilitation efforts has skyrocketed. Psychological services in rehabilitation must be expanded and improved, which is a priority consideration in serving the mentally ill and other rehabilitation clients.

The rehabilitation counselor has been rightly called the key to effective rehabilitation work since he is the center of activity, the coordinator, and often the developer of services to his clients. The responsibility for the success of various steps in the rehabilitation process rests upon the counselor's shoulders; psychological and related services are no exception.

Psychologists are engaged in a wide variety of activities, many of which relate directly to the goals of the vocational rehabilitation program. The rehabilitation counselor must develop professional psychological resources in much the same way that he develops community resources. Of the wide array of services offered by psychologists, three which the rehabilitation counselor will be particularly interested in include the following:

1. General psychological evaluations—relatively superficial but broad spectrum screening evaluation.

2. Speciality psychological evaluations—narrow in-depth evaluations (diagnosis of learning disabilities, determination of abilities, aptitudes and interests, and description of personality patterns of handicapped clients).

3. Individual and group adjustment counseling.

Rehabilitation counselors are becoming increasingly aware of the need for making the most effective use of psychological services during the counseling process. Therefore, the new rehabilitation counselor should acquaint himself thoroughly with the services provided by the psychologist and the role each of these services plays in the rehabilitation process. He can then provide the most needed services to his client at the appropriate time in the professionally appropriate manner.

Indications for Psychological Evaluations

Quite often the new rehabilitation counselor is in a quandary concerning when he should obtain additional psychological data. He feels, as a counselor, it is his responsibility to evaluate his client in order to counsel him. While he can agree on the necessity for psychological evaluation in the rehabilitation process, he needs some rather specific guidelines relative to securing such evaluation. The most obvious response to this question is, "The counselor should secure a psychological evaluation when he has a specific question regarding his client's personality or personal attributes." More specifically, the counselor should obtain a psychological evaluation when he is developing a rehabilitation plan which will be of long term. If a long-term plan is developed, some basic assumptions are made relative to mental ability, interests, aptitudes, and emotional stability. These assumptions should be checked out early in order to help insure the ultimate success of the plan. If the assumptions are not verified by means of a psychological evaluation but are found erroneous, a great deal of the client's time and energies can be wasted. Similarly, if an expensive rehabilitation plan is being developed, a psychological evaluation should be obtained for almost the same reasons.

Many psychological evaluations are obtained at the beginning of the rehabilitation process during the diagnostic phase when the individual's eligibility is being established. A psychological evaluation should be made in cases in which eligibility is based upon mental retardation, functional retardation, and behavioral disorders.

In developing the rehabilitation plan, the counselor needs to have a fairly complete understanding of the client's functional educational level, mental ability, aptitudes, and interests. If this needed information is missing, it should be obtained. If part of the information the counselor has is unclear, ambiguous or contradictory, the counselor should clear up the confusion with a psychological evaluation. For example, if the client has a reported educational achievement level or reported level of intellectual ability substantially lower than that required on a job that the client performed successfully, the counselor should clarify the obvious contradictions by psychological testing.

If the counselor suspects important talents, capacities, abilities, or disabilities which are unreported but have a bearing on the probable vocational objective, a psychological evaluation should be purchased to delineate these attributes. Also an evaluation should be obtained if the client has certain disabilities which will later materially affect his capacities, abilities, skills, or personality. For example, a client who is experiencing mild anaesthesia in his hands and fingers should be tested for manual dexterity prior to settling on a vocational objective calling for a manipulative ability. A client interested in electronics assembly work should be tested for color blindness.

Lastly, a psychological evaluation should be obtained if the client is exhibiting or has exhibited behavior the counselor does not understand. If the client's current behavior patterns are not predictable and are difficult to understand, the counselor should enlist the aid of the psychologist to explain the client's personality structure. If the client's past history is filled with events or actions the counselor cannot reconcile, such as unexplained job changes, frequent moves from one community to another, and a lack of organization to the client's vocational history, a psychological evaluation to describe the client's personality structure is in order to explain his behavior patterns.

Contraindication for Psychological Evaluation

Perhaps looking at cases when psychological evaluation is unnecessary would be meaningful. An obvious case in which a psychological evaluation is unnecessary is when the client recently has been successfully employed and intends to return to his particular vocation following the physical restoration and other rehabilitation services he will receive.

If the client has been successfully employed but is now unable to find similar work because of employer prejudice toward the handicapped, it is necessary for the counselor to use his counseling and vocational placement skills to convince the employers of the client's ability. In this case it would not be appropriate to obtain a psychological evaluation in an effort to change the client's vocational objective.

Psychological testing is not needed when a client has been successfully employed and the new vocational objective constitutes only a minor shift or the new job is directly related to his prior work. There is no need for testing when the client has developed a long and rich background of information regarding a particular industry or job family and when his new vocational objective, though not previously performed by him, is sufficiently related for the counselor and client to be safe in assuming he can meet the demands of the job. A separate but related case concerns the client having a long and rich background of educational information and experience, and the client plans to study or work in areas related to his background. Evaluation is not needed in this case.

In essence, a psychological evaluation is needed when the client's behavior is to be predicted over a long period or his behavior is difficult to predict over a short period of time. An evaluation is not needed when the client's behavior is understandable and predictable or if he has established a related pattern of vocational growth over an extended period of time.

At times, counselors will threaten to deny rehabilitation services if a client refuses to submit to the testing and interviewing of a psychologist. In many instances, if the client continues to refuse, the case is closed—"The client is not motivated." Even though this occurs much less frequently than it has in the past, it is appropriate to discuss. As rehabilitation counselors become more professional and more aware of the needs of clients, they will be more attuned to the motivating factors operating in the client. If the client refuses services which the counselor offers, the counselor should seek to understand and modify behavior through counseling rather than being threatened and defensive himself and reacting in a punitive manner toward the client.

REFERRAL FOR PSYCHOLOGICAL SERVICES

When securing psychological services, the counselor should ask himself some basic questions: What specific knowledge can be obtained from the psychologist which will be of value in the rehabilitation counseling process? What data can he (the counselor) obtain and what data should he request from the psychologist? When these questions have been asked and answered, the counselor is better prepared to make an intelligent referral to the psychologist. As mentioned above, there are numerous types of psychological evaluations; therefore, it is inadequate for a counselor to merely refer a client for a "psychological evaluation." If he is expecting highly specific definitive information from the psychologist, the rehabilitation counselor must set definite limits for the psychologist and provide him with the appropriate background information. Gandy's referral form, if used, will tend to increase materially the quality of psychological reports the counselor receives. This referral form should constitute the minimum information forwarded to the psychologist; however, generally little more than a request for an evaluation is sent.

REFERRAL FOR PSYCHOLOGICAL-VOCATIONAL EVALUATION

FROM: .... DATE: ....
TO: ....

IDENTIFICATION:

Name of Client ....
Social Security No. ....
Address ....
Sex .... Age .... Race .... Marital Status................
No. Dependents ....

SOCIAL-VOCATIONAL-MEDICAL:

Economic Stratum ....
Family Environment ....
Formal Education ....
Usual Occupation ....
Vocational Success ....
Leisure Activities ....
Physical or Mental Impairments ....
General Health ....

BEHAVIORAL OBSERVATIONS:

General Observations (appearance, mannerisms, communication, attitude, motivation) :

....
....
....

REASON FOR REFERRAL:

Statement of Problem ....
....
Specific Questions ....
....
....
Enclosures: ....
....

Note: This form was taken from Gandy, J.: The Psychological-Vocational Referral in Vocational Rehabilitation. Unpublished Master's Thesis, University of South Carolina, 1968.

Much of the information called for on the form is already in the case folder so it is easily accessible to the counselor. In order to select the appropriate instruments and interpret them, the psychologist needs the social-vocational-medical background information. Therefore, to facilitate the work of the psychologist and relieve the client of having to answer the same questions repeatedly and to increase the effectiveness of the psychological interview, the counselor should make a concerted effort to supply the psychologist with all pertinent information.

An individual's economic status, home situation, the degree of vocational success he has experienced and the physical or mental impairments he has will have a direct and major bearing on his behavior and personality. Test responses and results have to be evaluated in comparison with the above factors. If this information is not provided to the psychologist, he will have to interview the client at some length. The more time he spends in this duplicative effort, the less time he has to evaluate the client.

The counselor generally has had several contacts with the client before the client is referred to the psychologist. Also, the counselor is a professional who is skilled in observations; therefore, it is of particular value to the psychologist to have access to the observations the counselor has made. These observations can be quite meaningful since the counselor sees the client under a variety of conditions and the psychologist sees the client only in the testing and interview situation on one occasion.

Perhaps the most important information the psychologist should receive, a statement of the problem which prompted the counselor to refer the client to the psychologist, is usually not given to him. In order to specifically meet the needs of the counselor, the psychologist should have this statement since it will, in many cases, determine the particular instruments the psychologist will use. In conjunction with this statement of the problem, the counselor should outline the specific questions he wants answered by the psychologist. By considering these questions, the psychologist can further tailor his evaluation to the specific needs of the counselor.

Lastly, a good referral should include other reports, evaluations and examinations which have a direct bearing upon the psychological evaluation. These would include other psychological evaluations, social evaluations and reports, psychiatric data, the general medical examination report, and some medical examinations by specialists.

Selection of a Psychologist

After deciding upon what information the counselor himself will obtain and what information will be expected from the psychologist, the counselor has to select a psychologist. The counselor can obtain psychological data himself or he may rely upon a psychometrist (an individual skilled in the administration and interpretation of psychological, vocational and educational tests; an individual trained at a lower level than that of a psychologist), a psychologist in private practice outside the agency, a staff psychologist, or a consulting psychologist (these latter two will be discussed later). Generally, if he selects the psychometrist, the staff psychologist, or the consulting psychologist, the agency will describe the mechanics of referral in a policy manual or procedure manual. Therefore, here we will concern ourselves only with using the psychologist in private practice.

When the counselor is attempting to do part of the psychological study himself, it is very important for him to recognize his limitations in the field of evaluation. Certainly few counselors are skilled in psychological evaluation to the degree that they are able to use a wide variety of instruments. All counselors, however, should be able to use skillfully a small number of tests comprising a specific battery. When the counselor is inexperienced in the type of testing which he feels should be done, he must be able to secure the services of a qualified psychologist.

When obtaining the services of a psychologist in private practice, the counselor should have at hand a list of psychologists who are well known for their competency and who are experienced in working with handicapped persons. It is generally felt that psychologists who belong to the division of clinical psychology, the division of counseling psychology, or the division of psychological aspects of disability of the American Psychological Association will be interested in the field of rehabilitation and will be most helpful to the counselor. However, the counselor must recognize that psychologists, like other professionals, have areas of special interest. A psychologist who is knowledgeable concerning the emotionally disturbed or the mentally retarded may be relatively inexperienced in testing the physically handicapped.

When the client is sent to the psychologist, he is referred on an individual basis just as he is for a general or speciality medical examination. The payment is made according to a fee schedule developed by the agency and usually the state or local psychological associations. As with a new physician, a psychologist in private practice who is being utilized for the first time should be contacted. The counselor should discuss the vocational rehabilitation program, its goals, its procedures for referral, reporting, payment and the agency's fee schedule.

The Psychologist's Report

After the referral of the client, the counselor has every reason to expect and should demand speedy service for his client. This speedy service entails both a prompt appointment to see the client and a written report of the finding submitted. While the report should be received within ten days of the client's appointment, quite often it takes longer; however, if it routinely takes longer and at times exceeds three weeks, the counselor should discuss the problem with the psychologist so that he may receive better service or change psychologists. When the counselor receives the psychological report, it should cover five basic areas:

1. Clinical observations of the psychologist
2. Test administered
3. Results and interpretation of results
4. Specific recommendations
5. Summary

The observations of the psychologist are important since they provide the flavor of the evaluation and, without them the evaluation would be quite sterile. These observations will comment on the client's emotional behavior, appearance, motivation, reaction to the testing and so forth.

The tests which were administered should be spelled out for two reasons; first, most fee schedules are based upon the number and type of tests administered; but, more importantly, the counselor needs to know upon what data the psychologist is basing assumptions and making recommendations. In the reporting and interpreting of results, the counselor should find the results of all the tests given with an explanation of their importance. This section is highly technical; however, it should be very logical since this is where the psychologist builds his case. If some of the test results are not noteworthy or are not used in the diagnosis and recommendations, this fact should be mentioned and explained in the interpretation section. Essentially this is where the psychologist logically bridges the gap between his clinical observations, the test results, the diagnosis, and recommendations he will make. Above all the sections should be very sensible and understandable.

In the recommendations section, the psychologist should make a number of suggestions which are addressed to the specific referral problem and the questions the counselor asked on referral of the client. Recommendations should be stated clearly and concisely. If the counselor does not understand them, he should never hesitate to call the psychologist for clarification. The summary is a short, clear summation of the evaluation stated in nontechnical terms.

Use of Psychological Evaluation

After receiving the report, the counselor is confronted with how to use the evaluation. The use of the data will be easier if psychological evaluations are viewed as an integral part of counseling and closely related to all other rehabilitation services and not as an isolated event or service. The evaluation can be used in counseling sessions to aid the client in better understanding himself and in identifying his major problem areas. Additionally, the counselor can use the psychological evaluation as a counseling tool to aid the client in developing insights specifically related to his relative strengths and limitations and in helping him in making reasonable plans and decisions.

In interpreting the test results to the client, the counselor should develop short, clear, concise methods of describing to the client the purpose of the tests he took and the meaning of the results; but, by all means, the counselor should communicate only on the level at which the client is fully "with" the counselor. A most effective means of interpreting test results is relating test data in meaningful terms to the client's behavior. A trap to avoid is becoming overly identified with the client's test scores. They should be presented in a manner that will allow him to question, reject, accept, or modify the presentation and interpretation without having to reject the counselor. The counselor should not project his own subjective feelings into the results he is using.

Cautions in Using Psychological Test Scores

While psychological testing plays a vital role in the rehabilitation process, there are some cautions which need to be exercised in their use. It should be remembered that test scores are just that —only test scores. The indications are a product of the interpretation of the scores. Tests are only an *aid* to the counselor; they should never become the prime reason for a program of action in a client's rehabilitation. They are too fallible. They are too susceptible to human error to be relied upon completely. While scores are valuable in indicating vocational areas which merit consideration, the counselor should remember that tests are rather weak in industrial validation. But most importantly, it should be remembered that the individual can adjust to several occupations. Inherent in testing philosophy is the concept that an individual is "predestined" to only one occupation.

DEVELOPING MODELS OF PSYCHOLOGICAL SERVICES FOR STATE REHABILITATION AGENCIES

As the scope and commitment of vocational rehabilitation has expanded to include services to the culturally disadvantaged and those with behavioral disorders, so has the reliance on and need for psychologists in rehabilitation work. Psychologists who are trained at the doctoral level and who are aware of rehabilitation objectives and procedures are needed urgently.

The number of psychologists employed in vocational rehabilitation is limited. In order to obtain psychological services on a statewide basis, many vocational rehabilitation departments have generally taken one of three approaches in developing models of psychological services. The approaches might be labeled as (a) the consultation model, (b) the strict panel model, and (c) the supervising psychologist model.

Description of Models

The *consultation model* is relatively simple in structure. The department of rehabilitation must develop cooperative relationships with psychologists who are employed by institutions or who are in private practice. Usually rehabilitation area office supervisors contact these individuals and ask that they serve as consultants in psychology to the vocational rehabilitation program.

There are some problems with this approach. Many rehabilitation workers are not knowledgeable about the selection of qualified psychologists, and many psychologists are unaware of the objectives of rehabilitation. Unless there is considerable effort on the part of rehabilitation personnel and psychologists to develop understanding, the relationship between the rehabilitation department and consulting psychologists can be strained. This type of working relationship results in complaints from rehabilitation personnel that they are not getting the type of information they really need from psychologists. In addition, psychologists may not become fully involved and committed to the objectives of the rehabilitation programs. In addition, there is often confusion about fees and the selection of psychologists for various types of work such as psychotherapy and psychological evaluation of clients with catastrophic disabilities.

The *strict panel model* is the second approach which is used by some departments of rehabilitation. In this model, a part-time state consultant in psychology is usually hired. The state consultant in psychology and the rehabilitation department, in cooperation with the state psychological association, selects a panel of psychologists who represent various phases of professional psychology. The panel rules on the qualifications of psychologists who apply to perform various service functions for the vocational rehabilitation department and specifies areas of competency of individual psychologists. The state psychological consultant for the vocational rehabilitation department usually chairs the panel. Panel members develop a list of psychologists and describe services psychologists are qualified to offer to the vocational rehabilitation department.

This approach can be criticized as duplicated effort if the state has a certification or licensing board. Such boards examine the credentials of psychologists and determine areas of competency. The state licensing or certification board also is concerned with violations of ethical standards. The strict panel model can be very useful in states where no state board of examiners has been appointed.

The *supervising psychologist model* is a third approach which is used by departments of vocational rehabilitation. This model requires the employment of a full-time psychologist who serves as state supervisor of psychological services. The supervising psychologist has statewide responsibility for developing effective working relationships with other psychologists employed on either a full-time or part-time basis. He recommends psychologists for work with the rehabilitation department. He may also act as chairman of a panel of psychologists which meets to consider special psychological problems in vocational rehabilitation. The panel can also help in developing cooperative relationships between the rehabilitation department and consulting psychologists.

The supervising psychologist helps rehabilitation staff members develop understanding of concepts that will be of value to them in their work in vocational rehabilitation. He should participate actively in in-service training activities for professional rehabilitation staff members. He visits area offices and facilities in order to work with consulting psychologists and rehabilitation personnel.

In addition, the supervising psychologist assures that psychologists working for the rehabilitation department maintain standards of practice in accordance with the laws of the state and with standards established by the American Psychological Association. He may also plan training programs for them in order that they may develop improved understanding of the complexities of vocational rehabilitation work.

These models and general variations of them have been used by most state rehabilitation departments, although some departments have not yet developed psychological services on a statewide basis.

Of the three described models, the supervising psychologist approach seems most effective, mainly because it allows an individual who is a psychologist to devote a substantial portion of his time to psychological services within the department of rehabilitation. A supervising psychologist should hold a doctoral degree in psychology or a closely related field. He must be carefully selected. He has crucial responsibility for the effectiveness of psychological services in an important statewide social service program.

STATE REHABILITATION ADMINISTRATORS' VIEWS ON PSYCHOLOGICAL EVALUATION

The rehabilitation process relies, of course, upon a thorough understanding of the rehabilitated client. Counselors develop this understanding by careful evaluation and study of medical, social, psychological, and vocational components.

According to Hardy and Cull (1969) the widening range of vocational rehabilitation services, along with the increasing complexity of disabilities with which rehabilitation has become involved, heightens the need for more comprehensive evaluation services in the rehabilitation process. Even though a high level of evaluation is essential to providing adequate services to the rehabilitation client, obtaining pertinent and topical psychological information has been a continued source of frustration to the rehabilitation counselor. Not only does obtaining psychological information present a problem to counselors who have difficulty locating psychologists to evaluate their clients, but the psychological evaluation of clients presents a challenge to the rehabilitation administrators who must plan budgetarily for the provision of psychological evaluation.

Considerations in Obtaining Psychological Evaluations

The dilemma of handling psychological evaluations is a topic of frequent discussion by counselors and administrators. A basic question seems to be how the rehabilitation counselor can obtain an adequate psychological evaluation of his client without paying prohibitively large amounts in psychological fees for the increasing numbers of clients who need this type of evaluation.

Rehabilitation counselors and administrators generally acknowledge that from their experience, psychological examinations are extremely important in overall planning in the rehabilitation process. A study by Sindberg, Roberts and Pfeifer (1968) has confirmed this acknowledgment by indicating that, in terms of the usage of recommendations of psychologists, reports are definitely useful in the rehabilitation process. More than half of the recommendations of psychologists were followed completely or were followed to a large extent by rehabilitation counselors involved with the cases in the rehabilitation process.

Administrators Sampled

This current study is concerned with reactions of state rehabilitation agency directors relative to satisfaction with psychological services obtained from psychologists in private practice and the use of rehabilitation counselors in obtaining psychological information. All state vocational rehabilitation agencies were surveyed during the summer of 1969; of the ninety-one questionnaires sent out, fifty-five or approximately 60 percent were returned. Thirty-two of the fifty-five questionnaires which were returned indicated that state agency administrators do not believe that rehabilitation counselors should be prepared to administer a basic battery of psychological tests. Of the administrators responding to the questionnaire, 49 percent (or twenty-seven) did believe that rehabilitation counselors should be trained to administer interest tests, 47 percent (or twenty-six) felt they should learn to give aptitude tests, and 44 percent (or twenty-four) believed that they could administer intelligence tests with training.

Results

All fifty-five administrators who participated in this study stated that private psychologists are their primary source of psychological evaluations. Almost half of those persons returning questionnaires indicated that their state agency had hired psychologists on a full-time basis. Forty-three of the fifty-five agency administrators indicated that they were generally satisfied with the adequacy of reporting and professional services offered by outside psychologists. The most often expressed reasons for dissatisfaction by the twelve agency administrators who were not satisfied with outside consulting psychologists were (a) reporting was not sufficient for rehabilitation purposes and (b) there was an unacceptable time lag in getting material from the psychologists. Agency administrators concerned with programs serving blind individuals stated that psychologists in private practice often were not trained to evaluate blind persons. This observation apparently supports Allen's (1958) statement that less than 3 percent of all psychologists work in the area of mental deficiency and only 2.5 percent are engaged in programs for the physically handicapped.

A majority of the administrators (58%) indicated that rehabilitation counselors should not attempt to administer a basic battery of tests because counselors lack an understanding of the principles of testing and evaluation. Additionally, thirty stated that in their opinion counselors lacked the time necessary to achieve effective testing and evaluation.

In states that recommend that the counselor have a counselor's test kit for his personal use in evaluation of clients, the following tests were most often recommended:

1. *Tests of Intellectual Functioning*
   Peabody Picture Vocabulary Tests
   Wechsler Adult Intelligence Scale
2. *Tests of Academic Achievement*
   Wide Range Achievement Tests
3. *Tests of Vocational Interest*
   Kuder Performance Record-Vocational
4. *Tests of Motor Dexterity*
   Purdue Peg Board
5. *Tests of Vocational Aptitude*
   General Clerical Test
   Test of Mechanical Comprehension

In some states, the Otis Self-Administering Test of Mental Ability and the Revised Beta Examination are being used in lieu of the Wechsler Adult Intelligence Scale and the Wechsler Intelligence Scale for Children. The following comment from a state director on the Eastern Seaboard indicates the general thinking of state administrators concerning the use of a counselor test kit, "We feel very strongly that counselors should be able to administer basic pencil-and-paper tests requiring level B[2] competency and preparation. We strongly urge that they not become involved with projective techniques and complex personality inventories."

Results of this survey seem to indicate that about 42 percent of the state agencies are moving toward having counselors use tests to make initial screening judgments of their clients relative to some of his basic needs and toward gaining an understanding of the client. Also, it appears that these screening procedures being utilized by rehabilitation counselors are helpful to them in making decisions which concern whether the client should have further evaluation by psychologists or should be involved in extended evaluation. Since fees for psychological services represent a substantial portion of the case service budget in the state agencies' overall budget, it seems practical to screen many of these clients through the use of a counselor's testing kit along with evaluating other data from the social and medical areas which may be available in order to make basic decisions regarding the rehabilitation process for individual clients. After such screening, the number of clients referred to psychologists for in-depth psychological testing and evaluation can be substantially reduced. This procedure would seem to allow for improved services to all clients since much of the money expended for psychological evaluation could be spent on other case services and comprehensive psychological testing could be completed only when, in the counselor's opinion, it would be necessary for the rehabilitation of the client. As a result of this study, it is the opinion of the authors that agency administrators have confidence in their counselors and generally believe that they can depend upon them to make the complex decisions which are required regarding the variety of types of psychological evaluation needed.

SUMMARY

In summary, it was found that almost half of the state agency administrators felt counselors should be equipped to administer interest tests, aptitude tests, and intelligence tests; however, a majority felt administration time requirements precluded counselors' routine administration of a basic battery of tests. While over half of the agencies have employed full-time psychologists the major source of psychological evaluations in all cases was from psychologists in private practice. Although a large majority of state directors were satisfied with this arrangement, the main dissatisfactions concerned the relevancy of evaluations to vocational rehabilitation and the time lag in getting reports from psychologists.

Effective rehabilitation work requires comprehensive evaluation of clients. Psychologists offer invaluable information to the total vocational evaluation effort. The fullest and most effective use of their services by state rehabilitation departments is of high priority.

REFERENCES

Allen, W. S.: *Rehabilitation: A Community Challenge.* New York, Wiley, 1958.

American Psychological Association: *Ethical Standards of Psychologists.* Washington, 1953.

Cull, J. G., and Hardy, R. E.: State agency administrator's views of psychological testing. *Rehabilitation Literature,* 1970.

Cull, J. G., and Wright, K. C.: Psychological testing in the rehabilitation setting, *Insight,* 1970.

DiMichael, G.: *Psychological Services in Vocational Rehabilitation.* Washington, D. C., U. S. Government Printing Office.

Hardy, R. E., and Cull, J. G.: Standards in evaluation. *Vocational Evaluation and Work Adjustment Bulletin,* Vol. 2, No. 1, January, 1969.

Lerner, J.: The role of the psychologist in the disability evaluation of emotional and intellectual impairments under the Social Security Act. *Am Psychol,* Vol. 18, No. 5, 1963.

Sindberg, R. M., Roberts, A., and Pfeifer, E. J.: The usefulness of psychological evaluations to vocational rehabilitation counselors. *Rehabil Lit,* Vol. 29, No. 10, October, 1968.

University of Arkansas: *Psychological Evaluation in the Vocational Process,* Fayetteville, Arkansas, In-service counselor training project for vocational rehabilitation counselors in Arkansas, 1957. Monograph 3.

CHAPTER VI

BEHAVIOR MODIFICATION PRINCIPLES WITH DISADVANTAGED AND DEPRIVED

K. EILEEN ALLEN

INTRODUCTION

MUCH HAS BEEN WRITTEN about the young disadvantaged child during recent years. The literature yields innumerable assertions, many of them conflicting, about these children and every aspect of their development, their learning abilities, and the impact of poverty (Durham, 1969; Hellmuth, 1967; Jensen, 1969; Kagan, 1968). The literature also reveals innumerable curriculum models based on these disparate notions as well as contentions that they are effective (Hellmuth, 1970, Vol. 3). On some issues, however, there seems to be emerging a degree of consensus. A few of these issues bear directly on behavior modification principles and the disadvantaged child. In order to provide a context for the discussion to follow, a brief examination of these issues seems warranted.

89

THE DISADVANTAGED CHILD AND ASPECTS OF
BEHAVIOR ANALYSIS

A Child Is a Child

One rather obvious item is that disadvantaged children do exhibit an extensive array of developmental irregularities, developmental lags, and developmental disabilities. They also have what seems to be more than their fair share of problem behaviors— sometimes too few of what are considered to be socially valued behaviors, sometimes too many of certain socially deplored behaviors. On the other hand, there is a growing tendency to agree that a child, regardless of how he is labeled—disadvantaged, deprived, slow learner, hyperactive, withdrawn, immature—is still a child, responding and behaving in much the same ways that all other children respond and behave. Like all other children, with the exception of those who are severely handicapped, he can be observed to run, jump, shout, verbalize, share, quarrel, hit, laugh, cry, tantrum. These and a myriad of other behaviors are the essence of the developing child regardless of his socioeconomic background. The point has been made clearly, over the past several years, that young children are more alike than they are different, that differences are more a matter of degree than of kind (Gantt, 1972), and that *every child* has many, many strengths to serve as building blocks for healthy growth and development.

The so-called hyperactive child is an excellent case in point. Innumerable referrals on disadvantaged children list hyperactivity as a major concern. However, this kind of referral symptom is equally popular among clinicians who are seeing children from every other social milieu. A good case in point was James (Allen, Henke, Harris, Baer, and Reynolds, 1967), a middle class child from a professional family, whose counterpart can be found in every subgroup of children. The behavior modification program for James as described below would be equally effective for a disadvantaged child or any other type of child.

At the start of the study James was close to his fifth birthday. He appeared to have a well-developed repertoire of physical, social, and verbal skills, yet he rarely settled down to any sustained activity; he had all of the behavioral symptoms of the "classic hyperactive." During the baseline period he flitted from activity to activity as much as eighty-two times during each fifty-minute session of free activity time. He really moved! The overall average for the baseline period was fifty-six activity changes per fifty-minute session with an average duration of fifty-five seconds per activity. Study of the data revealed that the child's flitting from one activity to another consistently produced consequences from the teachers as they attempted to encourage, suggest, or structure more lasting activities for him.

After collection of baseline data had been completed, the following contingencies were put into effect: (a) all teacher attention was to be withheld until the child had remained with an activity for one continuous minute; (b) at that moment, a teacher was to go to the child and give interested attention and support to whatever activity he was engaged in; (c) the teacher was to stay with the child for the duration of the activity, but to withdraw attention the moment he left; (d) the teacher was to stay away, busy with other things, until the child again engaged in an activity for one continuous minute.

The one-minute criterion was chosen as a first approximation to increased span of attention, since baseline data indicated that the child could occasionally hold on an activity for that length of time. Records indicated that the contingencies resulted in an immediate decrease in number of activity changes. During the eighteen days following baseline the average number of changes was twenty-seven per session, with an average duration of one minute fifty-one seconds per activity, twice that of the baseline period. At this point another change was made in contingencies: the criterion for presentation of teacher attention was increased to two minutes of sustained activity. This produced some increase in number of activity changes initially with subsequent rather dramatic decreases. By the end of the school year the child often spent fifteen, twenty, or twenty-five minutes in one activity, making as few as four or five activity changes per free play period. His mother reported that he was more settled at home, too, though no data were collected there.

Concentrate on What Is Right with the Child

Recognition of adaptable first approximations to a desired behavior, as in the case of James, brings up another important aspect of a behavior analysis approach that has emerged frequently in working with young disadvantaged children—looking at each child from a "health" model rather than a pathology or "disease" model. Instead of concentrating on all of the things wrong with the child, a much more fruitful approach is to concentrate on all of the things right with the child. Usually the things right with the child far exceed the things wrong with him if actual data are kept on the child's responses. Using this approach, many child-care workers have come to alter their culture-bound notions of what is right and wrong and have thus developed a more healthy and positive attitude toward those responses that may be highly desirable behaviors for that child in his particular social milieu. Take, for example, the question of the kind of verbal behavior that young disadvantaged children bring to the preschool and how teachers often fail to reinforce this essentially healthy behavior. In fact, they often do just the opposite. Sometimes unconsciously, and sometimes deliberately, they give strong disapproval for the type of language the child uses. This results, in many cases, in the child who simply quits talking and is subsequently labeled as nonverbal. The health model as exemplified in a behavior modification approach does just the opposite—it views the existing verbal repertoire as a strong and healthy underpinning for helping the child to acquire additional verbal skills. Though not talking about behavior modification per se, there are many behavioral principles such as starting with the child's existing repertoire, shaping, and differential reinforcement implicit in the following quotation from Crosby (1967):

> The discovery that family dialects are valuable, that they communicate, and that they have deep emotional roots, implies that they should be encouraged and cultivated by the school. Deprived youngsters can learn to distinguish between those words that offend and those that add color and vigor to their expression. At the same time, they must learn that each person needs to command several dialects and that informal standard English is simply another dialect that is important to

them. They need to learn that it is the situation which determines which dialect is important.

When a more positive approach such as the above is used in modifying or extending the behaviors of the disadvantaged child, whether in the area of language development, social behavior, or academics, there is greater assurance that most of the time the child will experience success rather than failure. And this, of course, is another important behavior modification principle that is implicit in almost all programs that have dealt effectively with the developmental problems of disadvantaged children—arranging the learning environment so that the child does experience success each step of the way, for it is often said that the disadvantaged child has a poor self-image with little respect for his own self-worth. Such concepts do not last long in a good program where the child is experiencing repeated success rather than repeated failure. Such an approach, the hallmark of a good behavior program, has been another significant factor in providing more effective programs for disadvantaged children.

Early Identification and Avoidance of Labeling

Still another issue on which there is now fairly general agreement is that of early treatment; the earlier the identification and intervention program is initiated, the better off the child will be. Much has been written on this subject but of particular bearing to this discussion are those studies which suggest direct observation and analysis of behavioral data as a means for early detection and early intervention (Allen, Rieke, Dmitriev, and Hayden, 1972). Out of work along these lines has come also an ever-increasing skepticism if not actual disavowal of the whole labeling procedure which so often arises when inferential data rather than direct measurement become the basis for identification and treatment.

Examine, for example, the case of a five-year-old girl in a Head Start center for mentally retarded children. She had been tested just before her fourth birthday and received an I.Q. score of 42 on the Stanford Binet. Little was expected of the child and she was treated as mentally retarded by everyone except for one aide who was extremely uncomfortable with the label. As the aide observed, worked with, and developed rapport with the child, she recorded many instances of high-level problem-solving behavior and many instances of unique and inventive ways in which the child occupied herself with materials. On the basis of these records, the aide convinced the head teacher that she, too, should make some systematic behavioral observations. The head teacher observed similar and even more indicative instances of highly intelligent behaviors. Armed with this information, the staff asked repeatedly to have the child retested; finally, seven months later, this was accomplished. Again the child's score was very low—41. But the staff's belief in her potential, based on their direct observations, remained unshaken because in the seven-month waiting period for retesting, they had observed many additional intelligent behaviors on the part of the child. She had begun to talk more volubly, to interact with children, and to engage in a number of preacademic activities, even though she had displayed none of these behaviors in either of the testing situations where she had been unresponsive and uncommunicative. The staff increased their efforts to have the child removed from the class for mentally retarded preschool children. The following fall they succeeded in having her placed in a behavior management class. Within a few months she was indistinguishable from her intellectually normal peers. At midyear, a psychologist took several opportunities to interact in a friendly fashion with the girl in the classroom. A third I.Q. test was then administered. It yielded a score of 118. This test, it might be mentioned, was administered not to corroborate the child's now obvious intellectual functioning, but simply to lay the ghosts of the invalid scores in her folder.

The Interdisciplinary Approach

One more generally agreed upon conclusion has to do with the much greater efficacy of an interdisciplinary approach in the diagnosis and treatment of young disadvantaged children who appear to be developing in less than optimum fashion. Increasingly prevalent, at least in a number of the better funded and better administered programs, has been such a team approach. An example of one such program is that offered by the Child Development and Mental Retardation Center at the University of Washington. In this situation the Clinical Training Unit and the Model Preschool in the Experimental Education Unit provide joint training and practicum experience to graduate and undergraduate students from ten disciplines: education, psychology, social work, pediatrics, nursing, nutrition, dentistry, physical therapy, audiology, and speech pathology. One part of the training is a conjoint course in which students from the various disciplines participate in the diagnosis and management of developmental problems in young children. The unifying theme among the ten disciplines is the use of behavior modification tactics. Regardless of his discipline, each participant in the course learns to observe, record, and analyze behavioral data. Students then utilize these data to devise management programs for individual children which are carried out under the supervision of the faculty team (Haring, Hayden, and Allen, 1971). That such training does result in a truly interdisciplinary approach is well-illustrated in a recent study in which a young handicapped child was taught to walk (Knapp, O'Neil, and Allen, in press).

The child, referred to as Suzi, had been severely neglected and deprived during her earliest years. Eventually the grandparents were awarded custody of the little girl. The fact that the child had a severe neuromuscular dysfunction and did not walk resulted in the grandparents being overly protective and overly indulgent of her, through their great love and concern. In collaboration with the physician, the physical therapist, the social worker, the preschool teachers, and the school nurse, a behavior modificaion program was conducted to teach Suzi to walk and to teach the grandparents to allow her to acquire independence in locomotion. The grandparents, especially the grandfather, had a much more difficult time of it than did Suzi. It was agonizing for him to not indulge her every whim to be carried and waited upon. Particularly agonizing were the many occasions when he was not allowed to prevent her from falling nor pick her up and comfort her when she did fall. The team's program was successful, however. At the end of six months, Suzi, who had never so much as stood on her own two feet, was walking sixty steps unaided and smiling happily every step of the way. Grandfather too was ecstatic and most boastful of her accomplishment.

APPLICATION OF REINFORCEMENT PRINCIPLES

Effective Reinforcers for Young Children

With this fairly general discussion of the disadvantaged child and certain aspects of behavior analysis it is now appropriate to turn to actual application of reinforcement principles. Inasmuch as these principles have been thoroughly explored elsewhere in this text they will not be reviewed here in any depth. However, there necessarily will be some reiteration and elaboration in order to provide a specific context for the procedures as they relate to the young disadvantaged child. With this in mind it is well to start by taking another look at the reinforcers that have proven to be highly effective with the vast majority of young children.

The most powerful determinant of behavior in all young children is the attention of significant adults in the environment (Harris, Wolf, and Baer, 1966). To date, this is the single, most unifying theme found in the early childhood behavior modification research. Exactly what is adult social reinforcement? Put very simply it is the common everyday social behavior that most adults engage in as they work with young children. Generally speaking these include the adult responses in the following list:

> Making verbal responses and comments appropriate to the situation such as approval, praise, appreciation.
>
> Standing or sitting close and looking at, watching, nodding, smiling, listening, showing genuine interest.
>
> Providing physical contact such as a pat, hug, or holding a hand.
>
> Giving support on equipment, pushing a swing, joining in a child-directed activity.
>
> Bringing the child special supplementary materials or providing a special activity with an adult.

The foregoing adult behaviors are generally conceived of as positive reinforcers. Such things as scoldings, sharp reprimands and other forms of less benign adult responses are popularly thought of as negative reinforcers. However, under careful scrutiny it becomes apparent more often than not that these supposedly negative adult behaviors may not be serving the intended purpose. Vance (1973) described the paradox most aptly in relation to the management of highly disruptive, aggressive child whom she called Brad.

> Often a consequence that a teacher assumes is unpleasant and therefore punishing is really a reinforcer. For instance, verbal criticism of Brad when he attacks children or disrupts ongoing activities will probably result in increased frequency of his inappropriate behaviors. In such a case, verbal criticism is thought to be the presentation of an unpleasant consequence. Verbal criticism is frequently used by adults in the sincere belief that the application of such unpleasant consequences will decrease the frequency of a particular behavior. Often adults fail to realize that their criticism of a child is really a means of relieving fear, anger, frustration, or guilt on the part of the adult. But often this "unpleasant consequence" is really a "pleasant consequence" to the child. It is a form of adult attention. Any form of adult attention is highly rewarding to most children. Remember, it is the individual child who determines his own reinforcers, not his teacher.

Punishment, as a consequence to undesirable behaviors, should be shunned entirely except in a few rare instances when behaviors are totally unmanageable or likely to be physically injurious. Even then it should be used only as a temporary expedient. Bucker and Lovaas (1967) discuss the necessary use of punishment with long-term autistic children. The effects with other types of children are less predictable, however. Evans (1971) has this to say:

> . . . the consequence of punishment varies from no effect to a slight decrement of response strength to virtual suppression of the punished response (as well as other types of responses in the punished organism's repertoire). The application of punishment has yet to be shown effective in eliminating (or "stamping out") a response, and the side effects of punishment are typically quite undesirable. The preferred and most effective behavioral modification strategies are those based upon positive reinforcement, nonreinforcement, and negative reinforcement.

Following this very brief discussion of punishment and adult social reinforcement, it is well to turn now to a general discussion of specific procedures for conducting a behavior modification program for young disadvantaged children. The most frequently employed setting is a preschool situation and most of the examples which will be cited are from this type of setting. It is well to keep in mind, however, that the procedures are applicable anywhere—day care, neighborhood groups, the child's home, treatment centers of all kinds. To be kept in mind, too, is that while "teacher" is the label used in this discussion for the adult (s) providing the management, the adult could be any other professional or paraprofessional or parent providing a program for young children.

The ABC's of Behavior Modification

In the interest of brevity and for the sake of simplicity in training a staff to run a behavior modification classroom or treatment situation, the procedures may be viewed as an ABC approach:

A for antecedent conditions or stimulus events;
B for behavioral responses of the child;
C for consequent conditions or reinforcing stimuli.

A and C, of course, are environmental events that precede and follow B, the child's responses. If B is to occur (or in some cases, not to occur, as when dealing with maladaptive behaviors), then A and C must be prescribed according to a systematic contingency arrangement.

Thus, stated in overly simplistic terms, A may be thought of as what the teachers do *before* they would have a child respond: arrangement, selection, and presentation of activity and materials, whether at a desk, a table, in the block corner, at the easel, in the play yard, or wherever. C, too, may be thought of as what the teachers do (or do not do), *immediately following* the child's response: as mentioned earlier, they may smile, praise, touch the child approvingly or disapprovingly, provide him with additional materials or snack or a favorite toy or deprive him of some activity. Whatever they do or fail to do in A and C will have direct and immediate effect on B, the child's behavior, for this is the essence of the basic reinforcement paradigm. In the presence of A (usually called a discriminative stimulus or S^D) there is a high probability that B will increase if it is followed immediately and systematically by C, the reinforcing consequence.

Teachers, however, in arranging a behavior modification program for a child start not with A, but with B, the behavior of the child. No attempts are made to change B in the beginning. The first step is simply to observe the child and his overall behavioral repertoire and to write down in objective fashion what the child actually does. Out of this overall observation of the child the teachers begin to note appropriate responses as well as specific learning deficits and specific behavioral excesses.

When this has been accomplished the teachers are ready for the second step, that of pinpointing target behaviors and recording the frequency of their occurrence as well as the event immediately following their occurrence. Usually the initial period of pinpointing and recording (referred to as the baseline period) goes on for several days until a reliable assessment of the rate of the target or pinpointed behaviors is obtained. For example, a behavioral deficit that emerged from one baseline period on a four-year-old boy was a very low rate of verbalization: only eleven one-syllable, undifferentiated utterances over the entire period. On the other hand, the observer counted fifty-three times when the observed child clung to a teacher, crying and whining. The latter behaviors invariably resulted in the child getting something he wanted from the teacher—a drink, a toy, or a ride in the rocking boat.

Armed with these data the teachers were then ready for the third step—an actual modification program for at least two aspects of the child's behavior which appeared to be crucial to his overall development. The teachers knew how frequently his verbalizations occurred, and these they elected to *increase*. They also knew how frequently clinging and whining occurred and these they elected to *decrease*, inasmuch as the latter behaviors were incompatible with the former. In other words, for some children, if they can get what they want by clinging and crying, there is little point in going through all of the frustrating effort required to get it verbally.

The baseline data also provided the teachers with another piece

of valuable information: what events were reinforcing consequences for that particular child. It was obvious that the teachers'
attention and their presentation of various materials or activities
were highly reinforcing consequences for whining and crying
which was occurring at a high rate. The program, then, was outlined to completely reverse these contingencies of reinforcement.
Henceforth the teachers were to quietly but firmly disengage
themselves and move away from the child when he clung and
whined. When he was not clinging and whining one or another
was to go to him and present him with cues (antecedents) that
might evoke a verbal rather than a whining response. For example, if they saw him approaching the rocking boat, which had
been an antecedent event for much of his clinging and crying, a
teacher moved to him quickly before the onset of the maladaptive response and slipped in a new antecedent: "Mark, would
you like to ride in the boat? Say, 'boat.' " If he made an approximation to the word he was immediately lifted into the boat and
rocked vigorously for a minute or so. Then the teacher might
stop the boat, but before the child began to whine for more she
would say, "Do you want to rock some more? Tell me 'more.' "
Again, even a primitive approximation to the word resulted in
another rocking session. Every antecedent condition in the preschool situation which had formerly resulted in clinging and crying was handled in the same way. The key always was in the tim-
ing of the reinforcing consequences: immediate and consistent
withholding of reinforcement for those target behaviors which
were to be reduced; immediate and consistent presentation of reinforcement for those behaviors which were to be accelerated.

Of course, the teachers did not want Mark to stop at one word
utterances and so gradually, after he had acquired a sizable repertoire of object names, the target behaviors became more complex: first, two word phrases—"rock boat," then the addition of
the article—"rock the boat"—and the preposition "rock in the
boat," until finally Mark was saying, "Smith, wanna rock inna
boat!" All through such a program, reinforcement comes to the
child as a result of his making a response that will extend his developmental progress. No reinforcement is available for those
maladaptive responses which interfere with his healthy develop-

ment; therefore, they drop out rapidly. In Mark's case, clinging and crying reached a zero rate within six days and stayed there.

Reinforcing Successive Approximations

The procedure for increasing Mark's verbal output that was just described is referred to as "shaping," a procedure which was discussed in an earlier chapter. Technically it can be defined as differential reinforcement of successive approximations to the target behavior. However, the question is often raised, "What do you do if the response never occurs? After all, a response must occur in order for it to receive a reinforcing consequence." No problem, actually, for regardless of how deficit a child is, some form of the behavior, perhaps only a primitive form, can always be found in the child's repertoire. Obviously such an assumption is predicated on the target behaviors having been wisely chosen on the basis of careful observation and recording. (One can not select running as an initial target behavior for a nonambulatory child.) If that early primitive response is pinpointed and systematically reinforced, new but closely related responses will begin to emerge. Among these can be found some response forms which more closely resemble the target behavior. These closer approximations are then reinforced and the earlier, less accurate approximation is no longer reinforced. With the strengthening of these newly emerging responses, still better approximations will begin to appear for the first time and reinforcement may be shifted to them. Thus a step-by-step program is always in progress toward a behavior never before seen in the child's repertoire. In Mark's case he was moved from a few undifferentiated sounds to sentences that got him the attention of a specific teacher and caused her to engage with him in desired activities. True, "Smith, wanna rock inna boat," complex verbalization that it was, did not have the ultimate refinements of perfect articulation and address of the teacher by the formal Mrs. instead of just plain Smith. On the other hand, such language was entirely functional for this child in enabling him to navigate in his social milieu; the staff therefore elected to go on to other pressing deficits in order to extend his skills in still other directions deemed useful to him.

Mark, of course, was a relatively easy child to work with inasmuch as adult social reinforcement and a variety of play activities were reinforcing for him. This is true for the majority of children in a preschool. The activities that are available are usually "high strength," that is, "preferred" play activities (Premack, 1959); thus it is relatively easy to arrange contingencies in a variety of situations so the child does emit the desired response in order to be able to do what he wants to do. Following are some everyday examples of contingency statements:

"Hang up your coat and then you can play with the dough."

"After you have put your blocks on the shelf you may go outdoors."

"Tell Sara, 'my trike' and then I will see that she lets go."

"Finish your puzzle before the timer goes off, so that you can feed the guinea pig."

The contingency is stated clearly and simply and then the adult holds firm until the child makes the required response. Oftentimes, especially when a child has been in the program for awhile and has come to recognize that the adults do not vacillate, many of the contingencies no longer require the accompanying verbalizations—the child finishes his tasks of his own accord and then goes to a play activity of his choice. Such a child is well on his way to becoming a self-managing individual.

When There Is No Discernable Reinforcer

Though adult social reinforcement and preferred activities are usually powerful reinforcers for the majority of children, there is the occasional child for whom finding a reinforcer is most difficult, taxing to the utmost the ingenuity of every adult in the group. One such example was Jody (Haring, Hayden, and Allen, 1971), a child who did not interact with or respond to any adult or child in the group. Neither did she play with any of the materials or equipment. She would not accept food from the snack basket nor would she eat any special treats that were provided, such as small pieces of candy, peanuts, ice cream, sips of pop.

Thus the teachers did not have a primary reinforcer (food or drink), social reinforcement was to no avail, and the child did not show interest in any of the play activities or high strength areas. Quite literally, the teachers were without a reinforcer, and a behavior modifier, with a child with problem behaviors but no reinforcer for that child, is in a bad way. However, no respectable behavior modifier ever admits that he has not got a reinforcer. He goes to his data and combs it and recombs it for a clue. Jody's data indicated that she did do one thing for fairly long periods of time. She stood on a chair, looking in the mirror that was on the school room side of the one-way viewing screen in the observation booth. Apparently, seeing her own reflection in a mirror was reinforcing for Jody inasmuch as she made the response of going to the mirror and looking into it over and over again.

With this clue the teachers rigged up an easel mirror that could be set on the floor or table or wherever they wanted her to use materials. Also, they masked off, temporarily, the lower part of the observation glass so she could no longer see into it, for that kind of looking was not leading to purposeful activity. Then, as they had done before, they placed Jody on the floor in the block corner, put blocks in her hand and helped her to do simple stacking. But now, each time she placed a block the teacher verbalized, "Look in the mirror, Jody. See Jody building with blocks." If she stopped stacking, the mirror was turned away and the teacher's back was presented until Jody resumed stacking. Then the mirror and the teacher turned toward her again. Within a very few days Jody was engaging in first approximations to play with a variety of materials, indoors and out. Gradually the mirror was faded out, first by putting a thin coating of Bon Ami® over it and then, finally, over a period of time, obscuring all reflection. With careful programming such as this, other reinforcers came to supplant the mirror—the teachers' attention and the play materials themselves.

Because some disadvantaged children do seem to "wall off" from adults, one other child might be mentioned. Karl (Allen, 1970) was a child for whom initially there were no discernible reinforcers, nor were there very many behaviors to build on. He appeared to be totally oblivious, totally unresponsive to everything in the environment. He simply sat about with eyes downcast. Therefore, it was most difficult to select even a very low level target behavior as a beginning. It was finally decided that getting him to look up and make eye contact when his name was spoken should be the starting point, for there is very little that a child can learn unless he looks at and attends to the person who is attempting to teach him.

Again, the staff was working with a child for whom there was no discernible reinforcer, not even looking in a mirror as Jody had done. Optimists that skillful behavior modifiers are, however (having had their optimism reinforced by their ingenuity and hard work on many previous occasions), they set to work attempting to get the child to respond to his name. The data for the first session was most discouraging; no responses whatsoever from the child. It was decided to slice even finer—that is, to reprogram, to drop back to a much more primitive approximation, to select even shorter range targets. The verbalization would be extended to "Karl, look at me," and while saying it the teacher would take the child's chin and physically raise it. The second step in the program would be to drop the physical cueing and use only the extended verbalization. Step 3, the initial target behavior would be to have him respond to just his name.

The data, as usual, yielded up specific guidelines for the teacher, but even more, it revealed two serendipitous events that finally proved to be the key to a successful program for this child. The first occurred in one of the very early sessions when the teacher reached over to tuck the child's shirt into his pants. In doing so, the teacher apparently tickled Karl inadvertently. The child smiled and wriggled a bit—the first responsiveness that had been seen. The teacher continued to tickle a little tickle each time an approximation to the target behavior occurred and the response began to increase rapidly. This brought the second serendipitous event into focus: as the teacher moved her hand to deliver the tickling as a reinforcing consequence, she noticed that the child followed the hand movement with his eyes. The teacher now had an additional antecedent event to pair with the cue of "Karl, look at me": each time the teacher gave the cue she raised her hand to the level of her own eyes and the child followed the hand's movement, thus facilitating and eventually (within seventeen days) establishing eye contact.

Providing a Positive Environment

Sometimes, of course, no specific program has to be put into effect other than providing the child with an environment that is less punishing and more reinforcing. Such was the case with Eleanor (Allen, Turner, and Everett, 1970), an almost five-year-old girl who was not succeeding in a regular Head Start classroom. Referral information described her as extremely withdrawn, nonverbal, and incapable of learning. Before moving her to the behavior modification preschool class for disadvantaged children, initial observations were made of Eleanor in her regular classroom. During this observation she did not smile, laugh, cry, or look directly at another person. She sat crouched for long periods, aimlessly fingering small objects. The observer heard her speak only three times, each utterance an almost inaudible monosyllable.

The observer was particularly struck by the general tenor of the classroom: strict, authoritative control, few free-play activities, frequent reprimands to children who spoke out of turn or moved about the room without explicit permission. On the first day of observation of Eleanor in the home classroom, the observer tallied twenty-seven teacher-initiated contacts, all of them reprimands or commands. On the second observation day there were twenty-one teacher-initiated contacts with Eleanor, again all reprimands or commands.

When the child entered the Behavior Modification class, the teachers were given no special instructions except to establish rapport with her as rapidly as possible. In the first class session she said almost nothing and interacted with children only 3 percent of the time. In the second session, she verbalized 25 percent of the morning, mostly in response to the teachers' noncommanding type comments, and interacted with children 18 percent of the morning. It was apparent that Eleanor could talk and could play with children, at least at a low rate, in an environment where these responses were sanctioned. It soon became obvious, too, that Eleanor was not incapable of learning as had been reported. With a carefully arranged sequence of preacademic tasks, Eleanor progressed in all areas of intellectual development. The decision was made that no specific modification projects would be initiated; thus, teachers could test the effectiveness of a stimulus-rich preschool environment in which the appropriate spontaneity of all children was routinely reinforced. For the first twenty sessions of her enrollment, Eleanor's verbal output averaged 23.5 percent each school session. Her social interaction with other children averaged 22 percent of each session.

Though these rates were an improvement over the home classroom performances, Eleanor was still less verbal and more isolate than many of her peers. Therefore, a modification program was initiated in class session 21. The contingencies were:

1. No adult reinforcement would be available to Eleanor when she was playing alone.
2. She would receive adult reinforcement when she was interacting with other children, with or without verbal accompaniment.
3. She would receive additional adult attention when she was verbalizing with other children.

Under these contingencies there was almost immediate improvement in Eleanor's verbal output as well as in her interaction with peers. When the data indicated that the desired verbal and social skills were well established, plans were made to return Eleanor to her home classroom. Unfortunately, the homeroom teacher did not participate in the behavior modification instructional sessions offered to her, but she did express eagerness to have Eleanor back in her class.

Eleanor returned to the home classroom after class session 30. The observer reported that Eleanor came in smiling and talking animatedly. Immediately, and shrilly, the teacher reprimanded her for talking and ordered her to sit down, which Eleanor did. She worked a puzzle, got up to exchange it for another one, and again the teacher sharply reprimanded her, this time for leaving her seat. During the first half hour Eleanor received nine reprimands for behaviors which are generally considered appropriate for four-year-olds in a preschool situation. By the middle of the first day, Eleanor had reverted to her earlier patterns of sitting mute and unresponsive during the school session. Over the next several days she became totally withdrawn as before. Efforts to train the teacher in modifying her own behaviors in relation to the child were unsuccessful. The following week Eleanor was returned to the Behavior Modification class where immediate recovery of both verbal and social responses occurred.

Prompting Appropriate Verbal Behavior

Differential reinforcement, as has been demonstrated in the foregoing studies, is certainly an important facet of an effective behavior modification program for young disadvantaged children. Sometimes additional special procedures are necessary such as "prompting" or "priming." Treatment in Doreen's case used both of these procedures (Allen, *et al.*, 1970). Doreen's case used years and nine months, was a child with what were described as low-order verbal skills—her speech mainly consisted of echolalic responses or unintelligible mumblings. Occasionally she was heard to emit a few "normal" utterances. The verbal data taken on the child were broken down into two categories: (a) appropriate verbalizations as specifically defined, e.g., intelligible words relevant to the situation, and (b) inappropriate verbalizations or vocalizations as specifically defined. The later included her whimpering cries, echolalic or parroted responses, and the unintelligible monologues that she carried on with herself. The baseline data taken in the home classroom indicated that she engaged in more inappropriate than appropriate verbal behavior and that the teachers tended to respond more to the inappropriate than they did to the appropriate. When Doreen entered the Behavior Modification class the teachers were instructed to attend as frequently as possible to her appropriate verbalizations and to attend as infrequently as possible to her inappropriate ones. Under this regimen, appropriate verbalizations began an irregular increase with inappropriate verbalizations slowly declining, again at an irregular rate. The latter eventually constituted a relatively small percentage of the child's total verbal output.

Concurrently, a program designed to reduce Doreen's echolalic responses was undertaken. Two adults participated in this part of the program, one to ask questions or to direct comments to Doreen, the other to supply her with appropriate verbal responses. For example, one teacher might ask, "What are you doing, Doreen?" Left to her own devices Doreen usually responded, "What are you doing, Doreen?" Under the new program, however, the second adult prompted her to an appropriate answer *before* she could echo the first teacher's question or comment. Gradually, the prompted responses were faded out as Doreen emitted fewer parroted responses and a greater number of spontaneously appropriate responses. By the end of the school year all echolalic responses had been eliminated.

The Terrible Twosome

So far the children that have been discussed have all been relatively quiet or withdrawn children. The next examples will deal with very difficult, disruptive, hard-to-manage children, for these, too, are found within the disadvantaged population, just as they are found within every other population of children. The first example deals with a pair of four-year-old boys who were ruling a preschool program and reducing it to chaos. Peer reinforcement (discussed in greater detail in a preceding section) is a most powerful consequence for some children, particularly when it comes to the shaping and maintenance of those behaviors which adults tend to find aversive. Most adults who work with young children have encountered, more than once, the twosome who were thoroughly disruptive to social or classroom situations. Such a pair is the subject of this example (Allen, 1972).

The two boys, both almost five years old, roamed the play yard and school room with but one purpose it seemed: that of creating havoc by taunting other children, interfering with ongoing projects, racing about aimlessly and destructively, and defying teachers at every turn. In addition, they had an extensive repertoire of bathroom words and behaviors which was continually expanding through their mutual reinforcement of each other's efforts. When apart, however, each child exhibited a perfectly normal range of social behaviors with children and adults. The major problem was that they were seldom apart unless they had quarreled and vowed never to play with each other again as long as they both should live. The teaching staff was in agreement that if the boys were to profit from their preschool experience their time together must necessarily be much reduced.

Therefore, two teachers were assigned to the children, one teacher to be responsible for one boy, and the other teacher for the other boy; but never was either teacher to attend to either boy so long as they were together. The moment they separated, however, no matter how briefly, each teacher was to go to her particular boy, giving him her warm, undivided attention. If at all possible, she was also to steer him subtly into the activities of the nearest group of children, provided his cohort was not among them. The moment the boys teamed up again, each teacher moved away from the scene. While these plans sounded practical, both teachers had strong doubts that their social reinforcement would be powerful enough to compete with the reciprocally reinforcing qualities that each boy seemed to hold for the other. However, within three days of the start of the management program the boys were spending less than 15 percent of their play time together, approximately 75 percent of it with other children.

Following twelve days of this condition the teachers reversed contingencies, attending to the boys only when they were together. They began to play with each other almost exclusively, as they had in baseline. This provided convincing evidence that the boys' play with peers was strongly under the control of its stimulus consequence, teacher attention. After six days of reversal, the teachers again began attending to the boys only when they were separated. At the same time they redoubled their efforts to reinforce purposeful activities with other children so that each boy might acquire a more powerful alternate set of peer reinforcers. Post checks taken at random throughout the remaining months indicated that such a goal had been achieved. Each boy was spending 58 percent to 77 percent of his time with other children, 13 percent to 21 percent with his former "best friend." Teacher attention was now at a rate commensurate with the amount received by other children and was presented noncontingently, with one exception: if the two boys engaged in one of their former disruptive acts together, the teacher withdrew.

It was certainly true that during the early stages of the shaping procedures a great deal of teacher time was devoted to the boys. The data on teacher attention indicated, however, that the boys had always received a disproportionate share of teacher attention. Prior to systematic control, it had been dispensed randomly in large quantities as the teachers attempted to rechannel the boys' activities, interpret their behavior to other children, interpret to the two boys the other children's anxieties in regard to them, and so on. These procedures, so traditionally a part of a good nursery school teacher's repertoire, were totally ineffective in light of the experimental evidence.

Extinction of Several Types of Disruptive Behaviors

The final example to be given deals with a severely disruptive child for whom time-out (isolation from all social stimuli) and primary reinforcers were required during initial stage of shaping. Like punishment, both of these consequences should be used sparingly and only as a temporary expedient in order to bring the child under social control. This study will be given in much greater detail than the preceding examples in order to demonstrate with greater specificity the many and varied contingency arrangements required for this type of child—a child who is all too frequently "written off" or relegated at a very early age to institutional care for predelinquents. The child, referred to as Townsend (Allen, *et al.;* Haring, *et al.,* 1971), was four and a half years old when he was transferred from a Head Start classroom to a Behavior Modification class.

Beginning at seven months of age Townsend had been in a series of foster homes, each of which had reported great difficulty in managing him. His Head Start teachers described him as excessively disruptive, hyperactive, noncompliant with adults, aggressive toward children, mentally retarded and emotionally disturbed. In addition, for several months the Head Start bus system had refused to transport Townsend because of his uncontrollable behaviors; therefore, the child was transported privately each day by his social worker in her own car.

Collection of data according to the system described by Bijou,

Peterson, Harris, Allen, and Johnston (1969) was begun after his transfer to the Behavior Modification class. There the teachers were instructed, during the baseline period, to replicate as nearly as possible the homeroom teachers' methods of handling Townsend: rechanneling his disruptive activities, comforting him during catastrophic outbursts, physically restraining him when he attacked other children, verbalizing his feelings. The maladaptive behaviors continued at a high rate during baseline conditions.

On Townsend's eleventh day in the new classroom a first step in behavior modification procedure was initiated. All tantrums, regardless of duration or intensity, were to be ignored, that is, put on extinction. Absolute disregard of the tantrum, no matter how severe it might become, had to be thoroughly agreed upon among the teachers inasmuch as there are data (Hawkins, Peterson, Schweid, and Bijou, 1966) which indicate that, when tantrums are put on extinction, extremes of tantrum behavior may temporarily ensue. Townsend's data were no exception to the classic extinction curve. His first tantrum under the nonattending contingency lasted twenty-seven minutes (average duration of previous tantrums had been five minutes), becoming progressively more severe up to the twenty-minute point. The classroom was cleared of all children and adults when it became obvious that the tantrum was going to be lengthy. The children were taken to the playground by a teacher and a volunteer while the other teacher was stationed immediately *outside* the classroom door. When Townsend quieted, the teacher opened the door to ask in a matter-of-fact voice if he was ready to go to the playground. Before the teacher had a chance to speak, Townsend recommenced his tantrum. The teacher stepped back outside to wait for another period of calm. Twice more Townsend quieted down, only to begin anew at the sight of the teacher. Each time, however, the episodes were shorter (six, three, and one minute, respectively). Finally, the teacher was able to suggest going out of doors. This she did in a thoroughly neutral fashion with *no* grimaces or recriminatory comments on the tantrum or the shambles in which she found the room.

On the second day of tantrum intervention there was one tantrum of fifteen minutes with two two-minute followup tantrums when the teacher attempted to reenter the room. On the third day there was one mild four-minute tantrum. No further tantrums occurred in the Behavior Modification class nor was there a recurrence when Townsend returned to his regular Head Start classroom.

Modification of behaviors categorized as generally aggressive and disruptive—hitting and kicking children, spitting, running off with other children's toys—was instituted on the sixteenth class session. Disruptive episodes of this type had been averaging nine per session. On the first day of modification the teachers were instructed to give their undivided attention to the child who had been assaulted while keeping their backs to Townsend. Nine episodes of aggressive behavior were tallied on this day. During the next eleven sessions, there was a marked decrease (an average of three per session). During the twelfth session, there was an upswing to seven episodes with a gradual decrease over the next four sessions until finally no more grossly aggressive or disruptive acts were observed. A zero rate was recorded for the remainder of the sessions.

During this period of withdrawal of adult attention for the two classes of maladaptive behaviors, Townsend began dumping his lunch on the floor and then smearing it around with his feet or hands. The teachers handled the situation the first few days by getting sponges and towels for Townsend and instructing him to clean up the mess. However, a teacher always participated in the cleanup. The food-dumping and smearing continued day after day. The teachers obviously were not realizing that their insistence on the cleanup and their assistance in the task were maintaining the food-dumping at a steady rate of one plateful of food and one glassful of milk per day. The teachers were, therefore, instructed to ignore the entire episode and to give their undivided attention to the other children who *were* attending to the meal. Songs were to be sung as loudly as necessary to override peer comments calling attention to Townsend's behavior. On the first session of extinction Townsend himself called attention to the episode repeatedly: "Hey, looka I done, I make a mess. Get a sponge, we gotta scrub." The teachers failed to "see" or "hear" any of this. Instead, they sang a bit more lustily, calmly finished lunch with the children, and helped them get ready for outdoors. When Townsend came over to the wrap area, he was matter-of-factly helped with his clothing, with no acknowledgement of his continuing suggestions that "We gotta clean up a big mess." On the following day he again dumped his plate. Teachers followed the procedure of the previous day; that is, they ignored it completely. That session marked the end of the food-dumping except for one isolated episode two and a half months later, which the teachers again ignored.

Use of Consumable Reinforcers

Another behavior modification project with Townsend involved the use of consumable reinforcers. As mentioned earlier, Townsend had been banned from the Head Start bus. The children were required by the bus system to stay in their seats and keep their seat belts fastened. Staying buckled in a seat belt was a behavior incompatible with the disruptive behaviors that had caused Townsend to be banned: attempting to open the doors while the bus was in motion, playing with the instrument panel, throwing himself upon the bus driver while the latter was driving. Therefore, staying buckled in the seat belt was the target behavior in the following program aimed at reinstating Townsend as an acceptable bus rider.

Day 1. Townsend was prepared in advance for the bus trip. The teacher explained to him that he would be expected to sit quietly and keep his seat belt buckled. "I don't keep no seat belt on me," Townsend replied. The teacher ignored the remark. When the bus arrived, the teacher got on the bus with Townsend. The bus driver snapped Townsend's seat belt in place and the teacher *immediately* put a peanut in Townsend's mouth commenting approvingly, "Good, you are sitting quietly, all buckled up snug in your seat belt." She then quickly dispensed peanuts to every child on the bus with approving comments about their good buckling habits. Continuous rounds of peanut-dispensing and statements of praise were continued throughout the fifteen-minute bus ride.

Day 2. The same procedure as on Session 1 except that one peanut was dispensed to Townsend and each of the other children at longer intervals—two to three minutes.

Days 3, 4, 5. Peanuts—several at a time—were given only three times at variable intervals. Townsend's social worker alternated with the teacher in riding the bus and dispensing the consumables.

Days 6, 7, 8. One or the other of the adults continued to ride the bus but told the children that the peanuts would be saved until they got off the bus.

Day 9. With the exception of the bus driver, no other adult rode the bus. Both the teacher and the social worker were stationed at Townsend's bus stop. The driver had been cued to praise the children for their good bus-riding behavior as he let them off the bus. In Townsend's case he was to say nothing if Townsend had not stayed buckled. When the teacher and social worker heard the bus driver praise Townsend, they voiced approval, too, and gave him a small sucker as they accompanied him to his house.

Day 10. The same as Day 9 except that this day only the teacher met Townsend at his bus stop.

Day 11. Only the social worker met Townsend. Instead of a consumable reinforcer she presented him with a small toy.

Days 12 and 13. The social worker met Townsend but gave only social reinforcement for his good bus-riding behaviors.

Days 14, 15, and 16. No one met Townsend, but the bus driver was reminded to give him praise and a hug as he lifted him off the bus.

From then on Townsend was on his own, although the social worker occasionally met the bus if she was doing a routine call on the family. If she had brought clothing or play materials for Townsend, she presented these to him as she took him off the bus. The teachers also continued to intermittently praise his independent bus-riding when he arrived at school.

Shaping Play Skills

Establishing appropriate classroom behaviors incompatible with his maladaptive behaviors was the area to which the teachers gave the greatest time, energy, and planning in Townsend's program. Data from the home classroom indicated that he had few play skills. Out of doors he was unsuccessful at tricycle riding, climbing, jumping, and ball-throwing activities. Frequently the unsuccessful attempt precipitated a tantrum. Indoors, the only sustained play activity in which he engaged was isolate play in the housekeeping corner. Investigation of the data revealed that he did not build with blocks, paint, do woodworking, or use puzzles or other manipulative toys except to dump them out, scatter them about, or grab them away from other children. Also, he had an exceedingly low rate of interaction with other children. They avoided him, apparently because of his deficient play skills and his high rate of aggressive behaviors.

It seemed futile to attempt to build cooperative play with children until Townsend had acquired some play skills. Therefore, the teachers began a step-by-step program of teaching play with each of the materials considered important in a regular preschool program. For example, a teacher helped Townsend to duplicate what at first were exceedingly simple block models. If he refused to participate in a play "lesson" he simply forfeited the attention of all adults in the classroom. The moment he returned to the play materials, the attention of the teacher was again immediately forthcoming. In order to avoid Townsend's acquiring only stereotyped play patterns, he was also reinforced for all divergent or unique uses of materials and equipment as long as the divergence was within the broad limits acceptable to preschool teachers. Throwing blocks, while surely a divergent use, was considered inappropriate. This program of shaping play skills was concurrent with the extinction of maladaptive behaviors previously described. Therefore, even though the consequence of any one of Townsend's maladaptive behaviors was immediate withdrawal of adult social reinforcement, social reinforcement was readily and *unstintingly* available to him for any approximation to appropriate behavior.

Between Sessions 6 and 26 Townsend acquired an excellent repertoire of play skills with a variety of materials and equipment. It was decided, therefore, to change reinforcement contingencies: adult social reinforcement would be available only when Townsend engaged in constructive use of play materials *and* interacted appropriately with another child. The change in contingencies appeared to have a positive effect. Between Sessions 26 and 32 there was a steady increase in the rate of cooperative play.

Analysis of the data at this point indicated that it was an appropriate time to return Townsend to his Head Start classroom. Townsend's original teachers had visited the Behavior Modification classroom and had also been informed about each phase of the modification program. A joint staff meeting was held several days prior to the transfer in which all the guidance procedures and supportive data were reviewed. A member of the Behavior Modification team was assigned to Townsend's home classroom to continue the data collection and to provide necessary coaching of the teachers in maintaining the reinforcement contingencies. Coaching was supplied on Sessions 33 to 36 at which point the data indicated that Townsend's teachers were able to carry forward on their own. Not only were there no incidents of disruptive behaviors, but Townsend's social skills continued to hold at a high stable rate as measured by the amount of cooperative play. Several post checks were made throughout the remainder of the school year. Townsend continued to be a "normal" outgoing little boy, working and playing happily with an assortment of play materials and with a variety of children while requiring no more than what was considered an average share of the teacher's attention.

SUMMARY OF BEHAVIOR MODIFICATION PROCEDURES

The foregoing are but a few examples of the use of behavior modification procedures with disadvantaged children. As has been indicated, these tactics work equally well with all types of children. A number of behavior modification procedures were made explicit in the various examples that have been given. By way of conclusion these procedures will be reiterated:

1. Adults can readily employ reinforcement procedures to effect desired changes in disadvantaged children's behavior. To do so effectively, however, the adult must:
   a. assess children objectively (rather than subjectively or inferentially) so that specific behaviors can be selected as acceleration or deceleration targets;

   b. keep continuous records on these target behaviors;

   c. analyze the records and use them as a basis for program planning and continuous assessment of the effectiveness of the program.

2. The most severe maladaptive behaviors are responsive to their immediate consequences. For example, Townsend's tantrums were eliminated when they were systematically ignored.

3. Every adult involved in a child's environment is potentially a powerful social reinforcer. Thus, every adult who interacts with children in the preschool situation must carefully monitor his responses to each child. When systematic monitoring is not exercised, progress will be slower and more irregular.

4. Modification of only one or two of a child's behaviors at a time is essential to a successful modification program. The adults' responses may become scattered and unsystematic if too many contingencies must be kept in mind for each child.

5. Because significant adults do have powerful reinforcing properties, consumable reinforcers need be used only sparingly to shape appropriate behaviors in most preschool children.

6. The regular preschool environment abounds in natural reinforcers—play materials, snack time, outdoor play, special games and activities. Preschool teachers must make these reinforcers work *for* the child by making them available contingent on responses that will enhance the child's progress.

7. Physical or verbal punishment rarely need to be employed even when behaviors are as maladaptive as Townsend's food-smearing. (However, withdrawal of adult social reinforcement for an inappropriate response can be considered a form of mild punishment.)

8. Reinforcement of successive approximations to the target behaviors (shaping) is essential to achieve successful behavior modification. Reinstatement of Townsend as a bus rider is one example of shaping procedures.

9. A careful step-by-step reduction in the amount of reinforcement (learning the schedule) is necessary if a response is to be self-maintained. A behavior modification program cannot

be considered finished until the child is on a self-maintenance reinforcement schedule, e.g. that commensurate with the normal environment.

10. Though the extinction process (withholding reinforcement) is a highly effective means of freeing a child of his maladaptive response, it does not automatically provide an alternate set of behaviors. Therefore, it is critical that teachers give their attention to desired behaviors (or approximations thereof) so that the child may acquire a functional response repertoire.

11. Behavioral disorders in young children are primarily a function of the social environment rather than of some mysterious malaise within the child. Thus, gains in developing a repertoire of adaptive responses will be maintained only to the extent that subsequent environments reinforce appropriate rather than inappropriate responses.

A behavior modification program as described above requires a great investment of themselves on the part of the adults who work with young disadvantaged children. They must have alertness, perception, ingenuity, creative thought, flexibility, time, effort, and skill in working well with other staff members. However, the time so spent in planning and preparing each day's activities pays rich dividends in children's progress and in teachers' satisfaction. As each child successfully expands and improves his repertoire of skills and as these become intrinsically reinforcing, he requires less and less in the way of external praise and "rewards," and his total behavior shows qualities usually summarized as self-confident, happy, bright, creative, capable, and secure. Behaviors such as these, which are considered the hallmark of sound personality development, bring each child and the adults in his life immediate satisfaction and make more probable his love of learning and his sense of self-worth during his years of growing up.

REFERENCES

Allen, K. E.: The application of behavior modification principles to the learning deficits of handicapped preschool children. Paper presented at a Special Study Institute for Directors of Exemplary Early Childhood

Centers for Handicapped Children, Quail Roost Conference Center, Rougemont, North Carolina, July, 1970.

Allen, K. E., Henke, L. B., Harris, F. R., Baer, D. M., and Reynolds, N. F.: The control of hyperactivity by social reinforcement of attending behavior in a preschool child. *J. Educ Psychol, 58*:231-237, 1967.

Allen, K. E., Rieke, J., Dmitriev, V., and Hayden, A. H.: Early warning: Observation as a tool for recognizing potential handicaps in young children. *Educational Horizons*, pp. 43-55, Winter 1971-72.

Allen, K. E., Turner, K. D., and Everett, P. M.: A behavior modification classroom for Head Start children with problem behaviors. *Except Child, 37*:2, 119-129, 1970.

Bijou, S. W., Peterson, R. F., Harris, F. R., Allen, K. E., and Johnston, M. S.: Methodology for experimental studies of young children in natural settings. *The Psychological Record, 19*:172-210, 1969.

Bucker, B., and Lovaas, O. I.: Use of aversive stimulation in behavior modification. In M. R. Jones (Ed.): *Miami Symposium on the Prediction of Behavior: Aversive Stimulation.* Coral Gables: U of Miami Pr, 1967.

Crosby, M.: Elementary school programs for the education of the disadvantaged. In *The Educationally Retarded and Disadvantaged.* The Sixtysixth yearbook of the National Society for the Study of Education, Part I, pp. 168-84. Chicago, National Society for the Study of Education, 1967. (Distributed by the U of Chicago Pr, Chicago, Illinois.)

Durham, J. T.: Who needs it? Compensatory education. *Clearing House, 44*:18-22, 1969.

Evans, E. D.: *Contemporary Influences in Early Childhood Education.* New York, HR&W, 1971.

Gantt, W. N.: Language and learning styles of the "educationally disadvantaged." *The Elementary School Journal*, pp. 139-142, December, 1972.

Haring, N. G., Hayden, A. H., and Allen, K. E.: Programs and projects: Intervention in early childhood. *Educational Technology*, pp. 52-61, February 1971.

Harris, F., Wolf, M., and Baer, D.: Effects of adult social reinforcement on child behavior. In Hartup, W. W., and Smothergill, Nancy L., (Eds.) : *The Young Child.* Washington, D. C., National Association for the Education of Young Children, pp. 13-26, 1966.

Hawkins, R. P., Peterson, R. F., Schweid, E., and Bijou, S. W.: Behavior therapy in the home: Amelioration of problem parent-child relationships with the parent in a therapeutic role. *J Exp Child Psychol, 4*:99-107, 1966.

Hellmuth, J. (Ed.) : *Disadvantaged Child,* Vol. 1. New York, Brunner-Mazel, 1967.

Hellmuth, J. (Ed.) : Compensatory education: A national debate. In *Disadvantaged Child,* Vol. 3. New York, Brunner-Mazel, 1970.

Jensen, A.: How much can we boost I.Q. and scholastic achievement? *Harvard Educational Review, 39*:1-123, 1969.

Kagan, J.: On cultural deprivation. In Glass, D. (Ed.) : *Proceedings of the Conference on Biology and Behavior.* New York, Rockefeller, pp. 211-250, 1968.

Knapp, M. E., O'Neil, S. M., and Allen, K. E.: Teaching Suzi to walk. *Nursing Forum* (in press).

Premack, D.: Toward empirical behavior laws: I. Positive reinforcement. *Psychol Rev, 66*:219-233, 1959.

Vance, B.: *Teaching the Prekindergarten Child: Instructional Design and Curriculum.* Monterey, Brooks-Cole, 1973.

APPENDIX

JULIE: A CASE STUDY*

Subject and Setting

Julie was three years and eleven months old at the time of her initial enrollment in the Model Preschool. She was an unusually small child for her age though there were no untoward medical signs except that of arrested hydrocephalus in early infancy. The medical follow-ups indicated no evidence of subsequent physical or neurological impairment. Developmentally, she exhibited poor large motor skills and infantile speech patterns. In addition, she displayed an extensive repertoire of inappropriate and maladaptive social behaviors toward children and adults. With children, her most conspicuous responses were avoidance or attack. With adults, she was totally noncompliant. She screamed "No" to any request, however mild; any insistence by an adult (parent or teacher) provoked a full-fledged tantrum in which she threw herself face down on the floor, kicking and screaming hysterically.

Her previous school placement had been a preschool for emotionally disturbed children in the psychiatric department of a children's hospital. The staff there felt that Julie had made some progress but that she might progress more rapidly if she could interact with a more normal peer group than was available in the hospital preschool setting. Two members of the Experimental

---

* This study was presented originally at the Third Annual Conference on Behavior Analysis in Education at the University of Kansas in Lawrence, Kansas, May, 1972.

Education Unit in the Child Development and Mental Retardation Center preschool staff observed Julie in the psychiatric setting and they agreed to enroll her in a preschool class at the EEU. In this class were sixteen children, half of whom were classified as normal, the other half as handicapped. The handicapping conditions varied: emotional disturbance, mental retardation, orthopedic involvement, language impairment. Classroom personnel were a head teacher, an assistant teacher, and an intern advancing a master's degree in special education. Several other adults were in the classroom each quarter—students from various disciplines for whom the preschool staff provided graduate and undergraduate training.

Procedures

The basic Washington Social Code (Bijou, Peterson, Harris, Allen, and Johnston, 1968), with a number of variations, was employed as the data system. Data were recorded at ten-second intervals for twenty to seventy minutes during free play indoors. Length of sample time varied with the amount of personnel on hand each day. Specifically, data were collected on 1) quality of social behavior, indicating whether the child was engaged in cooperative, parallel, or isolate play; 2) amount of verbal behavior with peers; 3) amount of time not engaged in purposeful activities (e.g. wandering, watching, rocking, or thumbsucking, apart from a play activity or material); 4) amount of disruptive behaviors such as screaming, having a tantrum, running off with other children's possessions; 5) number of attacks (kicks, hits, or bites) that made physical contact with another child; and 6) amount of teacher attention, defined as any interval in which a teacher touched, spoke to, or presented Julie with material of any kind. Six days of baseline data were collected; on the fifth day a new category of maladaptive behaviors was added, throwing and dumping play materials and equipment.

At the end of six days, the Head Teacher declined to continue baseline, arguing convincingly that Julie's steadily increasing disruptive behaviors and ever more ferocious physical attacks were interfering drastically with the other fifteen children's school program. Several of these children were three-year-olds adapting to their first group experience. Experimentalists engaged in classroom studies know how imperative it is for successful research to have the teaching staff agree to the experimental procedures. It is sometimes necessary to be less rigorous than one would like in order to maintain teacher cooperation. Thus, a compromise was reached and Phase I commenced.

Phase I. The intervention tactics used in Phase I were a compromise, as mentioned above, between the wish to achieve a more stable baseline and the insistence that something had to be done. After examining several possibilities, the teachers agreed to operate negatively on only one behavior, the one they felt was most traumatizing to the other children—Julie's physical attacks. She was to be put in time-out for each attack. They contrived a time-out spot by placing two sets of heavy lockers in a partially closed "V" position. When the child was put in time-out, the "V" was pushed to a fully closed position, providing complete isolation within the classroom setting. Two more categories of data were added: amount of time Julie spent in time-out and amount of tantrum time during time-out. Another revision was made in the procedures: the teacher collecting the data acted as the time-out agent to insure that every physical assault received an immediate negative consequence. This teacher also dispensed positive reinforcement according to routine procedures in effect for all children—intermittent social reinforcement of appropriate behaviors. (In Julie's case, bare approximations to appropriate behaviors received positive reinforcement.) All other disruptive behaviors—dumping, throwing, snatching, screaming, and having tantrums—were ignored so far as possible. A series of language sampling observations was also scheduled at this time in order to assess potential qualitative improvement in Julie's verbal repertoire.

Phase II. The second set of intervention procedures, labeled "activity decision required," was aimed at reducing Julie's random wanderings about the room. The staff agreed that she most often engaged in disruptive behavior or physical assault during her aimless cruising. The procedure used was that each time Julie left an activity she was required to state where she was going to play next. Usually the teacher offered two or three suggestions: "There is room for you at the easel, or you can go to the puzzle table, or play with the blocks." If Julie refused to state a choice she was led to the locker area but not put in time-out. The teacher stood with her back to Julie, preventing her return to the main play area until she indicated verbally where she would play. Such decisions were heartily reinforced by the teacher who then accompanied Julie to the area of her choice and helped her to get started in play. Every effort was made during this period to teach Julie how to use play materials, for she had not even rudimentary skills with blocks, manipulative toys, creative materials, or dramatic play activities. Time-out for physical aggression was still in effect during Phase II.

Phase III. Julie's throwing and dumping of play materials continued to be a major disruption in the classroom. One reason, of course, was that while teachers could do a heroic job of ignoring her, it was almost impossible to prevent peers from reinforcing Julie with negative verbalizations when she swept their half-finished puzzles off the table, dumped the contents of their paint cans on the floor or on them, or poured water over their sleeping dolls. In fact, argued the teachers, Julie was becoming so aversive to all the children that it would take until Doomsday for her to be accepted as a member of that peer group unless further steps were taken immediately to reduce her obnoxious behaviors. Thus Phase III—time-out for all throwing and dumping episodes in addition to Phase I and Phase II conditions: 1) timing-out physical attacks, 2) ignoring screaming and tantrums, 3) requiring a play-choice decision, 4) intermittently reinforcing approximations to appropriate play, and 5) teaching use of play materials.

Phase IV. Because the children continued to shun Julie, a fourth phase, structuring cooperative play activities was instituted to insure that Julie would be included. For example, certain children were designated to play with her for part of the free-play period in a particular area: "John and Julie and Sara and Shelli are to play in the housekeeping corner." The rationale for this phase was the expectation that children, who were temporarily legislated to play with the semi-reformed Julie, would discover that she had shed many of her aversive properties and that teachers thus would have the opportunity to reinforce Julie for appropriate play with peers and to reinforce the children for playing cooperatively with Julie.

Results

Baseline period. During baseline, Julie's physical attacks on children rose to a high of sixty-eight during one sixty-minute observation period while throwing and dumping episodes reached a peak of seventy-four. Disruptive behaviors rose to 48 percent of the time; the amount of time not engaged in purposeful activities climbed steadily to 88 percent. Amount of verbalizing to peers was negligible, the high being 6 percent. Cooperative interaction with peers reached 30 percent, but was steadily declining, and amount of time spent alone was as high as 77 percent. Teacher attention to Julie averaged 15 percent during the baseline period.

Phase I (Time-out for physical attacks). Time-out for physical attacks resulted in an immediate and drastic decrease in the attacks. Over the five-day Phase I period, the range was two to seven episodes. Concurrently, throwing and dumping episodes decelerated to a low of five episodes in two observation periods. Julie's disruptive behaviors also decreased markedly to a low of four episodes. (Neither of these behaviors, it must be remembered, was under treatment during Phase I.) Amount of time not engaged in purposeful activities dropped to 34 percent on one day; however, much of Julie's time was spent in time-out during this period, so that she had much less time available to her for "cruising." Verbalizations to peers increased slightly to 12 percent. Cooperative interaction with peers remained at approximately the same average, 25 percent, while isolate play decreased. Again, this decrease was largely due to the time Julie was spending in time-out—she simply had less time at her disposal for isolate activities. Teacher attention to Julie in Phase I increased slightly to an average of 24 percent.

Phase II (Activity decision required). Even though Phase I produced a decrease in several of Julie's undesirable behaviors, the teachers were concerned about how much time she spent cruising about aimlessly when not in time-out. Therefore, Phase II was initiated, requiring Julie to state where she would play next and keeping her hemmed in a corner of the room until she did so. Teachers also continued the Phase I conditions of time-out for physical attacks, ignoring all disruptive episodes, and intermittent positive social reinforcement for appropriate behavior. Physical attacks dropped to a near zero rate and stayed there. However, Julie's throwing and dumping episodes rose sharply, reaching a peak of fifty-six episodes on one day. Disruptive episodes continued at roughly the Phase I low rate. During the first nine days of Phase II percentage of time not spent in purposeful activities was very high, from 50 percent to 85 percent. None of this was cruising time, however; it was time Julie spent in the corner deciding where to play next. Over the next nine days of Phase II, the amount of time not in activities varied markedly, although on four days she spent 10 percent or less of her time not engaged in activities. Since she was spending so much of her time in a corner of the room during these first nine days, verbal behavior and cooperation with peers dropped sharply but both showed good increases during the latter half of Phase II—especially verbalization to peers. It rose to 25 percent on one day. Teachers did not give Julie any attention when she was hemmed into the corner except for periodic cues to her to tell them where she would next play; therefore, teacher attention, except for the first part of Phase II was only a little greater than the typical Phase I rate. Julie also spent some time in actual time-out after making a physical attack on another, but this seldom went above 10 percent for any days except for one or two "bad days."

Phase III (time-out for throwing and dumping). Because Julie's throwing and dumping episodes were much too frequent during Phase II, the teachers decided on the negative consequence, time-out, for these responses. It produced an immediate and stable decrease to a zero rate which Julie maintained for the rest of Phase III. Physical assaults (still subject to time-out in this phase) stayed at a near zero rate; other disruptive behaviors also dropped to and stayed at that rate. Verbalizations to peers remained at a fairly good level—from 5 percent to 18 percent per day; cooperative interaction dropped to a little less than its former level. Isolate play, however, decreased considerably, indicating that Julie was spending much more time near other children or in parallel play with them. Teacher attention increased during Phase II to an average of 29 percent per day. After an initial increase in time-outs for throwing and dumping, there were no time-outs at all during the last seven days of the phase.

Phase IV (Structuring cooperative play). By the end of Phase III, Julie, according to the teachers' judgment, was not engaging in a sufficient amount of cooperative play. They began, therefore, actually to structure at least one situation per free play session in which they instructed Julie and several other children to play together in a specific activity. They made no requirements about the length of "legislated" interaction. This program did not increase Julie's cooperative play appreciably, although on several days she did go above 25 percent. However, the amount of isolate play decreased markedly, indicating that Julie was spending a great deal of time in proximity to children—a good first approximation to cooperative interaction. Her verbalization rate also continued at an appropriate level, although there was some fluctuation.

During Phase IV, Julie's physical attacks stayed at a near zero rate as did her throwing and dumping and disruptive behaviors. Time not in activities stayed well below 10 percent except for one day. In this phase, teachers discontinued the decision-making contingency. Teacher attention averaged 23 percent although several children were sharing in this attention since cooperative play was to receive adult social reinforcement. The time Julie spent in time-out was little though it was still required occasionally. She no longer had tantrums in time-out, however.

Discussion and Conclusions

Though Julie's disruptive and physically aggressive behaviors were at a low level during her first few days in the classroom, these began to appear at an accelerated rate once she was thoroughly adapted to the new situation. The teachers' anxieties over the other children's well-being led to abandoning one of the objectives, that of ascertaining the effect on Julie's overall behavior

of simple exposure to a more normal peer group. It seems unlikely, however, that she would have improved without specific
intervention; she was simply too aversive to both children and
adults. Because of her aversiveness, of course, most social reinforcement from peers was directed to her undesirable behaviors.
It is very difficult to get a group of preschool children to reinforce differentially a child with Julie's repertoire, especially when
half of the children are themselves management problems. Furthermore, even if the teachers had been willing to program the
children to do so, the extinction of Julie's maladaptive responses
would probably have been too slow and arduous a process.

After taking baseline data, the teachers chose one behavior—
aggressive physical attacks—as a first target behavior to modify.
However, data were kept continuously on many other responses
in order to ascertain what, if any, correlated changes might occur. It is interesting that while throwing and dumping and disruptive behaviors decreased during Phase I (time-out for physical attacks), the rate of throwing and dumping increased again
within a few days though an increase of disruptive acts did *not*
occur. In fact, these last responses disappeared almost entirely in
the course of treatment even though they were never subjected
to specific intervention.

In addition to the behaviors classified as disruptive, one other
behavior, never exposed to specific intervention, Julie's verbal interaction with peers, showed marked improvement. Not only did
amount of verbalizations increase spontaneously, quality also
was somewhat improved. These qualitative changes are documented in a series of language samples taken on the child during
the course of the study.

Another prediction, that Julie's rate of cooperative play would
increase spontaneously once she became less aversive to children
and had acquired some play skills, was not borne out. A specific
program (Phase IV) was required to achieve that goal. Even
then, the quantitative rate of increase was not remarkable, although the improved quality of her interaction with peers was
noteworthy. These improvements are readily observable on a series of videotapes that span the study from start to finish. These
tapes have been assembled into a video case study to provide ad-

ditional documentation of the dramatic changes in Julie's behavior.

This study, as well as several others in progress, seem to indicate that children with severe problem behaviors are not likely to improve without specific behavior management intervention. With such intervention, however, it appears that progress is rapid where there are normal peers to serve as models for appropriate behavior. Also, the "cost" in teacher time would seem reasonable. In Julie's case it exceeded by very little the typical amount that children receive in a well-staffed preschool. Thus, it may be assumed that other children are not being "short-changed." Data on the normal children indicate steady progress with no deleterious side effects. Additional favorable evidence appears in their parents' responses to the program. Without exception, all parents asked for a second year's enrollment for their child, or for a younger sibling if the older child was at kindergarten age.

Finally, this study yields some tentative answers to the question, "Can teachers realistically be expected to take data, program for, and manage so diversified a group?" In this study, the Head Teacher collected much of the data while supervising in the classroom. Such a dual role has been carried out by teachers in other studies (Turner, Allen, and Smith, 1972); therefore, data collection by the teacher is not unique. However, teacher-collected data are usually simple counts or duration measures of fairly discrete events, whereas the data system for this study was much more complex. The teacher recorded eleven aspects of the child's behavioral repertoire per ten-second interval over a twenty- to seventy-minute observation period each day, thus making 120 to 420 recorded observations during each class session.

Another noteworthy feature of this study documented vividly on videotape is that, in addition to supervisory and recording duties, the data-taking teacher also acted as the reinforcing agent for Julie. That is, the data-taking teacher dispensed much of the positive social reinforcement for Julie's appropriate behavior and served as sole agent for immediately putting the child in time-out for the designated inappropriate responses. It might be underscored that one of the reasons for assigning the recording teacher to this additional duty was to insure an immediate negative consequence. The other adults in the room, engaged in working with the other fifteen children, often failed to see Julie's undesirable response or could not disengage themselves from an activity they were involved in rapidly enough to provide immediate negative feedback.

While it cannot be stated definitively how and in what numbers to combine normal and handicapped children in a single classroom, a series of studies such as the one described should provide a foundation for designing a long-term, comprehensive research program to ferret out the answers. Answers are needed for we do atypical children a severe injustice if we keep them out of the educational mainstream. Grouping atypical children together, segregating them from normal peer models, often seems to increase their atypical behaviors. Behavior analysis has demonstrated that it can help to remediate many behavior problems; surely it can be expected to yield empirical data that will help meet the urgent need to better educate handicapped children.

REFERENCES

Bijou, S. W., Peterson, R. F., Harris, F. R., Allen, K. E., and Johnston, M. S.: Methodology for experimental studies of young children in natural settings. *The Psychological Record, 19*:2, 177-210, 1969.

Allen, K. E., Turner, K. D., and Everett, P. M.: A behavior modification classroom for Head Start children with problem behaviors. *Except Child, 37*:2, 119-127, 1970.

Turner, K. D., Allen, K. E., and Smith, P. K.: Modification of an autistic child's verbal and hyperactive behaviors (mimeograph).

CHAPTER VII

THE USE OF MODELING TECHNIQUES IN REHABILITATION OF THE JUVENILE OFFENDER

VICTOR J. GANZER

••

••

THE PURPOSE of this chapter is to describe how the concept of observational learning, or modeling, can be translated into an objective and viable vehicle for teaching various skills to clients who require some kind of social or vocational rehabilitation. Proceeding from a definition of modeling and its place in theories of social learning, this chapter briefly will review research on modeling, describe the development and application of modeling principles in the rehabilitation of male juvenile delinquents, and discuss some potential uses of modeling techniques in other rehabilitation programs.

THE CONCEPT OF MODELING

Modeling, or observational learning, is a central concept in theories of social learning (Bandura, 1969b). Observation of the behavior of others may have three different effects (Bandura and Walters, 1963).

The first is a learning effect. An observer may acquire (learn) a variety of responses simply by observing another person's (the

130

model's) behavior. This is true regardless of whether or not the observer imitates or matches the model's response following its occurrence, and regardless of whether or not reinforcement, either to the observer or model, is contingent upon any aspect of the behavior. There is considerable evidence that the observation and imitation of modeled behavior plays a major role in the acquisition of inappropriate as well as adaptive behavior, and that this is true in whatever sociocultural context the learning occurs (Bandura and Walters, 1963; Bandura, 1969a). An enormous diversity of behaviors is learned through the observation of models. These behaviors include vocational skills, various motives and aspirations, sex appropriate roles, and numerous kinds of verbal and nonverbal responses. The category of models includes many types of persons: parents, adults, one's peers, and symbolic and film mediated models such as are observed on television and in motion pictures.

The second effect of observing modeled behaviors derives from the consequences of the model's actions. The inhibitory responses of an observer may be strengthened or weakened depending on whether the model's behavior is rewarded or punished.

The third effect may be termed response facilitation and does not involve new learning or response inhibition. For example, a person may pause to look up into a tree if he observes another engaged in this activity.

Imitation as a concept in social psychological theory may be traced back to the psychologist Lloyd Morgan who, as early as 1896, was concerned with modeling phenomena. Since that time, other writers have considered imitativeness to be an instinctive or constitutional process, a phenomenon derived from Pavlovian classical conditioning principles, and more recently a special subclass of operant responses in which the concept of reinforcement is useful.

Aronfreed's (1969) research on vicarious learning and internalization provides an example of the importance of observational learning and imitation in contemporary social psychological theories. Aronfreed is concerned with the internalization of social role norms in children, which is the process of adopting these norms as one's own. For Aronfreed, observational learning is a mechanism or vehicle by which internalized behavior control is obtained.

A prototype for much current research on modeling was a series of experiments carried out by Bandura (1962) which demonstrated the importance of modeling effects in the transmission of novel responses from adult models to nursery school age children. In these experiments, children were exposed to films of adult models who behaved in different ways toward a large air-inflated plastic doll. One modeling sequence depicted the models behaving very aggressively and abusively toward the doll, while in another condition the adult models exhibited no aggression. Children who observed the aggressive behavior subsequently displayed a significantly greater number of imitative aggressive responses than did children in the nonaggressive modeling condition. Children in the latter condition rarely if ever aggressed toward the doll. These studies are especially suggestive in that they indicated that film mediated models also were effective in transmitting various patterns of behavior to the young observers.

Bandura has conducted other studies which have shown that the consequences contingent upon the model's behavior, such as reward or punishment, will produce differential effects on the subsequent behavior of observers (Bandura and Walters, 1963; Bandura, 1965). In this way, principles of reinforcement have been combined with observational learning and imitation to provide very convincing demonstrations of the importance of these concepts for the psychology of learning and behavior modification.

MODELING AND BEHAVIOR MODIFICATION

It was mentioned that theoretical and experimental developments of the concepts of modeling and observational learning are not new. Also not new is the therapeutic application of modeling procedures to the modification of maladaptive behavior. Modeling has been employed as a therapeutic tool within a variety of experimental and clinical settings. One of the earliest applications of modeling principles to behavior modification was undertaken by Jones (1924) in an effort to modify phobic behavior in children. Her technique for eliminating phobias was to expose a phobic child to other children who behaved in a fearless manner toward the feared object. The observation of children interacting with the object was in most cases sufficient to reduce the phobic observer's anxious and avoidant responses. Conversely, Jones demonstrated that fears rapidly could be acquired through similar observational processes.

Another early modeling study was conducted by Chittenden (1942). Chittenden was interested in measuring and modifying assertive behaviors in young children. Observation of the free play behavior of preschool children identified two types of assertive behavior: dominating (the direct application of force against another child), and cooperating (nonforceful influence) responses. Children who scored high on the dimension of domination participated in a series of play periods in which they observed small dolls enact social roles similar to the ones in which they themselves experienced difficulties. The role modeling situations de-emphasized domination of others as a play technique. The dolls served as symbolic models to facilitate the children's understanding of social situations. The experimenter also served as a model and helped the children to understand and select appropriate responses to various situations. Samples of behavior collected subsequent to the training period indicated that actions of children trained in cooperative social techniques were significantly less dominant than those of comparable children who had served as a control (no treatment) group.

A therapeutically useful modeling technique, termed Fixed Role Therapy, has been developed by Kelly (1955) for use with adults who are interested in modifying or strengthening certain personality characteristics. The client first is required to construct a descriptive characterization of himself. The self-descriptions subsequently are studied by a panel of therapists who suggest ways of modifying them to help the client eliminate inappropriate behaviors and maximize the use of positive assets. A new role sketch or self-characterization is then presented to the client, who is given modeled demonstrations of the new role behaviors. Through imitation and practice the new behaviors gradually are assimilated into the client's repertoire and generalized to the extratherapeutic environment.

Lazarus (1966) developed a behavior modification technique

which is similar in some respects to that of Kelly. Lazarus terms his approach Behavior Rehearsal and employs it with patients who are deficient in some type of assertive behavior. Typically, his patients are individuals who are unable to make assertive or aggressive responses in situations where such behavior would be appropriate. In the treatment situation the therapist serves as a model, playing the role of someone toward whom the patient reacts with excessive fear, inhibition, or anxiety. The patient first observes responses that would be appropriate in the situation, then practices responding to the therapist's role behavior in a more uninhibited and aggressive manner. More recently McFall and Lillesand (1971) demonstrated that subjects who lacked assertiveness in refusing reasonable requests could be trained to become more assertive. Subjects first listened to a tape recorded model who refused another's request and subsequently practiced, with coaching from the experimenter, similar refusal behavior.

A final example of the therapeutic application of modeling procedures is the work of Lovaas (1968) on techniques of teaching verbal and nonverbal behaviors to schizophrenic children. Children were exposed to a successive set of discriminations that required them eventually to imitate an adult model's vocalizations. The verbal imitation training phase employed response-contingent positive reinforcement to establish and strengthen matching behavior. An important finding was that imitation eventually became self-reinforcing. Children would imitate words in the absence of external reinforcement. Lovaas devised a similar training program to establish socially appropriate and self-sufficient behaviors in the children. It is of note that Lovaas considered the therapeutic use of modeling and imitation to have been crucial to the success of his program.

Modeling has been used as a vehicle for behavior change in other areas of research. Examples include Poser's (1967) use of modeling procedures to train behavior therapists. Geer and Turteltaub (1967) employed fearless models to reduce the fears of snake phobic female college students. Bandura, Blanchard and Ritter (1969) developed similar methods to modify dog phobic behavior in children. DeWolfe (1967) demonstrated that student nurses became less afraid of contracting tuberculosis as a result of their association with unafraid nurses who served as models with whom the students could identify. Olson (1971) found that preferences for magazines among adult male schizophrenic patients could be modified by exposing the patients to models who expressed different kinds of preferences. In a different context, Sarason, Ganzer and Singer (1972) have shown that Ss who are defensive about admitting to negative personal characteristics and problems in an interview situation can be influenced to make more problem-oriented statements if they first listened to a tape recorded model who discussed his problems in an open and honest manner. Marlatt (1971) demonstrated similar effects through the use of live models.

The above summary of research on modeling is by no means inclusive. It was meant to serve two purposes: (1) to illustrate the variety of behavior which has been successfully modified through the provision of various kinds of observational learning opportunities, and (2) to provide theoretical and empirical justification for applying observational learning procedures as rehabilitation techniques. We may now describe the development, procedures, and results of a modeling project which was concerned with the rehabilitation of juvenile offenders.*

The Cascadia Project

In different ways psychoanalytic, psychological, and sociological theorists have considered observational learning and the imitation of modeled behavior to be important explanatory concepts in accounting for the development and maintenance of delinquent behavior (Sarason and Ganzer, 1971). Similarly, a guiding principle in the research reported below was that if parents or significant others functioned as models of inadequate or deviant behavior, then impressionable observers such as children might

* The modeling research reported in this chapter was supported by grants from the Social and Rehabilitation Service of the Department of Health, Education and Welfare; and from the Law and Justice Planning Office, Planning and Community Affairs Agency, Olympia, Washington. Professor Irwin G. Sarason of the Department of Psychology, University of Washington, was the Project Director. The author served as Associate Project Director.

well imitate and acquire various deviant behaviors. Conversely, the provision of adequate and prosocial models for children who have learned to behave maladaptively might be expected to facilitate the learning of new skills and more socially adaptive responses.

This research sought to attain two general objectives: (1) Working from the premise that rehabilitation is facilitated and recidivism is reduced by strengthening the juvenile offenders' social response repertoire, the project sought to teach institutionalized male delinquents more appropriate social skills and ways of coping with problems which they would encounter during their institutional stay and after release. The first objective was to demonstrate that the teaching of appropriate behaviors could be effectively accomplished through the systematic provision of relevant observational learning opportunities. (2) The second objective was to evaluate modeling techniques in terms of how easily they can be learned and applied by persons unfamiliar with behaviorally oriented rehabilitative methods. The urgent need to develop and utilize the potential skills of line personnel is a focal issue in the community mental health movement (Cowen and Zax, 1967). The development of simple standard procedures for training people in the use of role modeling techniques might represent a significant step toward achieving this goal.

Background

The initial research in which observational learning opportunities were provided in an effort to increase the social-interpersonal skills of institutionalized male juveniles was conducted at Cascadia Juvenile Reception-Diagnostic Center located at Tacoma, Washington.* This institution, which is described more com-

* Former Superintendent Robert Tropp, Superintendent Wilham Callahan, Assistant Superintendent Keith Gibson, and Cottage Supervisors Lawrence Castleman, James Gibbeson, and John Sanguinetti and their staffs at Cascadia Juvenile Reception-Diagnostic Center contributed importantly to the conduct of the research described in this chapter. Completion of the project would not have been possible without the assistance and cooperation of Cascadia staff psychologists Sarah Sloat, V. M. Tye, and Ralph Sherfey; the Washington Division of Institutions, Juvenile Parole Services, the Office of Research, and the superintendents and staffs of the state's juvenile institutions.

pletely elsewhere (Sarason and Ganzer, 1969; 1971), is a facility of the State's Office of Juvenile Rehabilitation. Cascadia serves as the initial reception, treatment, and diagnostic center for all children between the ages of eight and eighteen who are committed as delinquent by the State's Juvenile Courts. It houses approximately two hundred in twelve self-contained residential cottages. The average length of stay for children in the diagnostic program is six weeks.

The ingredients of a "modeling situation" were at this point only generally conceptualized. First, it would be a small group situation, consisting of at least two models or group leaders (in this project, graduate students in clinical psychology training) and four to six boys. Second, the purposes of the group meetings would be to teach the boys some behavior or skill in which they were deficient. Third, the teaching would be carried out by the models who would demonstrate (model) various roles and behaviors while the boys observed. The final step in the learning process would be the boys' imitations of the modeled behaviors which, when accompanied by social reinforcement (e.g. praise), would further the learning process and the development of new skills.

Development of Modeling Procedures

Since information on previous work involving group modeling techniques with institutionalized adolescents was not available, it was necessary to build the procedures virtually from the ground up. The four psychology graduate students who were to serve as the models began preliminary work on the project by meeting informally with small groups of boys in order to better understand the juvenile offender. Some of the purposes of these informal meetings were to develop ideas of what were the boys' problems and major concerns and to determine how the models could best interact with them in order to maximize their influence and desirability as persons with whom they would want to identify. Another purpose was to establish the project in the institution's residential cottages as an accepted part of their day-to-day operation since boys often regarded strangers and innovations with suspicion and mistrust. As a further safeguard against arousing boys' antagonism and defensiveness, the project was introduced as being under the auspices of the University of Washington and *not* connected with any aspect of the institution's diagnostic process.

Many informal conversations were conducted and tape recorded over a period of several months. The sessions focused on the boys' problems, their perceptions of the adult and peer worlds, their needs, goals, feelings about themselves, and their identities in general. Informal content analyses were performed on the recorded material, and major problem and interest areas were noted and summarized. Subsequent groups of boys were asked to spontaneously role-play some of the problems. For example, the problems that teenagers have in dealing with authoritarian adults served as one topic around which spontaneous role-playing behavior was elicited. One boy or one of the assistants would play the role of an authoritarian teacher, and another boy would act the role of a teenager who was being disciplined. Or, two boys would role-play a dialogue in which one boy tried to convince the other not to experiment with narcotics. These and many other areas of importance to adolescents were role-played and the performances were tape recorded.

Further study of the boys' spontaneous behavior in these situations resulted in a series of revised and expanded dialogues which were typed in script form. The scripts were similar to those used by actors when learning various parts for plays. Depending upon the content and situations, roles for two to four people were written into the scripts. The sixteen to twenty of these scripts which were developed in this manner may be categorized into three or four general content areas. Some dealt with the problems teenagers often have in coping with authority. For example, one script dealt with how to appropriately interact with police officers; and another focused on appropriate behavior during a job interview. A related content area concerned the importance of planning ahead, which also involved some aspects of impulse control. Other scripts were based on the problem of negative peer pressure: how to recognize it, what it means, and various ways to cope with it. Another general topic concerned ways of making a good impression on others, not in the sense of manipulating somebody, but rather with aspects of dealing with people through acceptable and prosocial means. Most of the materials in some way dealt with the problem of impulsive (primarily aggressive) behaviors and various ways to recognize and appropriately express them.

The models practiced the various roles included in the scripts. These practice efforts were tape recorded, replayed, and the behavior of the models as well as the content of the scripts were further modified. Most of the scripts were tried out in groups with the boys as an audience. Their reactions to and opinions of the material regarding its realism and appropriateness were obtained. In a very real sense, the contents of the modeling procedures were developed largely by the boys themselves; they defined their problems, and the research staff worked with them on possible solutions.

Several common problems which other workers have noted as being particularly characteristic of delinquent youth became apparent during this preliminary work. These problems concerned the boys' motivations to work in groups and their often very short attention span. Learning through observing modeled behavior involves these two important variables. It was initially estimated that the boys' general level of attention could be maintained for approximately twenty minutes to one-half hour. Several techniques were instituted to increase this short and fluctuating attention span. One was the provision of a soft drink for each boy about half-way through an hour's session. While initially perceived as a "bribe" by many of the boys, the soft drinks soon were readily accepted as something that the models wanted to share with them. Another, and perhaps the most important, method of maintaining attention is the actual amount of physical activity which the modeling situations require. Models and boys are on their feet and actually moving about the room a great deal during the sessions. This physical activity, combined with the heavy emphasis on affect and nonverbal expressive gestures, did a great deal to facilitate motivation and attention to the content and purpose of the group sessions. Since many delinquent boys are primarily action and movement oriented and rely considerably less on verbal skills, this dimension of the group procedures has proven to be very important. Another method of maintaining interest was the replay of the audio, and later the video, tape recordings after the boys had imitiated various roles. This feedback was of considerable interest to the boys since it afforded them the opportunity to correct elements of their own behavior. Another method of maintaining attention was to ask one of the boys to summarize the situation that first had been enacted by the models. Boys did not know beforehand who was going to be asked, so it was necessary for them to be attentive in order to answer the questions satisfactorily. The fact that each boy knew that he would be expected to imitiate the model's behavior also promoted increased attentiveness. It was estimated that these procedures were able to hold boys' attention and interest for an hour or more.

The Main Experiment

The subjects were 192 male first offenders between fifteen and eighteen years of age. Half of them were drawn from each of the two cottages in which the research was conducted. Sixty-four boys each participated in modeling groups, guided discussion groups, and the control group. Subjects were comparable in age, intelligence, chronicity of preinstitutional delinquent behavior, and diagnostic classification.

All boys were administered a battery of tests upon admission to the cottages. The tests included self-report trait, attitude, and self-concept measures. A number of dimensions of their behavior were rated by cottage staff on two specially devised behavior rating scales. These instruments are more fully described elsewhere (Sarason and Ganzer, 1971). Boys who arrived at the cottages on nearly the same days were selected in groups of four or five to serve as experimental group subjects. This procedure allowed the group members to participate together for the same number of sessions without having them disrupted by losses or additions of new boys. Additional admissions also were tested and served as a pool from which the control group (i.e. no special treatment) subjects concurrently were drawn.

Boys in the modeling groups participated in sixteen hour-long sessions which were conducted four times a week during a four-week period. Procedures for conducting the groups were very uniform, and the sequences of events which occurred during the sessions were virtually the same. Each session was attended by at least two models and four or five boys. One complete script was used for each meeting. One of the modeling scripts which deals with a home problem situation is presented below as example material.

Home Problem

Scene I

INTRODUCTION: Almost all teenagers differ with their parents on the rules and restrictions that are set down. For example, hair styles and getting hair cuts, clothes, choice of friends, and hours to be home are important sources of conflicts. Most kids get into power struggles with their parents on at least one of these issues with the result that no one usually wins. Kids see parental standards as restrictions on their freedom, and often overreact to this by fighting or simply disobeying. Parents often overreact, too, and today's scene is about a typical family fight, the ways it might start, and some of the ways it might be prevented. There are three parts of this scene: in the first part the situation ends up in a family fight, in the second part a fight is also started but the boy's behavior will probably have more positive results, and in the third scene the fight is averted.

SCENE: *It's Saturday evening and John, a parolee, is home with his mother and father. John's mother is in the kitchen working and his father is in the front room watching television and drinking beer. John comes out of his room with his coat on and is walking toward the kitchen door to leave, as his mother confronts him. Notice how John helps set up a fight between his parents and doesn't get his problem settled.*

(Model Only)

Mother:	"Where do you think you're going?"
John:	"Out."
Mother:	*(angrily)* "What do you mean, 'out'?"

John: *(also angrily)* "I mean 'out'!"

Mother: "You're not going anywhere! I'm getting sick and tired of you thinking you can take off anytime you want to. It'll do you good to stay home now and then."

John: "Man, it's Saturday night—everybody goes out on Saturday night. All you expect me to do is stay home. Who wants to stay home all the time anyway?"

Father: *(from the other room, looks into the kitchen)* "Shut up out there."

John: *(walking into the front room)* "Why? Why can't I go out?"

Father: "You settle that with your mother. I'm trying to watch television."

John: "You always say that. Why don't you *ever* see my side of something? You always side with her."

Mother: *(walking into front room)* "You're crazy. He doesn't side with anybody. He just sits in his chair and drinks beer all night."

Father: "Don't start that crap again. I'm getting sick and tired of your bitching."

Mother: "Don't you yell at me. You never take any responsibility for that boy."

        (Parents start fighting between themselves. John leaves the room, runs out the back door, slams the door, and takes off.)

COMMENT: John was *set* to react negatively because he *knew* he'd be questioned.

Scene II

SCENE: *The scene is the same as Scene I except that John speaks to his mother first before heading for the door. He still has his coat on.*

(Model)

John: "Mom, I'm going over to Jerry's for awhile."

Mother: "What are you going to do at Jerry's?"

John:	"Oh, just mess around."
Mother:	"What do you mean *mess around?* The last time you and Jerry went out and messed around you both got arrested. You stay away from that kid. He's a bad influence."
John:	*(angrily)* "What do you know about it, you don't even know him. I don't tell you how to pick your friends, so don't try to tell me."
Mother:	*(angrily)* "That settles it. You're not going anywhere. All you and Jerry are going to do is go out and get in trouble, and end up in another institution. Haven't you got enough of a record as it is?"
John:	*(trying to control himself)* "Do you have to keep throwing that record bit up to me all of the time? How am I supposed to prove that I can stay out of trouble if all you do is throw that up to me and never give me a break?"
Mother:	"Well, you're *not* going anywhere."
John:	"Man, it's Saturday night—everybody goes out on Saturday night. All you expect me to do is stay home. Who wants to stay home all the time anyway?"
Father:	*(from the other room, looks into the kitchen)* "Shut up out there."
John:	*(walking into the front room)* "Why? Why can't I go out?"
Father:	"You settle that with your mother. I'm trying to watch television."
John:	"You always say that. Why the hell can't you *ever* see my side of something? You always side with her."
Mother:	*(walking into front room)* "You're crazy; he doesn't side with anybody. He just sits in his chair and drinks beer all night."
John:	"Oh, *shit,* here they go again."
Father:	"Don't start that crap again. I'm getting sick and tired of your bitching."

Mother:	"Don't you yell at me. You never take any responsibility for that boy."
John:	*(walks out of room into bedroom)*
COMMENT:	Okay, that's one way to handle a parent problem. Now here's another way.

Scene III

SCENE: *The scene is the same, but John's approach is different than in Scenes I and II, and he doesn't put his coat on first.*

(Model)

John:	"Mom, would you mind if I went over to Jerry's for awhile?"
Mother:	"Well, I don't know. What are you going to do?"
John:	"Well, we'll stay there for awhile, then I guess we'll go down town and either go to the dance or shoot some pool or something. I'll be home when I'm supposed to.
Mother:	"Well, the last time you and Jerry went out and messed around you both got arrested. You stay away from that kid. He's a bad influence."
John:	"Ah, mom, you don't even know him. *(Laughs)* Besides, do I tell you how to pick your friends?"
Mother:	"That's not the point. You and Jerry *did* get in trouble, and they sent you to that state institution."
John:	*(trying to control himself)* "I know, but I wish you wouldn't keep throwing the record thing up to me all the time. How am I supposed to prove that I can stay out of trouble if all you do is throw that up to me and never give me a break? I'm *not* going to get into any trouble."
Mother:	"Well, I don't know. Go ask your Dad and see what he thinks."
John:	*(walking into the front room)* "Dad, do you mind if I go out for awhile tonight?"
Father:	"What? . . . Well, I don't know. You settle that with your mother. I'm trying to watch TV."

(starts to get angry, but doesn't say anything, turns around and goes back into the kitchen)

John: "Well, he doesn't seem to care one way or the other. He said to ask you."

Mother: "Well, okay, but you'd better be home on time."

John: "Okay, okay, I will. See you later."

(Imitate II and III)

MAIN DISCUSSION POINTS:

1. How are these three ways of dealing with a family problem different?

2. John's belligerent attitude helped set the family fight up.

3. Notice how easy it is to get a fight "snowballing" when everyone is mad.

4. Discuss possible influence of expectancy effects. John's mother communicated that she *expected* him to get into trouble. Does this have any influence on someone's behavior?

5. Leaving only temporarily solves his problem; both parents will be mad when he returns, for disobeying them. Besides, it's very easy to get into trouble or do something destructive when you take off from home in a bad mood.

6. Again John didn't get anything settled, but he used a little different approach in Scene II.

7. Going to his room and waiting until the fight subsides is a better way of coping with the problem than just taking off and leaving home.

8. Even if waiting and trying again doesn't work for John, it would be a good idea to wait and discuss the problem with the JPC, since continuing to struggle with the parents over matters like this usually doesn't get anywhere.

9. In Scene III John was more honest in details about what he was going to do; he didn't get angry, especially when the question of his record was thrown up to him by his mother. This is a difficult item for most parolees to handle, and it frequently occurs in the family.

10. Trying to be reasonable with parents of course doesn't guarantee that a situation like this will always have a better outcome, but it increases the chances of it.

11. Point out that provoking a fight between the parents is a good way not to get anything solved. Discuss other ways of avoiding three- and four-way family fights—for example, not going to one parent saying, " (Mom/Dad) said I could go out," when it isn't quite true. (Sarason and Ganzer, 1971 pp. 1-4 of *Home Problem,* Scene II)

A detailed orientation and modeled example scene was presented to groups during their first meeting. Each subsequent session was conducted in the following sequence: (1) One of the models began the session by introducing and describing the particular scene that would be enacted during the session. The introductions previously had been memorized by the models. They served the purpose of orienting the boys to the group's work for that day and to afford them a rationale for the inclusion of the particular scene in the sequence. (2) The models then role-played the particular scene for the day while the subjects observed. Since the scenes were usually separated into two- and three-part sequences because often they were too long to be retained with sufficient recollection for good single imitations, only a first segment initially was modeled. (3) One boy was called upon to summarize and explain the content and outcome of what he had just observed. (4) Models and subjects commented upon and briefly discussed the scene; then an audio or video tape segment of the modeled behavior was replayed. (5) Depending on the number and kind of roles involved, either two or three boys or one boy and one model then imitated the modeled behavior that they had just observed. (6) Following one or two imitations, a short recess was taken while soft drinks were served and one of the previous role imitations was replayed. Participants also used this time to comment upon each other's behavior. (7) After the recess the boys who had not participated then enacted the situations. Insofar as possible, each boy participated in each session. (8) One of these two or three performances was replayed and commented upon. (9) The group's final task involved comments concerning the material, aspects of its importance, and its general applicability in other interpersonal situations.

The efficacy of the modeling procedures was evaluated by comparing the participants' subsequent behavior with that of other boys who were involved in guided discussions of the same content material but without modeling or role-playing. That is, while modeling group boys observed and then imitated appropriate behavior in a family problem or job interview situation, boys in discussion groups would only talk informally about such behavior. Every effort was made to insure that the conduct of the discussion groups was in other respects as similar as possible to that of the modeling condition (e.g. breaks, use of feedback, number of sessions).

Following participation in the experimental sequence, all subjects were readministered the same battery of tests; and their behavior again was rated by cottage counselors. Control group subjects also were retested and rated after a comparable time interval. All boys were discharged from the institution within a week after this second assessment was obtained. Approximately 14 percent of the subjects were paroled back into their communities. The remaining boys were sent to other juvenile institutions, and behavior ratings again were obtained on these boys after a four-month period in residence. A longer term follow-up evaluation provided further data through personal interviews after parole discharge and through records of recidivism. Indices of recidivism were obtained on all subjects at a risk period of at least eighteen months after release to parole.

Evaluation of the Project

The major results of this research are summarized below. Omitted are the numerous statistical analyses that were performed on the more than forty dependent variables which were measured in the study.

1. Boys who participated in both the modeling and guided discussion treatments showed more positive or favorable changes in their attitudes, self-concepts, and rated overt behaviors than did control group boys.

2. Further analyses of these measures suggested that less socially adequate, more dependent boys who required greater direction and structure, responded most favorably to the modeling procedures.

3. Behavior ratings obtained during the four-month follow-

up evaluation were complete on 82 percent of the subjects. Comparison of these ratings with the second Cascadia behavior ratings revealed that most experimental group boys continued to maintain favorable behavior or continued to show improvement. Fewer control boys continued to improve, and more changed in a negative direction.

4. Personal interviews and retesting with a small sample of fifty-three subjects following discharge from parole suggested that more former modeling than discussion group boys remembered and applied the information and concepts that they had learned in the groups. They more frequently expressed favorable or positive attitudes toward their experiences in institutions and on parole than did either discussion or control group subjects.

5. Fewer experimental than control group subjects reported engaging in further delinquent activities while on parole.

6. Data on recidivism were obtained on all subjects. Recidivism was defined as: (a) the return of a boy to a juvenile institution, (b) conviction in superior court resulting in probation as an adult status offender, or (c) confinement in an adult correctional institution. These data indicated that the rate of recidivism for controls was somewhat more than twice as high as that for experimentals. The control group contained twenty-two recidivists whereas there were twelve in the modeling group and nine in the discussion group. The difference in proportion of recidivists among the three groups was significant (p + .06, Chi-square test). Both the modeling (p = .06) and discussion (p = .01) groups had significantly fewer recidivists than had the control group. While recidivism is not an infallible indicator of the success of a rehabilitation program, these data do suggest that the experimental treatments employed in this research did favorably influence the subsequent adjustment of the subjects in the sample.

EXTENSIONS OF THE MODELING PROJECT

One practical yardstick of the value of any rehabilitation program is the extent to which it is applicable in different situations and with different kinds of clients. Perhaps an even more important question is whether a treatment approach can be readily learned and effectively applied by other rehabilitation workers.

Could modeling techniques be utilized in institution settings other than Cascadia? How easily could models other than university graduate students be trained to conduct modeling groups? Would other models be as or more effective than had been the graduate students? While the modeling procedures showed several specific advantages over those employed in the discussion groups, modeling was not more effective overall than was guided discussion. Would a new procedure which combined the most therapeutic elements of the modeling and discussion approaches provide an even more efficacious rehabilitation technique? New variations of the original modeling groups were initiated and conducted at three other juvenile institutions in Washington in an effort to answer these questions.*

In addition it was hoped that the new modeling programs would overcome two factors which were viewed as major problems in the Cascadia research. One problem in the Cascadia project was that the graduate student-models were relatively unacquainted with the subjects, interacted with them for only four-week periods, and rotated their participation in different groups on a part-time basis. The unfamiliarity factor would not exist in the new groups because institution staff social workers and counselors would serve as models. The boys would be well acquainted with the models since they had known them for several months prior to participation in modeling sessions. It was expected that familiarity with and trust in the models would enhance the effectiveness of the modeling situations. The second advantage was that modeling groups would be made up of boys for whom parole was an imminent reality (e.g. in one to two months). The major focus of modeling groups always had been on the development of skills and coping behaviors which would facilitate postinstitutional adjustment. In the Cascadia research a problem arose because this emphasis seemed of little relevance to many boys, since for most of them institution release was an event that would not occur for many more months. In view of

---

* Echo Glen Children's Center, Greenhill School, and Mission Creek Youth Forest Camp were the facilities in which modeling groups were conducted. The support and participation of the administration and staff of these institutions is gratefully acknowledged.

the limited psychological reality of the future for most delinquent youth, the Cascadia project which was aimed at a period so far ahead often may have appeared irrelevant.

Training New Models

Approximately twenty social workers and staff counselors, both male and female, expressed interest in learning modeling techniques. Some of them were experienced in leading small groups, and some had never participated in group situations. Their educational backgrounds varied from high school graduate to the Master's Degree. However, they all had at least several months' experience in working with adolescents. A training period of four to six two-hour sessions was sufficient preparation time to enable new models to begin conducting their own groups. The training sessions in each institution followed a similar sequence. First the theoretical rationale underlying the techniques was explained. The development of the procedure, content of the sessions, and the role and function of models were discussed in detail. Audio tapes of previous Cascadia modeling groups were played and discussed as example material. Videotapes later were made of two groups, and their subsequent use as teaching aids further facilitated the learning process for new models. The scripts then were used in practice sessions which closely approximated the course of actual modeling groups. Models began to work in informal groups after two or three practice sessions. Research staff participated in some groups and frequently consulted with the models to discuss procedures and any problems that arose. The only apparent difficulty that was noted was an initial tendency of the models to miss various parts in the role imitations where boys needed cues because they had forgotten part of the dialogue. During particularly long imitations, boys often forgot parts of their roles; and models had to be alert to provide cues to enable them to continue their performances. This was never a major problem and was overcome after several group sessions.

Procedure Changes

It was mentioned that the evaluation of the Cascadia project failed to demonstrate that modeling was clearly superior to guided group discussion as a rehabilitative technique. It was for this reason that the most effective elements of both procedures were incorporated into the structure and conduct of new modeling groups. Six major changes briefly may be described. (1) Groups were conducted in a more informal and less highly structured manner. While the sequence of events which occurred during each meeting remained generally the same (i.e. modeling followed by role imitations), both models and boys were permitted more latitude in their adherence to the roles. (2) Considerably more discussion, both structured and informal, accompanied the modeling and role imitations. (3) Role reversals and improvisations more frequently were employed. For example, boys more often were encouraged to take the role of adult authority figures after they had imitated a subordinate role. These three changes were accompanied by more active efforts to involve boys in an ongoing process of critically appraising and modifying modeled roles in an effort to develop the most appropriate and relevant example behaviors and coping and problem solving techniques. This greater emphasis on making the group sessions more meaningful and relevant appeared to foster more group cohesiveness and provided an additional incentive for active participation among boys. (4) Groups were larger, containing six to nine boys, which required a reduction in the number of imitations during each session. (5) Meetings were longer, often lasting one and one-half or two hours each. Lengthier sessions were necessary because of increased group size, greater emphasis on discussion, and the development of new and longer three- and four-part situations. (6) Although varying among the institutional settings, the number of sessions conducted with each individual group was reduced from sixteen to eight or ten.

Some Results and Effects

At present over thirty different modeling groups have been conducted within the revised format outlined above. No formal evaluation has been made of the usefulness or effectiveness of the new procedures and groups. However, a number of subjective impressions were formed based on the observations of the author, the models and boys, and other institution personnel. Several of these observations briefly may be mentioned. Modeling groups contained boys who were accorded both high and low status among their peers. Low status boys frequently were scapegoated on campus and within their respective residential cottages. Group participation facilitated more positive interactions and stronger friendships among status-different boys, with the result that weaker boys gained in status through the protection and encouragement of the stronger boys. In all instances these effects were quite immediate, which in part attests to the rapid impact that modeling procedures have on group members. It was the feeling of all concerned that group participation had a salutory effect on the ability and willingness of the boys to communicate more openly with adults as well as with peers. It also was noted that boys in the groups formed closer interpersonal relationships among themselves.

A number of the boys experienced situations in which they were able to apply successfully new coping behaviors which they had learned in the groups. One boy with a history of assaultive behavior was one of the best participants. He as well as several staff counselors felt that his aggressiveness had been brought under better control, in large part because of his group experiences. Another impulsive boy employed several self-control techniques, which he had learned in a modeling scene dealing with controlling anger, to avoid becoming belligerent and being isolated by a classroom teacher. A boy who had been on extended leave returned to the institution, sought out his caseworker, and described how the job interview modeling situation had been a key factor in his ability to secure a job which had been promised to him upon release. Another reported how the dealing with authority materials which were used in groups had been a major factor in keeping him out of trouble during a month's leave from the institution. This boy directly stated that he would not have lasted successfully for that month without the benefit of his group experiences.

These reports were offered spontaneously by boys as evidence of the immediate usefulness of the procedures and serve as indications that they have had practical utility for group participants.

CONCLUSIONS

Previously cited research on the therapeutic application of modeling principles has demonstrated that they are useful in individual and group approaches to rehabilitation. They may be employed as either a primary or supplementary means of teaching new skills to clients, of strengthening existing appropriate but weak behaviors, and of modifying maladaptive responses. Furthermore, both live and filmed or videotaped models have been used to successfully achieve various therapeutic goals.

Modeling techniques are relatively simple, objective, and effective methods of modifying behavior. While the procedures specifically adapted for the present research only have been applied in the rehabilitation of institutionalized adolescent males between the ages of twelve and eighteen, there is no compelling reason to believe that, with certain modifications, they would be any less effective with females of that age or with adults of either sex. The approach has shown favorable results with boys of different ages, of different personality types, and in different institutional settings. In view of these findings, it may be concluded that the first objective of the research was achieved: there is evidence that rehabilitation programs can be strengthened through the use of modeling procedures.

The second objective, the evaluation of how easily the procedures can be learned and applied by institution personnel, also was partly achieved. A number of persons, who were totally unfamiliar with modeling techniques, learned and became comfortable enough with them that they were able to begin conducting groups after approximately ten hours of training. Training was accomplished through didactic discussion, live and videotaped modeled demonstrations, and rehearsal sessions in which new models practiced and sharpened their newly acquired skills. Modeling procedures are learned equally rapidly by persons with and without previous experience in working with small groups. The experience variable appears primarily important in that models who are familiar with group processes initially are more self-confident and skillful in leading discussions of modeled behaviors than are inexperienced models. However, these differences are much less obvious after as little as two or three hours of group participation. Also, effective models need not be persons holding advanced degrees in the behavioral sciences. The importance of this factor to rehabilitation and mental health work may be of considerable importance.

As is true of any technique, the use of modeling and role imitation procedures is not without problems and cautions. Conducting groups is time-consuming. Time means cost to any rehabilitation program. The development of relevant and interesting content for use in groups may take substantial time and energy. At least two and sometimes three models are required to initiate each modeling session, although one model is usually able to conduct a group after the initial phase. Models also usually spend additional time rehearsing their roles prior to each group meeting. However, the cost per group in terms of time seems balanced by the fact that models can be easily and quickly trained. This factor is one of the basic strengths of the application of these procedures in group work.

Other potential problems involve the specificity of modeled behavior. Models perform a specific sequence of observable verbal, affective, and motor behaviors. Care must be taken to select and develop the most appropriate example behaviors to illustrate the purposes of the modeled situation. The examples should have some relevance for each client in the group, and ingenuity often is required to come up with situations which meet this requirement. The specific nature of modeled behaviors also demands that generalization be provided for at some point during the group session. Clients probably will never engage in situations where they confront a problem or are required to exhibit a behavior exactly as it was illustrated in a modeling session. It is therefore necessary to provide for adequate generalization to insure that learned behaviors will be applied in a variety of similar settings. Both group discussion and the modeling of several similar but not identical situations may be used to facilitate generalization.

Role modeling techniques appear to work, but what are the important ingredients which make them successful? As is true of other approaches to therapy and rehabilitation, there seem to be a number of factors which contribute to the success of the procedures. Modeling is a method or vehicle for presenting information to clients. It also serves as a potent stimulator for group discussion. Discussions help assure that the purposes of the modeling are understood. The practice afforded by role imitations serves to sharpen observers' skills as well as to promote better retention of what is learned. Modeling always focuses and holds the attention and interest of group participants, in part because it is an action-oriented as well as a verbal procedure in which clients learn by observing and by doing. Beginning a group by modeling a sequence of behavior immediately focuses on relevant aspects of the material. Because of this feature, groups start off rapidly, and there is little groping or searching for topics to discuss. Modeling has the advantages of role playing in that participants can feel safe being in the role of another person, yet they are free to express their own characteristic attitudes and behavior. Modeling permits but does not require self-exploration, discussion of personal problems, or the achievement of insight. In this respect it has some of the advantages of traditional group therapy.

Finally, participation in modeling groups is fun, and this factor may be of particular importance for adolescents. Almost all group participants, models and boys alike, at various times indicated that they enjoyed the sessions. While most people learn and work more effectively if they are enjoying themselves, this may be particularly important for adolescents because many of them lack the self-discipline to persist at something they dislike. While modeling procedures continue to develop and evolve, they may be considered effective as methods of modifying behavior, both with respect to their impact upon the clients with whom they have been used as well as the ease with which they can be learned and applied by group workers.

REFERENCES

Aronfreed, J.: The concept of internalization. In Goslin, D. (Ed.) : *Handbook of Socialization Theory and Research.* Chicago, Rand, 1969.
Bandura, A.: Behavioral modification through modeling procedures. In Kras-

ner, L., and Ullmann, L. P. (Eds.): *Research in Behavior Modification: New Developments and Implications.* New York, HR&W, 1965, pp. 310-340.

Bandura, A.: The influence of punishing consequences to the model on the acquisition and performance of imitative responses. Unpublished manuscript, Stanford University, 1962.

Bandura, A.: *Principles of Behavior Modification.* New York, HR&W, 1969 (a).

Bandura, A.: Social learning theory of identificatory processes. In Goslin, D., (Ed.): *Handbook of Socialization Theory and Research.* Chicago, Rand, 1969 (b).

Bandura, A., Blanchard, E. B. and Ritter, B. J.: Relative efficacy of desensitization and modeling approaches for inducing behavioral, affective, and attitudinal changes. *J of Pers Soc Psychol, 13*:173-199, 1969.

Bandura, A. and Walters, R. H.: *Social Learning and Personality Development.* New York, HR&W, 1963.

Chittenden, G.: An experimental study in measuring and modifying assertive behavior in young children. *Monograph of Social Research and Child Development,* Vol. 7, no. 1, 1942.

Cowen, E. L. and Zax, M.: The mental health field today: Issues and problems. In Cowen, E. M., Gardner, E. A., and Zax, M. (Eds.): *Emergent Approaches to Mental Health Problems.* New York, Appleton, 1967, pp. 3-29.

DeWolfe, A.: Identification and fear decrease. *J Consult Psychol, 31*:259-263, 1967.

Geer, J. and Turteltaub, A.: Fear reduction following observation of a model. *J Pers Soc Psychol, 6*:327-331, 1967.

Jones, M. C. The elimination of children's tears. *J Exp Psychol, 7*:383-390, 1924.

Kelly, G. A.: *The Psychology of Personal Constructs: A Theory of Personality.* New York, Norton, 1955.

Lazarus, A.: Behavior rehearsal versus nondirective therapy versus advice in effecting behavior change. *Behav Res Ther, 4*:209-212, 1966.

Lovaas, O. I.: Some studies on the treatment of childhood schizophrenia. In Schlein, J. (Ed.): *Research in Psychotherapy.* Washington, D. C., American Psychological Association, 1968.

Marlatt, G. A.: Exposure to a model and task ambiguity as determinants of verbal behavior in an interview. *J Consult Clin Psychol, 36*:268-276, 1971.

McFall, R. M. and Lillesand, D. B.: Behavior rehearsal with modeling and coaching in assertion training. *J Abnorm Psychol, 77*:313-323, 1971.

Olson, R.: Effects of modeling and reinforcement on adult chronic schizophrenics. *J Consult Clin Psychol, 36*:126-132, 1971.

Poser, E. G.: Training behavior therapists. *Behav Res Ther, 5*:37-41, 1967.

Sarason, I. G. and Ganzer, V. J.: Developing appropriate social behaviors of juvenile delinquents. In Krumboltz, J. D., and Thoreson, C. E. (Eds.) : *Behavioral Counseling: Cases and Techniques.* New York, HR&W, 1969.

Sarason, I. G. and Ganzer, V. J.: Modeling: An approach to the rehabilitation of juvenile offenders. Final report to the Social and Rehabilitation Service. University of Washington, June 1971.

Sarason, I. G., Ganzer, V. J. and Singer, M.: The effects of modeled self-disclosure on the verbal behavior of persons differing in defensiveness. *J Consult Clin Psycho, 39:*483-490, 1972.

CHAPTER VIII

BEHAVIOR MODIFICATION AND DELINQUENT YOUTH

JAMES F. ALEXANDER

••

Examples of and Definition of Delinquency
Approaches in Treatment of Delinquency
Behavior Modification in Treatment of Delinquent
   Families
Conclusions
References

••

EXAMPLES OF AND DEFINITION OF DELINQUENCY

WITHIN ONE WEEK the Short Term Behavioral Family Crisis Program received the following referrals:

Debbie, fourteen-year-old daughter of lower middle class parents, was referred for the third time within a one-month period by her father for runaway and ungovernable behavior. There was also strong suspicion of sexual and drug activity, particularly in conjunction with her nineteen-year-old unemployed boy friend.

Ronny, a sixteen-year-old male, was referred by the school to the police after having been caught with marijuana. Mother, divorced and working two jobs, was contacted at work to appear at the detention center. Ronny was also suspected of heavy drug abuse, and within a two-year period of time his grades had fallen from A's and B's to D's and F's. His younger brother had already been referred to the court for shoplifting six months before.

Susan, a fifteen-year-old daughter of upper middle class parents (father was on the local town council) was apprehended by

158

the police when they busted a "pot" party in a park during school hours. Although Susan had no prior referrals, an older sister had been referred to the court two years earlier for ungovernable behavior and "illicit" sexual activities.

Duaine, a seventeen-year-old son of upper middle class parents, was arrested for "trespassing" (he had jimmied open a window with two friends in a summer cabin). Duaine had two prior referrals for runaway.

Karen, a sixteen-year-old daughter of lower middle class mother and stepfather, was apprehended for shoplifting. She had been gone from home for three days and was living in a "crash pad." She had one prior referral for running away.

Paul, a fifteen-year-son of lower class parents (mother and stepfather) was referred for "ungovernable" behavior. Suspected of being slightly retarded, Paul had numerous referrals to the court beginning at age six and was no longer acceptable in any public school. Two older sisters had extensive involvement with the court and family services division, both having conceived illegitimate children.

Mrs. T was a middle-aged divorced mother who worked with Mrs. P., a prior client in the program. She called to refer her family because of frequent overnight absences of her sixteen-year-old daughter and failing school performance by her fourteen-year-old son.

Definition of Delinquency

In these cases, as with most delinquency referrals, formal definitions of delinquency are somewhat academic as the definition has already been made by the referral source (police, parents, school, etc.). However, to develop appropriate strategies and programs for change, individual therapists* must have a conceptual framework for understanding both the problem and the tools for change. And while "behavior modification" and "delinquency" would appear to encompass relatively straightforward topics,

---

* The general term "therapist" will be used throughout the chapter to identify the behavior change agent and may include a wide range of professional and occupational identifications.

both represent fields which include several dimensions. The delinquency literature, for example, contains numerous classification schemes, including differentiations according to sex, socioeconomic class, family structure (broken homes, etc.), environment (urban-industrial, etc.) and legal visibility (i.e. reported behavior vs. "hidden" delinquency). As discussed by Gibbons (1970) and Cohen (1966) most of these definitions involve a "sociological" level of analysis, attempting to develop explanations for the *kinds and amounts of delinquency* observed in a society (Gibbons, 1970). However, most therapists must instead deal with what Cohen (1966) calls the "psychological" question: What processes are involved in the *acquisition of delinquent behavior patterns by specific youths?* Not only do sociological definitions fail to provide a framework for this level of analysis, they focus on factors generally beyond the scope of individual therapists working with individual delinquents.

Traditional personality and intrapsychic approaches have also been of limited utility. With minor exceptions, "Taken en masse, it is clear that while juvenile lawbreakers are sometimes hostile, defiant, and suspicious individuals, they are not markedly different from nonoffenders in terms of psychological adjustment" (Gibbons, 1970, p. 193). Further, the intrapsychic-personality models have failed to produce effective programs for changing delinquent behavior (Gibbons, 1970; Gordon, 1962; Teuber and Powers, 1951).

As an alternative, the behavior modification philosophy suggests a dependent variable approach which cuts across the traditional sociological and psychological dimensions. At the (molecular) level of specific cases, therapists must first identify the situations and events that produce and maintain those behaviors. At a more molar level of analysis two general classes of problem behaviors may be identified and labeled criminal and status delinquency:

Criminal delinquency includes "crimes" typically involving violence against persons and property which would generally be illegal irrespective of the age of the offender. Representing the main focus of the traditional delinquency literature, criminal delinquency includes many "gang" activities, homicide, rape, robbery, assault, burglary, larceny, and arson.

Status delinquency is often identified as "behavioral," or "soft," or "offenses illegal for children only." Including such behaviors as runaway, ungovernable, truancy, curfew violations, possession of alcohol and tobacco, female sexual delinquency (excluding prostitution), and most "soft" drug use, status offenses typically represent acts for which minors may be arrested but adults are not.

Though not as dramatic, status delinquency deserves far more attention than it currently receives in the research and intervention literature. Though delinquency is in general rising at a faster rate than the juvenile population, rates of status delinquency are literally exploding, particularly with females and in urban settings, to the point of representing roughly half of all delinquency referrals (Annual Report of the Juvenile Court, State of Utah, 1971; Ferdinand, 1964; The President's Commission on Law Enforcement and Administration of Justice, 1967).

Further, status offenses often represent early forms of delinquency which if unchecked may lead to the more criminal forms of behavior (Wolfgang, Figlio, and Sellin, 1972). Successful early intervention may thus serve to prevent both subsequent status and criminal offenses. With recidivism rates frequently reported around 50 percent (Annual Report of the Juvenile Court, State of Utah, 1971; Alexander and Parsons, 1973; Wolfgang, Figlio, and Sellin, 1972) and occasionally higher (Stumphauzer, 1973), such intervention would represent a tremendous social and economic savings.

APPROACHES IN TREATMENT OF DELINQUENCY

Treatment Approaches

Intervention contexts represent a second major dimension, overlapping but not isomorphic with the criminal-status dichotomy. Since criminal delinquency involves more direct physical harm, institutionalization, or its threat, may occasionally be relevant. In such cases, a variety of behavioral approaches are available, encompassing a number of specific operations (i.e. token economy, time out, contingency management) in institutions and other highly controlled "schools" and "homes." (See, for example, Burchard, 1967; Cohen, Filipczak, and Bis, 1970; Cotler, Applegate, King, and Kristal, 1972; Phillips, 1968). Such institutional approaches have at times demonstrated impressive ability to control and modify a variety of behaviors, but the serious problems of generalization upon reentry into the natural environment have yet to be systematically examined and successfully resolved. Further, particularly with status offenders, institutionalization is seen more and more as an unfortunate alternative to treatment in the natural environment (Harlow, 1970; Stuart, 1971; Wolfgang, Figlio, and Sellin, 1972). For example, Stumphauzer (1973) asserts "The incentives and behavioral control provided by behavior therapy programs are particularly well-suited for institutional schools" (p. 140). However, in discussing traditional institutional approaches, he concludes that, "Institutions for delinquents, or rather the people that support and run such institutions, have failed miserably" (Stumphauzer, 1973, p. 239). "What's more, this leads to the inescapable conclusion that intervention, or more importantly *prevention*, should take place in the natural environment (family, school, peer relations, social structure) of the youth and not in an artificial institution, from which he will be discharged to this same environment armed with newly learned antisocial behaviors" (p. 240). In a similar vein, Agras (1972) emphasizes that a great deal of deviant behavior is learned in the natural environment, thus the primary focus of change should be working with this environment. Yet in reviewing behavioral approaches to delinquency, all but one of the studies Agras summarizes deal with delinquents and predelinquents in institutional settings, as opposed to the home or other natural environmental settings.

Thus while behavioral treatment approaches represent a recent and increasingly widespread form of therapeutic intervention, an important deficiency in focus is apparent. This deficiency takes an even greater importance in light of the strong national trend to avoid institutionalization in delinquent cases. In Utah, for example, there has been a steady decline in referrals to institutional settings, and by 1971 fewer than 3 percent of all delinquency referrals resulted in institutionalization and only 10 percent in probation (Annual Report of the Juvenile Court, State of Utah, 1971). Comparable rates of 6.5 percent and 11 percent were found by Wolfgang, Figlio, and Sellin (1972) in Philadelphia. Thus it appears that the heavy preponderance of cases do not end up in institutional settings, yet the majority of the literature covers treatment in such settings.

However, several notable exceptions do exist, including studies by Schwitzgebel and Kolb (1964) and Thorne, Tharpe, and Wetzel (1967), though their data on recidivism are unavailable or disappointing. Further, impressive programs aimed at directly modifying families have been initiated by Patterson and his associates (Patterson, Cobb, and Ray, 1972; Patterson, Ray, and Shaw, 1968) and Stuart (1971). These programs provided the impetus for a carefully controlled behavioral family program with thirteen- to seventeen-year-old court referrals (Alexander and Parsons, 1973; Parsons and Alexander, 1973). In this project several parameters of family interaction patterns were significantly modified, and follow up recidivism rates were reduced to 26 percent, compared to the 47-73 percent rates of various comparison treatment and untreated control groups. While not completely eliminating recidivism, this inexpensive short term (three to six weeks) program demonstrated the potential for dramatically reducing delinquency by utilizing behavioral principles in a family context.

Advantages of Family Approaches

Even if family approaches to modification of delinquent behavior produce recidivism rates comparable only to institutional or individually oriented programs, several advantages identify it as the treatment of choice. In terms of cost, it is certainly less expensive than separate formal institutions and quasi-institutional settings such as ranches and "schools." Working with the family also provides potential preventive measures, particularly if the program is aimed at modifying family interaction patterns to produce more effective problem-solving styles (Malouf and Alexander, 1972). Specifically, as new developmental crises are encountered with the same child or with other children, production of a more adaptive style of interaction increases the likelihood of a satisfactory resolution of these crises.

Dealing with the family also allows the therapist to help the family respond more adaptively and perhaps even change many of the environmental factors thought by some theorists to have etiological significance in delinquent patterns. Additionally, working with the family can avoid, to at least some extent, the powerful "labeling" effects (i.e. secondary delinquency) that are highlighted in programs that involve removal from the home. Finally, the alternative of family intervention allows therapists to respond more to "crisis" situations, as this form of intervention simply requires less formal court action (i.e. time). Even if formal court adjudication is ultimately necessary, modification of family patterns can nevertheless have already been under way, providing a context for reentry by the delinquent at a later time.

BEHAVIOR MODIFICATION IN TREATMENT OF DELINQUENT FAMILIES

Behavior Modification With Delinquent Families

The phrase "delinquent families" reflects an important point of view in modifying delinquent behavior. Specifically, the focus is not on "families of delinquents," but on "delinquent families." The difference is not merely semantic, as the goal of therapeutic intervention must be changing the entire family system that produces and maintains delinquent behaviors. This attitude emanates from the theoretical position that social environments, not individual pathology, are responsible for deviant behavior (Haley, 1963; 1971). As Tharpe and Wetzel (1969) emphasize, ". . . The environment, in which the individual is embedded, is principally responsible for the organization or disorganization, the maintenance or change, the appearance or disappearance of any behavior (p. 7)."

However, theory alone is of secondary importance as a basis for this attitude. As is often the case, practicality (or feasibility) plays a more important role, particularly with an adolescent population. While a variety of techniques are potentially available for modifying delinquent behavior in the family context (e.g. therapist or parent imposed time out, punishment, shaping and fading), the nature of "the adolescent" severely restricts the alternatives available. For example, time out and extinction procedures (so successful with younger children) are generally disastrous with teenagers for reasons including their far greater physical and economic mobility (cars, bikes, etc.), greater physical strength (removal to a time-out room may be physically impossible for most mothers), greater peer "influence" and reinforcement for alternative unwanted behaviors (boy friends strongly reinforce "sneaking out" after curfew), as well as the powerful, and normal, adolescent developmental processes which include considerably less parental influence and control.

Thus the traditional operant concept of arranging the social environment (i.e. parents, teachers) to "operate on" the delinquent represents an unrealistic and generally ineffective approach.* As an alternative, numerous authors have, at least in theory if not in practice, emphasized reciprocity in dealing with deviant families (Alexander and Parsons, 1973; Parsons and Alexander, 1973; Patterson and Reid, 1970; Stuart, 1971). At the level of family interaction research, for example, Alexander (1973) found delinquent families to be generally less reciprocal than normal controls, and the little reciprocity delinquent families did demonstrate revolved around maladaptive, system-destructive behaviors. As a guiding principle, reciprocity implies that positive behaviors in turn elicit positive behaviors, either because it is an established family norm (as in adjusted families), or because specific therapeutic operations are instituted to initiate a pattern of "something for something."

As a basis for therapeutic intervention, reciprocity must operate at two levels. As will be discussed later, specific techniques such as contingency contracting must be governed by the norm of reciprocity (Stuart, 1971). At a more molar level, however, therapists must be able to conceptualize *all* family members important in modifying deviant behavior. The suffering wife, caught between an arguing father and son (the "apparent" problem), is just as crucial a focus of change as are the more obvious

---

* Institutional settings, with far greater control, are of course less restricted by these factors but, as mentioned previously, have sufficient other drawbacks to render them a less than desirable treatment approach.

problem interactions. In fact, modifying the interactions of less obviously problematic family members is often a more efficient and effective means of changing a maladaptive system. As a simple example, getting mother to apply reinforcers and sanctions directly rather than nagging father to "control the kids," may *automatically* serve to prevent a runaway producing father-child fight. In this example, an oversimplified "target behavior" approach would have forced the therapist to focus on the specific antecedents (father-child arguing), which may be more difficult to modify.

Thus, the goal of intervention is often to modify specific antecedent behaviors or consequent events that maintain delinquent behavior. However, as delinquents acts *per se* are relatively infrequent, the larger goal must be the modification of characteristic interaction patterns that provide a context for the occasional delinquency.

Families: What to Change

Again, some minimal definitions are necessary, due to the varied conceptual and practical approaches to defining families. For our purposes, the family may of course entail the traditional biological unit (father, mother, children) but can also include single parent families, step-parent combinations, foster home parents, relatives, and (occasionally) older siblings who have formal custody of delinquents. Each of these family forms has unique properties, potentials, and problems, yet programs designed to produce adaptive change must assess the contribution of each of two fundamental processes. Stated simply, delinquent families behave the way they do for some combination of ignorance and pathogenic need to maintain the *status quo* of the family.

In many instances, parents and teenagers behave the only way they know how based on their own prior learning experiences, cultural (including peer) expectations, as well as modeling and advice from "experts" on T.V., in the schools, at church, etc. One recurrent theme, for example, involves some act (dress style, language, school performance, heterosexual activity . . . the list can be almost infinite) which violates or threatens to violate some implicit or explicit norms or value of the family. A frequent parental response is to punish that act ("not in this house, you won't!") which in turn often sets off a sequence of reciprocated arguing, condemnation, and similar system destructive interactions (Alexander, 1973). In another recurrent situation, aversive behaviors ("mands," in Patterson's terms) such as nagging and complaining occur and are reinforced (mother "gives in," teenager cuts his hair, and so on). This given in to coercion is in turn reinforced by cessation of the aversive behavior, but the family members are now characterized by a pattern of getting what they want through coercion and occasionally high rates of aversive behaviors (Patterson and Reid, 1970). Such a pattern rarely lasts indefinitely, as this tactic tends to escalate to unacceptable magnitudes.

In both of these situations, parental response was "intended" to diminish unwanted behavior, but instead it served to maintain or even accelerate that unwanted behavior. Many theorists (Alexander and Parsons, 1973; Haley, 1963, 1971; Watzlawick, Beavin, and Jackson, 1967), however, view deviant producing interactions as more than the inability of parents to effectively control behavior. Specifically, deviant behavior is seen as serving important maintenance functions in family systems, i.e. delinquent behavior (or the interactions leading to it) often produces a relatively stable system held intact by that delinquent behavior. To return to our case example, mother often bickered with Debbie (resulting in running away), but it was only when Debbie began running away that father began coming directly home from work and stopped going out alone at night "with the boys." Thus Debbie's delinquency served to maintain more contact between father and his family, including his wife. If "by magic" Debbie had ceased her delinquent activities, mother would have again been faced with a functionally absent husband. Other examples abound, including Ronny's divorced father who only took child rearing responsibility for Ronny (including child support payments) after he "got into trouble."

The implications of this view place a more serious demand on therapists intervening in delinquent families. Specifically, we cannot simply apply techniques developed to change specific target behaviors, because even when successful the changes may not be maintained unless the impact on the entire system is considered and integrated into the program. To return once again to Debbie, one end-product of intervention was an agreement in which Debbie received freedom to go where she wanted, without questions, each day after school in return for a card signed by each teacher indicating she had done acceptable work for that day. Just as important, however, was the fact that father, not mother, was responsible for monitoring her contract (along with several others negotiated with the other children). In return for doing this (thus meeting mother's request for more involvement), father received no more nagging from mother (his request) as well as a bonus of going out alone once weekly.

In summary, then, programs designed to modify teenage delinquency are forced to (1) utilize a somewhat restricted range of behavioral techniques; (2) provide alternative ways for all family members to influence each others' behavior on a reciprocal basis; and (3) consider the possibility that delinquent behaviors serve important maintenance functions. If so, the specific behavioral changes produced must provide for the continuation, by more appropriate and adaptive means, of those functions.

The process of training families in behavioral contracting (Stuart, 1971) provides a context for meeting all three of these program needs. In addition to allowing therapists and families to focus on changing specific unwanted target behaviors, training in behavioral contracting also helps families to become a more efficient and effective problem solving unit (Malouf and Alexander, 1972); an "experience in form" in Stuart's (1971) terms which provides a basis for more effective interaction.

Further, as demonstrated in the example of Debbie's family, therapists can aid the family in negotiating contracts which provide for the maintenance of family functioning. In Paul's case, mother had wanted to work outside the home, but was forced to remain home to deal with Paul. With Paul's return to school and father's agreement to work with him (e.g. on the car) after school, mother was able to consider employment. In return for complying with their contracts, both father and Paul earned time alone with mother. Thus in this case, both father and Paul continued to have contacts with mother, but such contacts were no longer coerced by delinquent behavior (which mother formerly reinforced with attention, and father maintained by being unavailable).

These are but a few examples of the numerous contracts potentially possible to modify delinquent families.* The content of specific contracts are of course unique to each family, but the *process* of training families in behavioral contracting must contain several consistent aspects in order to insure lasting changes in family functioning.

In order to generate reciprocal and effective contracts, families must be trained in labile, effective communication styles (Parsons and Alexander, 1973). Specifically, therapists must model, shape, explain, prompt, and rehearse unambiguous communications that contain the following crucial elements:

1. BREVITY. Communications must be short to avoid overloading (overwhelming amounts of information) and the general aversive impact of long monologues ("sermons," "harangues," etc.). Not only are such monologues ineffective in producing positive change, they increase the likelihood of confusion and "acting out" rather than constructive verbal interchange. For the same reasons, therapists too must avoid long and complicated "explanations," no matter how accurate.

2. DIRECT. To avoid pathological cross generational ties (Haley, 1963), middleman positions, and distortions, messages must occur directly between the parties involved. Parenthetically, this principle also constitutes a rationale for seeing all family members in therapy. Behaviorally, the therapist models and reinforces "I-you" statements, while ignoring, punishing, and preventing talking through and for others, third person comments ("oh, he's always like that"), and vague or indirect comments (both hostile *and* affiliative).

3. SOURCE RESPONSIBILITY. As a general rule, responsibility for assertions and requests must be restricted to family members present. The police, church, God, friends, and "truth" are not

---

* See Stuart (1971) for an excellent discussion of elements of behavioral contracts and the assumptions underlying this process.

relevant, as successful contracts require changes *I* want and consequences *I* will be responsible for. Careful attention to this principle will help therapists avoid being trapped in coalitions with certain family members because of the "goodness," legitimacy, and benevolent intent of their assertions and requests. It also avoids futile contracts based on erroneous assumptions (for example that father shares mother's value of the importance of church attendance). Therapists and family members alike can take nothing for granted!

4. PRESENTING ALTERNATIVES. In addition to taking responsibility, family members must develop the habit of providing alternatives. In early contract negotiations therapists can model and prompt this process, demonstrating alternatives to meeting responsibilities and providing payoffs whenever possible. Meeting curfew, for example, can include coming home at a prearranged time, calling home one-half hour early to ask for an extra hour out, "averaging" a certain time (e.g. if out one night until twelve, adolescent must be home by eight the next night to "average" ten o'clock), or by coming home one hour before curfew in return for having the car. Payoffs, too, can include finances, independence, changes in interpersonal behaviors, and numerous other rewards. The atmosphere provided in presenting alternatives can avoid "non-negotiable" and unacceptable demands and both emphasizes and reflects the therapeutic concept that a variety of specific behaviors can serve to maintain a family function.

4. CONGRUENCE. Successful contract negotiation requires that family members send congruent messages at the verbal, nonverbal, behavior, and contextual levels. Father's assertion, for example, that he wants teenager to spend more time with him must not only be said in a nonhostile way, but father must make it contextually possible by being available. In addition to modeling and shaping this congruence in family members, therapists may also utilize this principle in training family members to recognize the impact (or function) of their behaviors (e.g. father's absence forces mother to assume primary responsibility, mother's constant questioning elicits less, not more, information from daughter, etc.).

6. CONCRETENESS AND BEHAVIORAL SPECIFICITY. Concepts such

as "being responsible" and "loving" must be translated into specific behaviors to be performed at specific times, for the actor and recipient must be able to agree precisely on required behaviors. Further, only overt acts are possible to monitor, a crucial element in behavioral contracting (Stuart, 1971). It is also generally more productive for therapist and family members to focus on contracts that create new alternative behaviors, rather than emphasizing the cessation of old ones. To smile, for example, is easier and more pleasant than to stop frowning, just as working together on a project is more productive than "stopping going alone to your room."

7. INTERRUPTIONS AND FEEDBACK. As clearly demonstrated by Parsons and Alexander (1973) family members must be trained to interrupt for clarification and provide feedback on the messages they receive. This process, of course, represents the receiver's reciprocal component of brevity and specificity, and together they produce much more labile and productive interactions, with fewer opportunities for distortion and apathy. Therapists, of course, model this process when gathering information (assessment) and initiating change in families. When families see this process producing order out of chaos and resolution out of incompatibility, they generally quickly adopt a similar style, with prompting and reinforcement by the therapist.

When Change Begins

One often overlooked aspect of behavioral intervention in family systems is the fact that the above elements of communication training can be instituted immediately upon seeing the family. Many of the traditional intrapsychic as well as the newer behavioral methods tend to begin with a more or less extensive diagnostic or initial assessment phase, followed by intervention based on this information. The present approach, on the other hand, initiates communication training immediately, even during initial data gathering. Therapists ask directive, pointed, concise questions, emphasize behavioral specificity rather than global evaluations, and often interrupt for clarification and feedback. They also begin movement towards reciprocity by eliciting input from all family members. In the initial assessment phase, therapists rely heavily on the process of labeling (Malouf and Alexander, 1972), in which the sequential pattern of events is slowed down and each member's contribution to the sequence is identified. As is inevitably the case, it becomes clear that more than one family member is necessary for any given sequence to occur. Identifying sequences also allows the therapist to avoid blaming, as all family members (including the good sibling who "tells on" the delinquent, the father who is unavailable to support mother, etc.) contribute.

This technique of focusing on family sequence rather than individual guilt can have a particularly powerful impact on the adolescent. Accustomed to being the problem in the eyes of parents, teachers and police, the adolescent now is seen only as a part of a sequence. This impact is heightened as the concept of reciprocity among all family members is emphasized in reciprocal contracting. As emphasized by Stuart (1971), the guiding principle in contracting is *quid pro quo* (Jackson, 1965); the contract must offer positive consequences for everyone involved. Thus in requesting a change in the delinquent's behavior, for example, parent must offer an acceptable payoff. Just as importantly, however, for every parent-to-adolescent request, the adolescent also may request a change in the parent's behavior, again in return for a positive consequence. To further emphasize reciprocity, every negative sanction placed on adolescent for failure to comply is matched by a negative sanction on parent for failing to comply.

It is at this critical point that family intervention can succeed or fail, as parents often strongly resist adolescent control of their behavior. Earlier training in communication and functional interpretations of behavior make this easier, but therapists can also facilitate this process with reciprocal parent-to-parent (or parent-to-teacher, etc.) contracting. If the therapist has been successful in shifting the focus from the adolescent to the family, parents have also identified desirable potential changes in each other's behavior; changes easily incorporated into reciprocal contracts. To maintain reciprocity a rule-of-thumb is one parent-parent contract for each parent-child contract.

Finally, resistance to contracts can be lessened by initially avoiding the major issue (s) that led to the delinquent offense and contracting instead around less crucial events (Alexander and Parsons, 1973), particularly higher base rate behaviors where change may more readily be apparent. This provides the therapist with an opportunity to evaluate and train basic communication and contracting skills without as much of the intense emotional involvement which surrounds the historically "basic" family issues. Success in these early contracts also creates a more positive set concerning the possibilities of change and the advantages of involving all family members in this change.

Adjunct Techniques and Skills

Good monitoring skills, often including formal record keeping, are essential in maintaining successful contracts. Clear records of concrete behaviors facilitate proper administration of consequences, provide cues about earning additional reinforcers, and set the occasion for positive social behaviors (smiles, comments, etc.) which can gain in reinforcing value (Stuart, 1971). Particularly in families characterized by pessimism, hopelessness, and skepticism, records can promote recognition of positive changes which may not have been otherwise noticed. Many family members who initially insist on immediate and complete changes become much more flexible in the face of consistent (though not complete) changes in target behaviors. Records also influence maladaptive and inappropriate labeling, as delinquent family members often enter therapy with the perspective that each other "always" or "never" does something, which leads to numerous and nonproductive arguments. Records demonstrate the perspectives are rarely entirely true. Further, when apparently good contracts fail, record keeping helps the therapist identify the problem, i.e. stimulus conditions, failure to meet the contract, or failure to reliably apply consequences. Finally, record keeping also provides temporizing alternative behaviors early in the process of intervention. When someone else fails to meet the contract, it is amazing how family members can avoid their formerly characteristic arguments if they have an alternative such as checking the monitoring form.

Another useful technique is the utilization of reliable cues or prompts. Delinquent family members are often proficient at "negative scanning" (Stuart, 1971), but "forget," "lose control," or are "busy" when critical events are to occur. Therapists, however, can reprogram the social and physical environment to avoid such impediments (traditionally called resistance). Other family members (e.g. forgetful father monitors school contract but mother accepts responsibility for reminding him), bulletin boards, phone calls, notes in lunch boxes and on car mirrors, and numerous other contrived devices are available to prompt behavior but often become unnecessary when it becomes apparent that the "forgetting" strategy no longer serves to impede progress.

A variety of additional change techniques are available to deal with specific behavioral or "emotional" deficits and excesses. While many of these techniques have traditionally been utilized in a one-to-one context, they may (and should) be incorporated into a family program. In cases of true behavioral deficits (responses not readily available even under appropriate stimulus and reinforcement conditions; examples might include study skills, speech fluency, and work-related skills), modeling, role playing, and shaping may assist in developing these behaviors, either as part of or adjunct to behavioral contracts. Such skills may be developed by the therapist on a one to one basis in the family context, or one or more family members (not always parents!) may be trained to apply the appropriate change techniques. In cases of excessive or inappropriate anxiety mediated responses (school phobia, jealousy, etc.) additional techniques such as desensitization can be useful.

The Larger Environment

Even though the focus has appeared to be exclusively on the family, in actuality many changes directly involve elements of the larger environment. As indicated previously, many delinquents lack critical school, employment, and interpersonal skills. While such skill training may be an integral part of reciprocal family contracts, therapists must often interface direct family intervention with services available from other agencies. Optimally, of course, family members can be trained in assertion skills, problem solving skills, and information gathering skills in order to integrate such services themselves.

Often the environment also can be brought directly into family sessions. Boyfriends, grandparents, neighbors, school counselors, and others often represent significant (and at times problematic) aspects of a family's interaction patterns. These people can be utilized as prompts, monitors, and reinforcing agents, and utilizing the concept of reciprocity can often be induced to make important changes themselves. Just as family approaches provide many more alternatives for change than one to one approaches, utilizing larger segments of the environment in turn may expand these alternatives even more.

CONCLUSIONS

The behavioral concepts and techniques described in this chapter represent a promising new approach for treating, and to some extent preventing, delinquent behavior. However, therapists must avoid reifying these principles, particularly in light of the failure to completely eliminate recidivism and other measures of delinquent and predelinquent behavior. On a comparative basis, behavioral approaches presently seem to provide the most powerful and efficient techniques, but refinements and even entirely different approaches are possible. As emphasized in Alexander and Parsons (1973), the burden of proof, at the level of well-controlled empirical demonstrations, must now lie with adherents of these alternative approaches. However, we cannot afford to continue the unfortunately common tradition in the mental health and criminal fields of becoming disciples of a given approach (including eclecticism!) and thereby failing to evaluate our work. Basic research and program evaluation is not only an exercise for "Ivory Tower" types; it also provides a vehicle for feedback and accountability.

REFERENCES

Agras, S. W.: *Behavior Modification: Principles and Clinical Applications.* Boston, Little, 1972.

Alexander, J. F.: Defensive and supportive communications in normal and deviant families. *J Consult Clin Psychol, 40*:223-231, 1973.

Alexander, J. F., and Parsons, B. V.: Short term behavioral intervention with delinquent families: Impact on family process and recidivism. *J Abnorm Psychol, 81*:219-225, 1973.

Annual Report of the Juvenile Court, State of Utah, 1971.

Burchard, J. D.: Systematic socialization: A programmed environment for the rehabilitation of antisocial retardates. *Psychological Record, 17*:461, 1967.

Cohen, A. K.: *Deviance and Control.* Englewood Cliffs, N. J., P-H, 1966.

Cohen, H. L., Filipczak, J., and Bis, J.: A study of contingencies applicable to special education: Case 1. In Ulrich, R., Stachnik, T., and Mobrey, J. (Eds.) : *Control of Human Behavior: II. From Cure to Prevention.* Glenview, Ill., Scott, 1970.

Cotler, S. B., Applegate, G., King, L. W., and Kristal, S.: Establishing a token economy program in a state hospital classroom: A lesson in training student and teacher. *Behavior Therapy, 3*:209-222, 1972.

Ferdinand, T. N.: The offense patterns and family structures of urban, village, and rural delinquency. *The Journal of Criminal Law, Criminology, and Police Science, 55*:86-93, 1964.

Gibbons, D. C.: *Delinquent Behavior.* Englewood Cliffs, N. J., P-H, 1970.

Gordon, S.: Combined group and individual psychotherapy with adolescent delinquents. *Corrective Psychiatry and Journal of Social Therapy, 8*:195-200, 1962.

Haley, J.: *Strategies of Psychotherapy.* New York, Grune, 1963.

Haley, J.: *Changing Families: A Family Therapy Reader.* New York, Grune, 1971.

Harlow, E.: Intensive intervention: An alternative to institutionalization. *Crime and Delinquency Literature, 2*:3-46, 1970.

Jackson, D. D.: Family rules. *Arch Gen Psychiatry, 12*:589-594, 1965.

Malouf, R., and Alexander, J. F.: Family crisis intervention: A model and technique of training. Paper presented to the First Annual Conference on Training in Family Therapy, Philadelphia, November, 1972.

Parsons, B. V., and Alexander, J. F.: Short-term family intervention: A therapy outcome study. *J Consult Clin Psychol,* in press, 1973.

Patterson, G. R., Cobb, J. A., and Ray, R. S.: A social engineering technology for retraining aggressive boys. In Adams, H. E., and Unikel, P. (Eds.) , *Issues and Trends in Behavior Therapy.* Springfield, Thomas, 1972.

Patterson, G. R., Ray, R. S., and Shaw, D. A.: Direct intervention in families of deviant children. Oregon Research Institute Research Bulletin, 8: no. 9, 1968.

Patterson, G. R., and Reid, J. B.: Reciprocity and coercion: Two facets of social systems. In Neuringer, C., and Michael, J. L. (Eds.) , *Behavior Modification in Clinical Psychology.* New York, Appleton, 1970.

Phillips, E. L.: Achievement place: Token reinforcement procedures in a homestyle rehabilitation setting for pre-delinquent boys. *Journal of Applied Behavior Analysis, 1:*213-223, 1968.

The President's Commission on Law Enforcement and Administration of Justice, *Juvenile Delinquency and Youth Crime.* Washington, D. C., U. S. Government Printing Office, 1967.

Schwitzgebel, R., and Kolb, D. A.: Inducing behavior change in adolescent delinquents. *Behav Res Ther, 1:*297-304, 1964.

Stuart, R. B.: Behavioral contracting within the families of delinquents. *Journal of Behavior Therapy and Experimental Psychiatry, 2:*1-11, 1971.

Stumphauzer, J. S.: *Behavior Therapy With Delinquents.* Springfield, Thomas, 1973.

Teuber, H., and Powers, D.: The effects of treatment of delinquents. *Res Publ Assoc Res Nerv Ment Dis, 31:*139-147, 1951.

Tharpe, R. G., and Wetzel, R. J.: *Behavior Modification in the Natural Environment.* New York, Acad Pr, 1969.

Thorne, G. L., Tharpe, R. G., and Wetzel, R. J.: Behavior modification techniques: New tools for probation officers. *Federal Probation,* pp. 21-27, 1967.

Watzlawick, P., Beavin, J. H., and Jackson, D. D.: *Pragmatics of Human Communication.* New York, Norton, 1967.

Wolfgang, M. E., Figlio, R. M., and Sellin, T.: *Delinquency in a Birth Cohort.* Chicago, U of Chicago Pr, 1972.

CHAPTER IX

THE USE OF BEHAVIOR MODIFICATION TECHNIQUES WITH THE MENTALLY ILL

DELOSS D. FRIESEN

••

••

INTRODUCTION

A FEW SHORT YEARS ago the mention of behavior modification divided people pretty sharply into two camps: for or against. Those trained in, or at least introduced to, a psychodynamic or phenomenological explanation of the human personality were usually opposed to manipulating the patient's behavior. On the other hand, the person embracing learning theory as the better explanation of human behavior (according to the medical or disease model) was usually comfortable with behavior modification.

Behavior modification is a process through which human behavior is altered directly by rewarding desired behavior and not rewarding unwanted behavior. This approach is based on the notion that behavior which is rewarded will increase and behavior which is not rewarded will decrease.

178

The medical model holds that behavior is the effect or the result of some deeper process or illness. Therefore, treatment of the behavior alone is superficial. When behavior is maladaptive it is often considered to be a symptom of some deeper problem. This model indicates that an attempt to cure a problem by changing the superficial behavior is analogous to an attempt to cure a brain tumor by treating the patient's headache and is perhaps fraught with as much danger. Even if not dangerous, treating the symptom without dealing with the root cause may prove to be fruitless. The medical model further argues that since the root cause is not removed a second symptom would take the place of the first. Therefore any attempt to change behavior directly is at best a waste of time due to the patient substituting one symptom for another and is at worst dangerous. Using this premise many workers in the mental health field have not used the technique of behavioral modification.

Other behavioral scientists feel that the medical model, while appropriate for most of medicine and for those psychological problems that are clearly organic in nature, does not fully explain the psychology of man. Such behavioral scientists believe that man learns his behavior whether it is a skill like tennis or a psychotic behavior such as pulling out all of one's hair. If behavior is learned rather than caused from some deep source, then it can be unlearned and some new more appropriate behaviors can be acquired.

Many mental health professionals attempt to resolve the conflict between the psychodynamic purist and the learning theory purist by using multiple treatment approaches. Severe psychotic symptoms respond to major tranquilizers, hassles in the family are reduced by family therapy, with traditional counseling and psychotherapy producing insight, more mature problem solving, and changes and clarification of values and attitudes.

It is true that as the patient's overt psychotic symptoms are brought under control by medication, his family starts to understand him better through family therapy, and he understands himself better because of psychotherapy and his behavior begins to improve. But the behavior has not changed enough. In other situations the patient's behavior itself is such a problem that other forms of treatment cannot be successfully employed. Some psychoanalytically oriented psychiatrists are using behavior modification to reduce the severity of symptoms so that regular analytical therapy can be effective. Modifying the behavior of patients is seen more and more as an important part of the treatment package whether used with other treatment modalities or separately.

Some patients, particularly the mentally retarded or those institutionalized for many years, have not responded well to treatments other than chemotherapy. Chemotherapy may reduce agitation or decrease hallucinatory behavior, but no drug has been discovered which increases politeness, coming to work on time, responsibility or personal cleanliness. Behavior modification techniques may not increase the I.Q. or decrease strange ideations, but if the patient's speech, dress and manners become more appropriate his probability of surviving outside the hospital is surely increased.

Behavior modification works! It does change behavior, but it takes some continual effort on the part of everyone who interacts with the patient: staff, family, employer, etc. Suppose, for example, that patient H.J. has had a psychotic break and now is recovering. H.J. does not dress neatly and lacks personal hygiene. His shirt is not tucked in or buttoned, his fly is unzipped, and often he reeks of urine. Even when all the psychotic symptoms subside he is not welcome in many homes or in places of employment. But the staff develops a rather complex program and in a few weeks has shaped his behavior so that he is now acceptably neat before breakfast (he may earn his breakfast by neatly dressing himself), does fairly well in the workshop working on a repackaging subcontract, and comes back to the ward to be praised for his neatness. In the evening he is able to spend at the canteen some of his points that he has earned during the day for being careful whenever he urinated. His progress is being maintained by verbal praise and spendable points from the staff.

Contrast the patient H.J. to a normally developing small boy who has personal hygiene problems with unzipped pants, polo shirt on backwards and is careless while urinating. He learns just the same way as H.J. The boy gets reinforced positively, rewarded for good behavior and punished for bad behavior. The difference between H.J. and the little boy is that little boys grow up. They develop an internal system of reinforcement. The little boy turned young man wants to be appropriately clean because he feels better that way and people respond more positively to him. No one praises a young man for having his shirt tucked in or for not having body odor, but subtle reinforcers in the environment plus internal feelings maintain the behavior. Unfortunately this is not so for many of the H.J.'s. If H.J. is moved to a board and room home staffed with those who do not use or understand the principles of behavior modification, his behavior may quickly revert back to its original state. This illustration cautions the user of behavior modification techniques to remember that behavior must be reinforced for it to continue to occur. If a patient's behavior is successfully shaped in a hospital environment but reverts to its original state when the patient returns to the family environment, the conclusion is not that behavior modification is ineffective but rather that the patient's behavior was not sustained by his environment. It does little good to use staff time to alter the behavior of a patient if it is known that the environment to which the patient will return is dedicated, even unintentionally, to keeping the patient ill.

BASIC PRINCIPLES OF BEHAVIOR PRINCIPLES

Two similar schools of psychological thought have influenced greatly the psychotherapeutic world; the works of Ivan Pavlov and B. F. Skinner. Pavlov's system, called classical conditioning, holds that learning takes place by the associating of a new stimulus to an already established stimulus response pair.

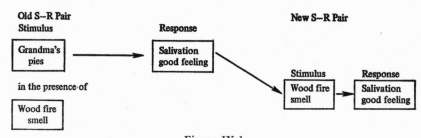

Figure IX-1

Classical Conditioning

The response to the pies was a natural one. After eating grandma's pies several times in the presence of the wood fire odor, the wood fire took on the capability of producing some of the same kind of sensations as when the pies were present. You can imagine an adult with this background frequently enjoying a fire in the fireplace.

Another example:

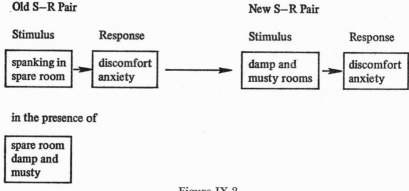

Figure IX-2

This kind of association is very common. Phobias seem to be explained very well by this classical model. We tend to remember an event such as a severe spanking but we forget the other cues that were present. Phobias seem often to be unexplained because we have been trained to look for symbolic meaning when, in fact, the explanation may be simple association, a case of classical conditioning.

Operant Conditioning

The second system, even more widely used as a theoretical base for behavior modification is Skinnerian, or operant conditioning. Operant conditioning uses a slightly different model. Instead of a stimulus followed by a response, operant conditioning posits a response which is followed by a reinforcement.

As examples:

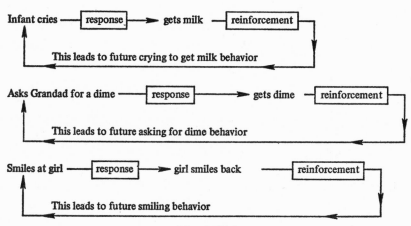

Figure IX-3

The operant approach does not ignore the stimulus but concentrates on the response and the reinforcement of that response. There are many factors which affect the rate at which one acquires learning using the | response | → | reinforcement | model.

The most general concept of operant conditioning is that *behavior which is rewarded or reinfor*ced *is likely to occur again.* A puppy which is purposefully ignored each time he whines soon emits a low level of whining behavior, but a puppy which is given attention (reinforcement) through food, petting, or even mild scolding continues or increases whining behavior. Behavior must be reinforced to occur repeatedly and on cue. Politeness, personal hygiene, work habits, punctuality, etc. are all behaviors which must be reinforced to occur consistently.

A second concept states that *the more quickly a behavioral response is reinforced the more likely the future occurrence of that behavior.* It is far more effective to praise a patient for having made his bed immediately upon completion of the task than to do it at the end of the day. A week later has almost no effect on future bed making. This is a difficult problem to manage in behavior modification programming. Immediate reinforcement does not occur after rounds, or at morning or evening reports, or meals, or after Mrs. Brown is restrained, or after inventory is finished. And yet there are times when nurses, psychiatric technicians, social workers, and rehab counselors cannot take the time to properly administer immediate reinforcement.

It is also important that staff be aware of the effects of inconsistent reinforcement. If cleaning a ward or workshop for inspection takes precedence over reinforcing some newly emerging positive behavior of a patient, the staff clearly finds the approval of the administration more reinforcing than the progress of a patient. There will be situations, of course, which demand action but the staff should be aware of the results of their behavior and behave in the direction with the most positive outcomes.

Points to Remember in Using Behavior Modification

Know what the reinforcers for your patients are. Most people respond to primary reinforcers such as food with the result of nicknaming behavior modification the "M&M Therapy." For many adults snack type foods such as potato chips and pretzels have value as reinforcers. Tobacco is frequently used. Alcohol, where legal for treatment purposes, is an effective reinforcer. Many behaviors improve with the anticipation of a couple short beers at the five p.m. ward bar. Some treatment facilities have constructed questionnaires which list a large number of items with potential reinforcement value. The patient then identifies those items which he would like to enjoy. While this approach has usefulness, it is often inaccurate. Patients may mark items as reinforcers which they care nothing about and omit ones they do care about. The best method for identifying reinforcers is to observe the patient. Things that the staff does not consider reinforcing may be powerfully reinforcing for the patient. For one patient to sit in a certain chair, watch a particular TV show, go for a walk, or have a nap may be reinforcing while a cigarette, a movie, or ice cream is reinforcing to another patient. Some tasks, such as work, are drudgery to be endured by one person but pure pleasure for a different person.

The power of any reinforcer varies. Satiation and fatigue also influence the potency of reinforcers. Many favorite foods have high reinforcement value because they are available infrequently. The Christmas Plum Pudding would lose much of its reinforcement value if it were served many times during the year. Even patients who like ice cream would grow tired of ice cream if given it ten or twelve times each day. If you are very tired a long walk is not appealing regardless of your desire for walks. If a patient has just had a big meal, a candy bar loses much of its power to reinforce. It is important for the mental health worker to have several items, tasks, or privileges available as reinforcers. By varying the reinforcers the patient will retain a high interest in the program. A common complaint regarding staffs operating behavior modification programs is that the reward works, the patient improves, but then the patient gets worse. Usually the patient has grown tired or lost interest in the reinforcer.

Primary and Secondary Reinforcers

With more normal patients, both in terms of symptoms and intellectual functioning, a secondary reinforcer differs from a primary reinforcer in that a secondary reinforcer is learned and is often symbolic and irrelevant. A primary reinforcer is immediate and direct. For example, a patient made his bed so he can have a piece of candy or has worked well at the bench for two hours to earn a cup of coffee. Money is a good example of secondary reinforcement—one does fifty units of work to earn five dollars. Secondary reinforcement can be immediate but it is not direct. One cannot eat five dollars, but it can be exchanged for something edible. Money, poker chips, stars on a chart, punches on a card, or tokens are all examples of this kind of secondary reinforcement. This economy system is discussed more fully later.

Secondary reinforcement has several very positive aspects as a therapeutic tool. It allows the mental health worker to reinforce desirable behavior immediately without having to be a walking general store. Because the tokens or chips are cashed in for something reinforcing, the patient usually has a variety of reinforcers to choose from, hence he may vary the reinforcer. If he tires of soda pop he may buy a game of pool. The most important long range aspect of secondary reinforcement (in some forms referred to as a token economy) is its normalizing effect. It allows the patient to get an immediate symbolic reward while training him to delay immediate gratification. Decisions must be made whether to buy candy and soda pop today or to save for a week and go out for pizza and beer. The concepts of working for a paycheck and then budgeting one's money are concepts which can be more easily taught within the structure of a token economy.

The Use of Social Reinforcement

Another type of reward is social reinforcement. Praise, greetings and salutations, smiles, affectionate behaviors, touching, and other verbal and nonverbal events are social reinforcers. They are learned reinforcers rather than natural reinforcers like food. Using Pavlov's model, a baby learns to associate the mother's smile with milk. Later, the mother's smile provides pleasure without the milk being present. Still later, through a process called stimulus generalization, a smile from any valued person will give pleasure. Social reinforcers are very important in that almost everyone can learn to respond to attention from others. The problem with some psychiatric patients, especially those from deprived environments is that they have not learned to respond positively to positive attention. These patients can be taught to respond to social reinforcers by pairing praise, attention, smiles, etc. with such primitive reinforcers as food.

Schedules of Reinforcement

While behavior must be reinforced to assure its reoccurrence, this does not mean that an act should always be reinforced every time. Let us consider first continual reinforcement. *To become learned a newly emitted behavior should be reinforced continuously.* If a chronically depressed patient is observed smiling, the smile is to be reinforced immediately and everytime it occurs. It is important for the patient to associate the response (smiling) with the reward. If the behavior emitted is only occasionally reinforced the organism will not make any association between the reward and the desired behavior. Once the person makes the response-reinforcement association, the behavior will continue at a high rate (if the reinforcer retains its potency). If, for example, ward and sheltered workshop personnel working together on

Mary's smiling behavior have reinforced her continuously, she will be smiling at a high rate. But if she goes home for a weekend, where no one reinforces her smiling, her smiling behavior will decrease to about zero when she returns. This process of a once learned behavior decreasing to near zero is called extinction. While the fastest way to learn a new behavior is to have that behavior reinforced every time it is emitted, continually reinforced behavior also extinguishes rapidly. It has been found that when established behavior is maintained on an intermittent reinforcement schedule the behavior will continue long after reinforcement ceases. Fishermen, for example, have been known to continue to fish many hours or even days without reinforcement. The task in designing a schedule of reinforcement is really two fold: using continuous reinforcement to establish the behavior, then switching gradually to intermittent reinforcement to make the behavior more resistant to extinction. John's coming to work on time has been reinforced everytime it occurred and John has been on time the last nine out of ten mornings. On the eleventh morning his punctuality is not reinforced and he may or may not be on time the twelfth day. The next day if he is present on time, reinforce him to reestablish the desired behavior. Reinforce for several days and then skip a day or two. The reason for switching to an intermittent schedule where reinforcement is given on an irregular basis is not to do away with the necessity of reinforcement, but to decrease the necessity for continuous reward. This is normalizing in that while the real world is based on rewards, tangible or intangible, rewards are not handed out everytime a behavior is emitted. Every smile is not responded to and few people will comment on pressed pants or shined shoes. There must be a minimum amount of reinforcement to maintain behavior otherwise people would not fall out of love, change political parties, or find new friends.

Shaping Appropriate Behavior

Sometimes a behavior is desired that is not being performed by the patient. It is possible by operant conditioning to produce a behavior which is currently not in the person's behavioral repertoire.

Successive approximation is a method to bring behavior closer and closer to the desired pattern through a series of progressive steps, each made possible by selectively reinforcing certain responses and not others. Thus responses which are closer approximations to the goal are reinforced and all other responses are not reinforced. Successive approximation is used in teaching any skill, from combing hair to skiing or piano playing.

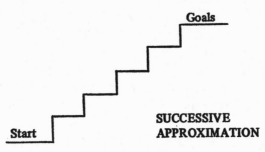

Figure IX-4

Suppose that Jane had not learned to comb her hair but appears to possess the motor and intellectual skills necessary to do so. Let us further suppose that Jane likes cornchips and can hold the comb. The task now is to shape her behavior through successive approximation. First, reward her with the cornchips and praise only when she holds the comb with the teeth pointing down—after that behavior is well established (repeatedly reinforced) move on to the second step. Now reinforce her only if the comb is brought within eighteen inches of her head. At first she will be confused as she is accustomed to being reinforced every time but it will not take many attempts and she can be reinforced. If eighteen inches is too difficult a step for her, make the goal easier. When she consistently brings the comb closer to her head move to the next step. Third, shape bringing the comb closer, perhaps moving from eighteen inches to twelve inches then to six inches and finally to touch the hair. The last steps will be to move the comb into the hair, learn to comb in the right direction, and to learn to style her own hair. These last steps may take as many as ten to twenty discrete steps.

While it is possible to teach Jane to comb her hair through

shaping alone it would make it much easier if the process of combing hair were demonstrated or modeled for her. *Modeling is observational learning.* Imitative behavior through modeling is an excellent short cut to acquiring new behavioral skills.

Positive or Negative Reinforcement and Punishment

Behavior is learned through negative reinforcement as well as positive reinforcement. Positive reinforcement involves a reward, whereas negative reinforcement is the avoidance or termination of a painful or annoying stimulus. Swatting a fly is an example of negative reinforcement. The response of swatting is reinforced by the cessation of the buzzing. Paying attention to an unruly patient so he will quiet down is also negatively reinforcing for you. The problem is that your behavior is positively reinforcing for the unruly patient for he has learned that the best way to get your attention is to be unruly.

Punishment is not negative reinforcement because there is nothing reinforcing about punishment in itself. *Punishment does not change behavior but merely suppresses it temporarily.* Punishment teaches the subject to avoid getting caught rather than teaching behavior change. Instead of using punishment to control undesirable behavior it is much better to reward positive behavior. Rather than to punish swearing behavior in the ward it is much better to reward positive conversation. Another problem in using punishment is that it must be given by someone. If a patient is desiring attention, a verbal tongue lashing may be highly reinforcing. Most people would rather be given negative attention than to be ignored. If punishment must be used to prevent a dangerous behavior from occurring it should be done as quickly and with as little personal contact as possible. Fifteen minutes in a stimulus free, quiet room would have fewer negative results than a ten-minute lecture or being belted to a chair in a public day room.

One type of problem frequently seen by the family of mental patients is inappropriate social and personal behavior. Greeting everyone that walks into the canteen may not seem strange to the hospital staff, but the same behavior at the local dime store will earn a phone call to the ward. The ward is often seen as one big happy family with every patient, except the withdrawn ones, knowing everyone else's business. This behavior may be functional for those people who will be spending the rest of their lives in the hospital setting, but it is not functional for those who are planning to leave. A method similar to shaping and successive approximation is discrimination learning. This is a high level process which tells us that behaviors are appropriate only in context. When a staff is getting ready to move a patient from the ward slowly into the community it is very useful to observe the patient in a workshop setting or at home or on a shopping trip. With the contextual cues altered the patient's behavior can more clearly be judged appropriate or inappropriate. Then the process of discrimination can be taught but it usually is necessary to involve in the learning process the mental health professionals who are in the intermediate phases of rehabilitation. Behavior must be shaped and reinforced in the setting where it occurs as well as back on the ward.

SETTING UP THE BEHAVIOR MODIFICATION PROGRAM

There are four simple points which serve to outline the behavior modification program. The acronym PAIR is spelled from (1) problem (2) antecedents (3) intervention and (4) results.

The first task is to scientifically define the *problem*. What exactly is the behavior in question? Not only what is the behavior but when and how much must be asked as well. Behavior is lawful and occurs for a reason. The knowledge of when and how much behavior along with other events in the environment can be used to find the cause for negative behavior. It is important to know how much behavior because (1) the patient may be really emitting the behavior less than you think, (2) he may be doing more and (3) his average rate must be known to determine the effectiveness of your intervention.

Let us suppose that Mary is staying at a halfway house and is working at a coffee shop run by the house. Mary has trouble with "nervous spells" and must go to the back room for a rest. She works a four and a half hour shift and gets a ten minute break after each one and a half hour period. It was decided to observe Mary three times each day, twenty minutes each at the beginning of the shift and after each break period. The problem is being able to work at the counter. The graph shows an average time at the counter of two minutes the first day, five minutes the second and four minutes the third. Mary was able to stay at her work station less than five minutes on each trial.

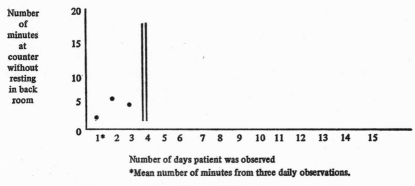

Number of days patient was observed
*Mean number of minutes from three daily observations.

Figure IX-5

The second letter in PAIR represents antecedents. In this situation antecedents are those events which went on just prior to and immediately after the client's inappropriate behavior. This takes more observation. Having the patient keep records if they are able to or at least tell you verbally contributes to your data. It is important to know what happened in the environment or at least what the patient thought had happened. In our example, Mary was watched both at her work station and in the back room. The following things were observed: (1) Mary had very poor eye contact and never smiled at the customer, (2) the customers often stared at her, (3) Mary reported that the customers were sending evil thoughts into her mind, (4) Mary was worse after a very blatant staring, (5) Mary always laid on the cot in the back room and (6) Mary complained to the other girls about her problem and they comforted her.

The third letter in PAIR stands for intervention. The strategy for intervention is determined by the data collected in the first two steps. It appears that the customers stare at Mary because she appears to be so frightened. This staring makes her even more frightened. She enjoys the back room as she gets to lay down and she gets attention. She likes the break time also. With this information a program is set up to modify her behavior. The conditions are now (1) for every customer she looks at when taking the order or smiles at just once, she gets a tip (poker chip) worth one minute extra breaktime, (2) the cot is removed, (3) if she leaves the counter because of nervousness she goes to the storeroom and sits where no one can listen to her story and (4) break periods can be taken in the back room with the other girls where it is permissible to visit. Along with this the coffee shop manager observes any behavior Mary emits while with a customer or other employees. Whenever she does something positive, he immediately reinforces her for what, however small, she does. This helps her calm down after dealing with a particularly obnoxious customer. The task now is to follow through on the strategy and to record the patient's progress and any other data that would be useful.

The fourth letter in PAIR represents Results. Now look at the progress and evaluate where to go from here.

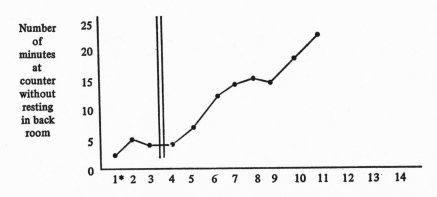

Number of days patient was observed

*Mean number of minutes from three daily observations.

Figure IX-6

It appears that the strategy works. The reinforcements seem appropriate for shaping new behavior, and the settings that were reinforcing inappropriate behavior have largely been removed. The scientist may want to know what part of the program was responsible for the change, but that it works is most important to the practitioner.

If the changes in the hypothetical case of Mary had not been as positive, a different strategy would be tried until progress was made. Even though as in this example, the behavior moves along nicely you are not finished. Usually you have followed a continuous reinforcement schedule. It is not practical to consider long term behavior maintenance on other than a variable intermittent schedule. So you substitute verbal praise once in a while for a token. Also you hope that the environment will begin to provide some reinforcement of its own. Some real tips and genuine smiles may take over. The end of the chart doesn't mean the end of the program. Modify it to suit the patient's needs.

THINK POSITIVELY

A natural tendency is for the staff to shape behavior by rewarding appropriate behaviors and punishing inappropriate ones. If this style of treatment is used the staff will try to find good behaviors (by the staff's definition) to reward and poor behaviors to punish but will usually find far more negative than positive behaviors. Aversive (selected-punishment) is an effective form of treatment for certain psychiatric problems in the hands of a competent professional. But if the whole staff uses aversive conditioning freely the attitude of negativism reduces the acquisition of positive behaviors. Besides, except in special situations, punishment does not change behavior it only suppresses it.

The question is what to do with negative behavior. *Most negative behavior should be ignored.* The greatest amount of inappropriate behavior continues to be emitted by the patient because it is reinforced by social attention. Psychotic, aggressive, annoying, self-destructive, etc. behavior usually causes some commotion. A fire in the wastebasket gets more people involved than a hundred good work passes. While the staff is the greatest giver of attention, much is also given by the family and the other patients. The cooperation of the family and others should be gained if the negative behavior is to quickly cease.

In addition to ignoring inappropriate behavior, another part of the procedure is to shape a positive behavior which is incompatible to the negative behavior. If a person is getting reinforced for reading, playing cards, or watching TV (acceptable behaviors) he cannot be pacing the floor (unacceptable behavior).

If the patient is about to do something destructive to himself or someone else place him in a stimulus free room (no bed, no chairs, no pictures, etc.) until the behavior has subsided. Use as little force as necessary to decrease the importance of this event in the patient's eye and as much force as necessary to get the patient under control quickly. In summary use positive reinforcement for desirable behaviors, ignore negative behavior, and introduce and reinforce positive behaviors that are incompatible with the negative behavior.

THE REINFORCEMENT ECONOMY

One of the most useful techniques in encouraging the patient is reinforcement economy. This is a system by where a patient earns points, funny money, or tokens and then spends them for the necessities and luxuries of life. The economy has a normalizing effect in that the patient experiences many of both the positive and negative consequences of their behavior.

The basis for any economy is income and expenditure. The patient must earn enough to pay for his necessities. He should be able to, by working harder or longer, earn enough for some luxuries. He should not be allowed to earn too much or establish a large bank account too easily as this weakens the system. The unit of exchange (money, points, or tokens) should not be loaned by the bank (staff) to the patients or from one patient to another. This practice teaches some patients begging behavior rather than work behavior.

It is best if the entire building, or at least ward, is on the same economy since everyone gets the same pay for the same job and is charged the same price for the same privilege. If possible the economy should be extended into the work setting and into the living setting if the patient is not full-time at the hospital.

The economy in a hospital, like that of the real world, is based upon supply and demand. Jobs that everyone wants, within reason, pay less than those no one wants. If apples are more desirable than oranges, apples cost more. Spending is encouraged. The more people spend the more beneficial behaviors they will perform to earn the currency.

All appropriate personal, social, and working behaviors can earn points. Bed making, tooth brushing, showering, clean underwear, smiling, "good morning," reading newspapers and magazines, proper use of fork, taking small bites, staying at work station, number of items assembled, coming back from coffee break on time, and remembering meals are some of the many behaviors which can earn points. Patients spend points purchasing things that have a high reinforcement value to them. Examples include coffee, cigarettes, soda pop, candy, snack foods, regular meals, bed (instead of a cot), TV, newspaper and magazine, games, walks, swearing, laying on bed during the day, inappropriate dress, sleeping late, or crazy talk.

Some of the items to be purchased, such as food, universally have a high reinforcement value. Other behaviors, like newspaper reading, will earn some patients points and cost others points. The difference is at what level the patient is performing that behavior. A college graduate who refuses to read a newspaper or magazine might get paid for it, whereas someone who reads excessively neglecting social interaction may have to pay for his reading.

In the spirit of trying to keep things on a positive note, fines are generally avoided as such. People are allowed to eat cigarette butts, hallucinate in the corner, or crazy talk to a technician. But these behaviors cost them money. The question of semantic game playing is valid here but there is more than just that. If the staff tells the patient he can talk to the clock for twenty points the patient often finds the behavior less desirable if it is permissible and if it costs something. If talking to the clock is really important there are other gains because the patient has to perform other desirable chores to earn the twenty points which allow him to talk to the clock.

A token economy can follow one of three models: (1) everyone receiving the same income and outgo for the same behavior; (2) everyone on a highly individual program tailored to his own needs; and (3) everyone following the same basic system with some individual programs for problem behaviors. The first type is the easiest to administer, the second type leads to the greatest behavior change, however, the third is the one most frequently used.

COMMON BEHAVIORS THAT CAN BE INCREASED OR DECREASED USING BEHAVIOR MODIFICATION

RECOGNITION OF ENVIRONMENT. A common complaint is that mental patients are lost in a fantasy world. This is worsened by not attending, at least verbally, to their surroundings. Patients should be reinforced (verbal praise, points, tokens, stars, etc.) for knowing what day it is, for addressing people by name, and being aware of things in the changes of the environment. Teaching appropriate behavior in context is the task. It is appropriate to compliment a nurse on her new dress once. Any comment more than once should be ignored. Similarly Dr. Jones may appreciate a "good morning" from Tom the first time but finds it inappropriate more than once the same morning.

IMPROVED SOCIAL INTERACTION. Rewards should be given for all positive forms of communication. One experimental program is the Model Interview. This interview is a fifteen minute discussion between the patient and the same technician, nurse, or counselor occurring several times a week. The purpose is to teach discussing things meaningful to both the patient and a normal adult. Crazy talk or psychosomatic complaints are ignored. The patients are encouraged to watch the news, other TV shows, or read the paper for a discussion focus.

A technique with a similar goal is to have a patient government with appropriate participation and good decision-making being reinforced. Patients can work in small groups planning ward activities and giving suggestions to the staff useful in treatment programs for other patients. The quantity and quality of the group's decisions and recommendations determine the points earned.

WORK BEHAVIORS. The most typical work behaviors which are reinforced are coming to work on time, staying at the work station, working while at the station, self-supervision, responsible use of rest room, amount of work, quality of work, and accepting orders and criticism. Points as reinforcement which can be used with points earned on the ward are the most effective, as the consequences of work behavior is coupled with those of living behavior.

PERSONAL HABITS. Bladder control, unless there is organic damage, can be brought under control. Positive reinforcement for dry clothes and a ten point charge for clean clothes in the event of an accident is often effective. For bed wetters, the pad which rings a bell at the first drop of urine is very useful. This wakes the patient up while they still have a full bladder. They can then be led to the bathroom (reinforced, of course). After repeated trials, most people will learn to awaken with a full bladder before the bell sounds.

Good table manners are reinforced but here other problems occur, particularly with chronic patients who have often developed disgusting eating habits. A shaping procedure is useful but takes a lot of time, as each patient must be worked with almost individually. When the patient slips in his behavior his food can be removed. Eating as best as he can is the prerequisite for having the food. Some mental health settings use small tables with white linens and flowers for the best mannered. The poorest mannered eat from steel trays with several steps for intermediate manners in between. As they improve they move from one group to the next until they are at the white linen table.

SITTING AND SLEEPING are usually behaviors which should be decreased rather than increased. Charging rather stiff fees for daytime bed and chair use helps. Making the ward a noisy place after last "get up" call discourages late sleepers. Chairs moved from back corners into busy day halls lose some of their appeal for chronic sitters. Of course, having activities which interest patients (incompatible responses) make staying awake better than sleeping.

ACTIONS THAT ANNOY STAFF. Every social worker, rehab counselor, and nurse has experienced the patient who has endless complaints and/or questions. Ignoring unimportant or fabricated concerns is usually enough. If it is not, questioning can be purchased on a sliding scale, which allows several free questions per day and has an increasing fee schedule for the dependent patient. Not only will this slow down the question, but for the dependent patient who hates to make decisions, independent behavior should be shaped. At first any kind of decision should be reinforced and, when decision-making is well-established, only those choices which are good ones should be reinforced.

CRAZY TALK. The relating of hallucinations, delusions, and strange beliefs is one of the most self-defeating of all behaviors. A patient can look normal and have good work skills; but if he cannot be on a new job ten minutes without telling everyone of his delusioned system, he is immediately suspect and avoided by others. This usually produces in the patient even stranger behavior. A decrease in crazy talk can be effected by ignoring it in any conversation and reinforcing those thoughts which are sensible. Discontinue any conversation which contains mostly crazy talk.

AGGRESSIVE BEHAVIOR. Mild appropriate aggressive behavior is encouraged as a normalizing function. Inappropriate behavior has consequences. Swearing can be decreased by placing the patient in a stimulus free room, rent charged of course, for unlimited swearing. Striking behavior can be handled in a similar fashion: a purchase of fifteen minutes with a punching bag not only makes the anger cost something but shows an alternative way for handling anger. A very low fee for the punching bag prior to overt aggression encourages hitting the bag rather than a fellow patient.

PHILOSOPHICAL OBJECTIONS TO BEHAVIOR MODIFICATION

While many issues could probably be raised, two points of objection are frequently raised to behavior modification: that it is control of human behavior and that it is bribery.

Behavior modification is seen as the control or manipulation of the patient. The behaviorist would not deny this, but would say the patient is being controlled already by reinforcing his current behavior, and it is causing the patient trouble. The family and hospital staff pay attention to his hallucinations. They reinforce his crazy talk. Ignoring his schizophrenic gibberish is not cruel but humane. To reinforce schizophrenic behavior is cruel as it causes people to avoid him and decreases his chances for independence.

The second most frequent objection is that behavior modification constitutes bribery. Bribery is the act of causing someone to do something against his own and/or society's best interests. A reinforcement schedule helps someone to do something toward their own and/or society's best interest. Except with the most disturbed patient, who already has most of life's choices made for him, most patients agree with the intent of a good behavior modification program. They want to get better. We all respond to reinforcement. Few of us would continue to work very long if our employers ceased paying wages. We would stop being friends to those we love if they gave us no social reinforcement.

Behavior modification could be used in a controlling authoritarian fashion, but in the hands of sensitive humanitarian mental health workers it is a powerful and beneficial tool.

SUGGESTED READING

Ayllon, T., and Azrin, N. H.: *The Token Economy.* New York, Appleton, 1968.

Deibert, A. N., and Harmon, A. J.: *New Tools for Changing Behavior.* Champaign, Ill., Res Press, 1970.

Gardner, W. I.: *Behavior Modification in Mental Retardation: The Education & Rehabilitation of the Mentally Retarded Adolescent & Adult (Modern Applications of Psychology Ser.).* Chicago, Aldine, 1971.

Reese, E. P.: *The Analysis of Human Operant Behavior.* Dubuque, Iowa, Brown, 1966.

Schaefer, H., and Martin, P. L.: *Behavioral Therapy.* New York, McGraw, 1969.

CHAPTER X

BEHAVIORAL GROUP THERAPY WITH ALCOHOL ABUSERS

STEVEN M. ROSS

●●●

Techniques and Terminology
Pre-Group Preparations
Group Meetings
Conclusions
References

●●●

THIS CHAPTER is an attempt to present a broad spectrum behavioral approach to group treatment of alcoholism. The emphasis will be on practical techniques which the reader can use regardless of his theoretical orientation. Theory, technical vocabulary, and academic arguments will be kept to a minimum, while references will be provided the reader to obtain more detailed information of various techniques, the research literature, and other sources.

The approach to be described is based on the assumption that alcohol abuse is a learning problem in that patients learn to either escape or avoid unpleasant events or gain access to pleasurable events through excessive drinking.

If patients learn to respond in these ways to various life events, it is possible to teach them to respond in ways other than drinking. The task of the group is to provide a setting where other behaviors can be learned, practiced, and strengthened. Unless there is more to be gained by not drinking than by drinking, it will persist. The group must, therefore, also help in generalizing the behaviors learned in the group to situations where they are most needed outside the group, for instance, in the community.

The group has special advantages for accomplishing these very difficult tasks, advantages which individual therapy lacks. (1) Members are able to learn from each other via observation and imitation; (2) members learn that their problems are not unique and they are not alone; (3) new behavior can be practiced and strengthened in the presence of a variety of people which more closely approximates "real life"; (4) group censure and support can exert more pressure to bear for change and strengthening of new behaviors; (5) patients learn that they are able to trust and help others; (6) more efficient use of the leader's time is made; and (7) more facets of problems and more problem solving techniques can be gained from group discussion.

Naturally, the total treatment of the alcoholic cannot occur in one therapy group. There are often medical, vocational, and recreational problems which must be left to other members of the treatment team. Oftentimes individuals must be prepared to function in a group and this preparation itself may take the form of one-to-one counseling or therapy. The leader must decide with each potential group member which problems should be brought up in group and which are better dealt with elsewhere. The key to this problem lies in pre-group preparations— deciding on the kind of group (composition, goals, commonalities of members, time limitations, size) and the assessment of prospective members (identifying behavioral assets, deficits, excesses).

In the sections to follow we will examine these pre-group functions in greater detail, but first it may be helpful to define a few terms which will be used, trying, of course, to adhere to my original promise of keeping technical vocabulary to a minimum. It is more the purpose of this section to provide the reader with a "cookbook" of techniques which he can draw upon regardless of the type of group he runs, than it is to teach a foreign academic language.

TECHNIQUES AND TERMINOLOGY

Baseline Rate

This term refers to the frequency, duration, or magnitude with which a particular behavior occurs naturally before any type of treatment takes place. Obtaining baseline rates before treatment provides us with some indication of how successful our treatment is, providing we continue to get data on the same behavior in the same way after treatment begins and ends. If someone drinks a fifth of scotch every day prior to treatment their baseline drinking rate would be a fifth per day (magnitude). Another way of measuring pretreatment drinking behavior might be to observe how frequently a patient pours a drink during a particular time sample. The third possibility, duration, might be determined by measuring with a stop watch how many total minutes during a time sample the patient had a drink poured for himself.

It is not necessary to obtain all three measures on any given behavior. For any given behavior, whether it is drinking, talking about family problems in group, or number of A.A. meetings attended, there is usually one best measure to get. A general rule of thumb is, if a behavior occurs frequently and lasts only a few seconds, e.g. fidgeting, eye contact, using a particular word, it is probably better to measure frequency of response. If the behavior occurs for several hours or minutes, e.g. tardy for group, feeling depressed, talking in group, it is probably better to measure duration of occurrence per session, per day, etc. Magnitude is probably best used when the behavior already is in some quantified form, e.g. number of ounces of wine consumed in a day or week, how fearful someone rates himself on a scale from 0 to 100. A much more detailed description of data collecting is provided by Jackson and Della-Piana (1971).

While it is not always feasible to obtain baseline rates and subsequent data on all problem behaviors for all patients because of practical limitations of time, personnel, cost, etc., it is possible to a greater degree than one might imagine, especially in a hospital or clinic or through home visits. At the very least, patients themselves can obtain data on their own behavior even if it is something as gross as counting empty bottles. In addition, many friends, family members, employers, and relatives are willing to help as collateral sources of data and general functioning. By comparing several baseline rates we can determine how reliable the measure is, providing the two observers did their data collecting independently of each other. The help of collaterals should never be enlisted without the full knowledge and consent of the patient lest his trust in the treatment program be undermined.

Functional Analysis

A functional analysis of behavior is an assessment of what cues set the stage for certain responses to occur and what happens immediately after the responses have occurred which strengthen (reinforce) them or weaken them. All of the behavior we emit which has some effect on ourselves or our environment is controlled by that effect. To change this behavior we must change the effect it has, or, we must practice new responses to the old cues. These notions are worth pondering for a few minutes because they are very important but very difficult to achieve.

Consider an individual who claims that he does not know why he drinks. He even says that if he knew why he drank he would not be asking for our help. It is very likely that this individual is telling the truth. He may be unaware of many events that lead to drinking and what the drinking "does for him." If he were to keep records of his drinking to include the following data: What Occurred Just Prior to Drinking, Date, Time, Place, Alone or Whom With, Amount Consumed, Type of Beverage, What Happened After Drinking, very definite patterns would emerge which would yield much information as to what cues the drinking and what functions the drinking serves. I have had copies of the above information made which I give to people seeking treatment and individuals they list as collateral sources of information. I call these data sheets the *Intake Record* and often require waiting list patients to complete them in order to qualify for treatment when a vacancy arises. This does not mean that if they have already stopped drinking they must start again to provide pre-treatment baseline data. However, if they do drink or even have an *urge* to drink they are to record the information as accurately as they can.

The patterns which emerge from intake data of this type are often very informative and can be very helpful in setting goals and generating group discussion. For example, an individual reports coming home from work tense and needing a drink to "unwind." Upon arriving home he finds his wife yelling at the kids and asking him to punish them for misbehavior. This may further upset him because he may not want to punish them for something that happened hours earlier and did not even involve him. Instead of having one drink he may have three. Instead of having the drinks *with* his wife and kids while chatting about the events of the day, he may bring the bottle to a secluded location of the house in order to escape the battle. His wife may then turn on him for shirking his responsibilities which results in another three drinks to drown her voice. By now dinner is ready but he is in no mood to eat and has a few more. He and his wife may sleep separately that night. He probably wakes up with a hangover (late because the alarm clock is in the master bedroom and he slept on the couch). Feeling terrible, he has a few to get him going and to give him courage to face the boss who is angry because he is late. At work people look at him twice because he is disheveled. He feels they are staring at him and talking behind his back. His job may be in danger which adds to the pressure he feels. He may try to be a model employee and perform perfectly that day. If he makes a mistake he becomes extremely upset with himself. At lunch he "has a few to steady his nerves."

This individual may be starting a binge or he may be in the middle of one. We could go on to describe the rest of his day, but let us stop at this point and look at a functional analysis of his behavior. His Intake Record shows that he first reported an urge to drink upon arriving home in order to unwind. There are two possibilities at this point. Does arriving home *itself* function as a cue for drinking or does the feeling of needing to unwind? Perhaps both do. Careful inspection of his intake pattern might reveal that he automatically drinks whenever he arrives home regardless of how he is feeling and regardless of how well he and

his family are getting along. Perhaps he has learned to drink upon arriving home because so much of the time his wife had a
drink waiting for him or because the family squabbling made arriving home an aversive event. Pre-group discussion might focus
on these possibilities: what else he might do instead of drink,
how the group might be of assistance if he brings the problem
up in group, and the fact that other group members can be expected to ask for his help for similar kinds of problems.

The second urge to drink or actual drinking that he probably
reported on his Intake Record was that additional drinking
which occurred after his wife accused him of shirking his responsibilities. Again, inspection of his Intake Record over time
might reveal that he almost always drinks after being criticized.
Furthermore, the criticism-drinking association is not limited to
his wife. The pattern may also reveal that even when his own
children, not to mention his boss, co-workers, and friends, criti-
cize him, he drinks or has a strong urge to drink. Criticism, then,
may also function as a cue for drinking and he may not even be
aware of it. The drinking which follows criticism may enable
him to calm down and forget the criticism which had been bothering him. In addition, the drinking may give him courage to tell
the criticizer to shut up. The section of the Intake Record which
asks, What Happened After Drinking? might, in fact, support
these hypotheses by showing that the individual felt more relaxed and forgot about the criticism or told the criticizer off.
Careful questioning by the group or by the leader, prior to the
group's starting, might reveal difficulties in assertion and extreme
sensitivity to criticism. Both of these problems would lend themselves to group treatment quite well and we shall provide some
concrete examples of how in later sections.

The third and fourth drinking episodes in our example were
drinking instead of eating dinner and drinking to get him going
in the morning. Let us examine number three. If our patient or
our home observer is keeping accurate records, he would have recorded under the column, What Occurred Just Prior to Drinking?, "Wife called out, 'Dinner is ready!' " Then, he would have
recorded the Date, Time, and specific room in his house for
Place. Under the next column, Alone or Whom With?, he would

have recorded, "With family." Next he would have recorded an estimate of the Amount Consumed and then the Type of Beverage. Finally, he would have recorded something under the last column, What Happened After Drinking? He might have recorded something in this last column such as "I wasn't bothered by her voice anymore, and I was glad she had cooked for me for nothing. Served her right." Again, looking at his intake pattern over a period of time might demonstrate similar ways of escaping aversive stimulation, that his appetite diminishes when drinking and that he uses alcohol to help him punish others, even when such punishment is not warranted. (If his wife deserved punishment for anything which is debatable because of insufficient information, it would be for telling him to punish the kids when he arrived home and then punishing him when he failed to do so. Instead of counter-punishing her or asserting himself, however, he ended up punishing her surreptitiously for cooking dinner, which was an appropriate behavior that he should have reinforced.)

The fact that he had a drink or two the following morning "to get going" is not uncommon. The hangover sets the stage and functions as the cue. The drinking itself allows the patient to escape the aversive headache, nausea, criticism, etc. It is also not uncommon for alcoholics to continue drinking to avoid the onset of withdrawal symptoms entirely.

The last drinking episode mentioned, having several at lunch to "steady the nerves," was cued by making mistakes on the job, by people looking at him, and by worry over his job being in danger. Examining his intake pattern would probably show that each of these is sufficient to act as a cue for drinking. Group discussion could focus on steps he could take to increase his job security and how he could be desensitized to making mistakes and having people look at him.

While we have been discussing an individual who claims that he does not know why he drinks, all that we have demonstrated applies equally well to those who *can* tell us why they drink. Often large discrepancies exist between what the patient thinks alcohol is doing for him and his actual behavior just before and just after drinking. In addition, cues which set the stage for excessive drinking may be unnoticed and it is easy to attribute the reasons to things which may have little to do with the total amount of drinking that goes on.

Reinforcement and Contracting

To reinforce is to present some verbal or physical reward af-er a response occurs. Anything is potentially a reinforcer. The only way one can be sure is to see the effect it has on the response which it follows. If it makes the response more likely to occur again under the same conditions, it is strengthening the behavior and is, therefore, a reinforcer. On the other hand, if a consequence to a response produces some verbal or physical event which decreases or suppresses the response, the event is punishing the behavior and is an aversive event. If drinking is followed by an Antabuse reaction, drinking is punished by that very aversive event.

It is easy to show that what may be reinforcing for one person in a group may be aversive to someone else. Someone who loves to talk and be the center of attention, for example, would probably talk at a very high rate (talking response strengthened) if the leader and the rest of the group sat and reinforced the talking behavior with rapt attention, continuous eye contact, nods of agreement, and requests for more detail. Another individual who finds talking in group aversive would probably talk as little as possible under the same conditions. Therefore, one should not assume that a reinforcer *is* a reinforcer until the effect has been observed.

Extinction refers to the process of withholding reinforcement from a response which has ordinarily been given reinforcement. The purpose of extinction is to diminish the response. If the group ignored an individual who had previously gained a great deal of attention by telling people how much liquor he can drink, two things would happen. First, his rate of such talk would probably increase (this can be expected and is called the extinction burst) but, if the group remained steadfast, his alcohol talk would soon begin to decrease, especially if the group gave him attention when he spoke of other, more appropriate topics.

Reinforcement is most effective when it is delivered immediately. When a response is new and still weak and unpracticed, reinforce each time the response occurs. To make the response durable, however, the schedule of reinforcement should be *thinned* and reinforcement should be given every second or third time the response occurs. At the same time, patients need to learn how to start programming their own reinforcers for themselves as part of improving self-control.

A convenient vehicle for teaching patients to program their own reinforcers, as well as for teaching realistic goal setting, is a written contract. Homme, *et al.* (1970), Knox (1971), and Stuart (1971) have described the procedure in detail on a one-to-one counseling basis. It is possible, however, to make the same kinds of commitments to a group or to bring up a contract negotiated on a one-to-one basis in the group and to discuss the commitment.

Several steps are involved in teaching patients to write their own contracts. First, the therapist or group leader and the patient decide upon some specific problem behaviors which can be improved on a daily or weekly basis. A level of performance is then agreed upon which *both* parties agree is fair, easily attainable, clear, and worthwhile. Next, consequences in the form of reinforcement are agreed upon for performing the behavior at the specified level. Both parties must agree that the reinforcer is acceptable in that it is given consistently and soon after the performance. The contract should also be positive in the sense that the parties are saying, "If you do this I'll do that" vs. "I will not do this if you do that." The contract is considered fair if the amount of work required of both parties or the amount of performance and the amount of reinforcement are of equal weight.

The second and third stages of teaching patients to write their own contracts, either with themselves or with family members, involves showing them how to specify target behaviors clearly so that there is no doubt or room for argument as to whether they occurred or did not occur. The same is true for teaching the patient to identify reinforcers which are all around him but which are unnoticed and taken for granted. The patient is then given guided practice in writing contracts, specifying first the behaviors and then the consequences agreed upon.

Exchange contracts between husband and wife are variations of self-contracting. They seek to teach partners how to reciprocally give in order to get and take the general form, "I'll do this if you'll do that." This is in contrast to a coercive or arbitrary form of interaction, for example, "Do it or else" or "Do it because I said so."

Contracts should be written, signed by both parties, and dated. The period for which the contract is in effect should be specified as well as the time when the contract will be reviewed for changes or extensions. In addition, there should be some provision for record keeping of the behaviors to occur. If the contract is negotiated between an individual and the group, all should sign and have access to copies. Progress toward performing the behaviors should be discussed in the group and support for following the contract given. Often it is helpful to provide fines or other consequences for failure to follow the contract and positive consequences for meeting the terms.

By writing and completing a series of short-term contracts, patients move toward specifying and attaining longer-term goals. Therefore, a fourth stage in contracting is teaching the patient to specify long-term goals and the methods by which he can attain them. While progress towards short-term goals is reinforced almost immediately with small rewards, this same progress and the same rewards are, in fact, serving the purpose of rewarding progress toward long-term goals. When a series of short-term or "mini" contracts is fulfilled, that in itself may be a long-term goal and the reinforcer should be of greater magnitude than for each of short-term contracts. To illustrate, a wife might want to redecorate or paint a house. The husband would like her to stop nagging him to do it. Both would like to take a vacation in a few months. A series of short-term exchange contracts might be as follows. Husband: I agree to paint for one hour during the week and at least four hours a day on weekends if my wife does not mention painting that day and if she gives me a choice of dinners for that evening. Wife: I agree to give my husband a choice of dinners and to not mention painting to him if he paints for one hour a day during the week and four hours a day on weekends. Additional consequences might also be specified in case of default: If my husband fails to paint the required number of hours on any day, he will prepare his own dinner and do his own dishes. The husband might add: If my wife mentions painting or does not provide a choice of dinners, I will not be required to paint that day. Both the husband and the wife may then agree to a longer-term goal: If the house is completed by (date) we will take a week's vacation in Canada.

Shaping, Fading and Prompting Responses

Shaping refers to a procedure in which a new response is learned by rewarding rough approximations to the desired response. An individual who has never been in a group before and who is unable to discuss intimate material can be reinforced initially just for talking. As time goes on, however, he can be prompted by the leader (who also prompts the rest of the group to do the same) for talk which comes closer and closer to the desired areas for discussion. As the desired responses are made and strengthened through group support and reinforcement, the leader fades his prompts out of the picture and lets the natural contingencies of reinforcement take over.

Psychodrama Techniques

A variety of techniques using principles of social learning theory have evolved. Many have been with us for years under different names. Moreno (1966), for example, has developed several techniques within the general context of Psychodrama. Sturm (1970, 1965) has translated these techniques into a behavioral format. While space does not permit a full discussion of all Moreno's techniques, some of the more frequently used techniques as they relate to a behaviorally oriented group will be presented.

Warm-up is a period in which the leader attempts to elicit a great deal of reinforcing interaction (smiles, acceptance, physical touching, attentive listening) and to discourage punishment or extinction (bored stares, disapproval, withdrawal). An atmosphere is created in which participation in the group and the group itself is seen as reinforcing and people can be spontaneous without fear of punishment.

Problem-presentation begins with the leader reinforcing the members' attempts to reveal personal problems which they are asking the group to help solve. Usually the group focuses on a problem that it agrees is relevant to their own lives. Often the leader serves as a model for members to imitate by stating that everyone, even he, has problems with which to contend.

Self-presentation is the next step in which the individual describes the setting and characters in detail in which the problem has most recently come up. The leader may also ask the individual to enact the various roles so that all present can get a better understanding of the cues which set the stage for various responses and what the consequences are.

Role-playing techniques are probably the most widely used of all those to come from Psychodrama. They enable group members to model appropriate behavior for others to imitate, to selectively prompt and reinforce each other for improved performance, and to see oneself from others points of view.

After self-presentation of the problem, the leader asks the patient to choose members from the group to play the major characters. In choosing the auxiliary cast, the patient is asked to choose whenever possible on the basis of an actual resemblance to a real character. In addition the auxiliaries are told to incorporate their own reactions into the role. If they are not quite sure of how to play them additional detail is given and several trial runs are made. Often the patient is asked to reverse roles either to show how the character needs to be played or to show the patient the other's position or point of view. When roles are reversed again to their original positions, patients often have new ideas of how best to respond to the other individual taking into account the other's expectations and perceptions.

Not only does role-reversal enable patients to understand better the behavior of others, but it also provides an opportunity for the patient to interact with "himself." By stepping back and looking at himself, patients are often surprised at their own behavior and are often quite receptive to prompts and suggestions from other group members as to how to handle the problem differently. These alternate ways of handling situations can then be rehearsed and rerehearsed with the group providing feedback as to how comfortable, convincing, and appropriate the patient seemed in performing the new behaviors.

Sometimes it is apparent that the patient is responding to cues or consequences which other members of the group feel are not there. Or, it may be that the group senses that the patient is avoiding saying or doing certain things which would be most appropriate. A technique for giving this feedback immediately and, at the same time modeling the appropriate behavior, is *Doubling*. The leader asks one or more group members to play directly alongside the patient and to first mimic his responses in order to start approximating his character. The next step is the dropping of simple mimicry when the auxiliary is ready and saying and doing what the patient is not saying and doing under the circumstances. The patient stops his enactment to observe the double and then imitates the double's behavior. He then observes the consequences of the new behavior on the character he is interacting with. He can also reverse roles at this point to compare his old behavior with the new behavior learned from the double.

While the double provides instant and simultaneous feedback of new behavior to be learned and imitated, the *Mirror* is the original "instant replay" developed long before video tape equipment. The patient is asked to leave the stage or area where role-playing is occurring and to watch while an auxiliary plays parts of the performance just enacted. The patient can then evaluate his performance while not in the midst of some other role. The auxiliary may also be requested by the leader to extend the new behaviors to new situations so that the patient can see the adequacy of his new responses in a variety of settings. In *Future Projection* the patient and other group members anticipate problems and practice solutions using the new behaviors for future events which are likely to occur or which the patient would like to see occur.

Sessions are usually brought to an end with additional reinforcement for the patient who enacted his problems and for the group as a whole. This is accomplished through *Group Participa-*

tion in which group members are called upon to share what they learned about their own problems while observing the enactments and providing feedback. In this way tangible progress is made public and the patient is reinforced for his efforts by knowing that he helped others in the group.

Assertion Training

This technique, developed by Wolpe (1958), involves training patients to appropriately express both positive and negative feelings. It is common for many of us, because of fear, to say nothing rather than to stick up for our rights or to tell someone off. Either we are afraid of hurting their feelings or we are uncomfortable because we do not know quite how to say it. Often feelings of resentment keep building and the fear of losing control and "blowing up" develops. In these cases alcohol enables the individual to either relax and forget the resentment or to tell the person what he thinks of them (with guilt and apologies often following when sober).

Assertion problems are frequently apparent when group members seem timid, relate experiences in which they did not know what to say, and have trouble expressing positive feelings such as love and respect as well as annoyance, irritation, and the opinion that their rights as human beings have been infringed upon. Role-playing techniques can be extremely useful in assessing the problem and treating it.

The leader, for example, can openly ask the group if any members have difficulty telling people how they feel or if they "keep things inside." If no one volunteers such information, standard scenes can be enacted with group members taking turns in the various roles and giving each other feedback as to how they came across. Wolpe asks patients to respond to such standard scenes as: walking out of a shop and finding you have been shortchanged one dollar; someone pushing in front of you in line; ordering a steak rare and the waiter brings it well done. Wolpe and Lazarus (1966, p. 41) provide a more complete list of possibilities. Additional scenes can be used depending on the actual experiences of group members once it has been established that some members really do have an assertion problem.

Desensitization

Systematic desensitization is another technique developed by Wolpe for the treatment of a specific problem, namely, excessive fear which prevents appropriate behavior from occurring. While the technique was originally employed in individual therapy as was assertion training, it has been successfully used in groups on many occasions. We must, however, make a distinction between groups formed purely for desensitization, assertion, or some other specific problem and more heterogeneous groups which include these techniques for some members. It is probably unwise to spend very much group time on a problem which has relevance only for a very few members. Therefore, unless the problem involves a theme which is troublesome for other members too and can be treated in a few sessions of role-playing, it is better to form another group for individuals having just that problem. An alternative would be to deal with it in individual therapy.

As originally developed, systematic desensitization involved first pinpointing precisely what it is about the situation which is causing the fear and what factors seem to make it better or worse. For example, a patient might become panicky if criticized by his boss in front of co-workers but only a little uncomfortable if criticized about his bowling score by friends. A hierarchy of scenes is drawn up ranging from the first scene which causes no discomfort at all to the last scene which makes the patient the most frightened. To insure that steps between hierarchy items are not too great, the patient is asked to rate each scene on a subjective hundred-point scale. The zero point represents absolute calm and one hundred represents the most frightened he has been. Hierarchy items, according to Wolpe, should not be any more than fifteen units apart.

Patients are then taught *deep muscle relaxation* which is believed to be a response incompatible with fear and which is a very useful technique in its own right for individuals who have trouble relaxing. After relaxation is achieved the patient imagines himself actually engaged in the first scene on the hierarchy. The scene is imagined several times first three to five seconds, then six to eight seconds and then usually ten to twelve seconds.

Relaxation is reinstated between each imagining. If no anxiety is signaled while imagining, the process is repeated with the next scene until the entire hierarchy is negotiated, a process which usually takes several months.

Often relaxation training and a small amount of *in vivo* desensitization can be easily incorporated into a group which has not been formed specifically for those reasons. Desensitization often is a by-product of role-playing almost any new behavior until it feels comfortable and can be accomplished by shaping and rewarding approximations to the goal behavior. For example, an individual with a fear of criticism can construct a hierarchy with the help of the group and then role-play each scene until it no longer causes discomfort. Each step in the hierarchy represents approximations to the final scene which may be a goal to then achieve outside the group. The group may actually give individual members homework assignments to carry out between meetings. One of these can be reporting on doing those things outside the group which the member has been working on in the group. It is important, however, not to give assignments for which the member is not ready or which will lead to failure. Members should not go beyond the hierarchy scene they have successfully completed in group.

Another way of doing systematic desensitization, assertion training, and relaxation training in groups is to carefully select group members who have one of those problems and work only on that problem in that group. Lazarus (1961, 1968), for example, describes group desensitization and assertion training. More recently Suinn and Richardson (1971) have developed an extension of relaxation training to provide a general competency for new anxiety provoking situations. These groups are time-limited and highly specific. The members all have the same problem, although they may be heterogeneous in other respects such as age, educational background, etc. For example, in a desensitization group, all the members might have a fear of height for which they are seeking treatment. In a ward of alcoholic patients there may be a half-dozen or more who have fears of failure or other specific fears. Often highly specific groups can be run simultaneously with other groups and individual therapy in a general ongoing alcohol treatment program. Frequent staff meetings are necessary to insure continuity of care across modalities.

Relaxation Training

First introduced by Jacobson in 1938, the procedure is relatively straightforward and can be mastered by most people in a few hours of training. There is considerable overlap with hypnotic techniques, especially some of the suggestions which some clinicians use to deepen the state of relaxation achieved. Each of the major muscle groups in the body is first tensed and then slowly relaxed beginning with the hands and forearm. The fist is clenched and the patient is asked to concentrate on the feeling of tension and to learn to discriminate when it is present in varying degrees in each muscle group. Similarly, he is asked to concentrate on the feeling of relaxation which seems to "flow into the muscle" when, after being held tense for about five seconds, it is slowly relaxed. The upper arms are usually done after the hands and forearms: the triceps by pushing the hands against each other very hard and gradually relaxing and the biceps by clenching the fist and tensing the upper arm and gradually relaxing. The muscles of the upper back, neck, face, stomach, thighs, calves, and ankles are all done in like fashion. If any tension remains in any muscle the patient is instructed to redo it until it feels quite relaxed. A calm relaxing voice on the part of the therapist is required, as is a quiet room with no distractions. While a reclining chair or couch is optimal, I have relaxed groups of eight patients on hard folding chairs by having them get as comfortable as possible by leaning way back with legs outstretched, head back, and eyes closed. No muscle tension should be required to sit or recline while listening to the instructions and arms should be resting comfortably at the sides.

After the muscles have been relaxed additional suggestions are given. For example, patients can be told to concentrate on their breathing: "Breathe deeply . . . (pause while patients inhale) and slowly . . . calm and relaxed. Muscles loose . . . no hurry . . . enjoying the relaxation you have achieved. Notice how you seem to get heavier in the chair and muscles seem to relax more each time you exhale." Another common suggestion is to ask patients to imagine lying in the sun and to feel the warmth of the sun on their skin. "Your muscles feel warm and relaxed. You may find yourself getting a little drowsy. Perhaps you can hear water lapping against the side of a pool." Another useful technique is to ask patients to think of a word which they can associate with the pleasant state of relaxation (not an alcohol-related word) and which they can think of when they are beginning to feel tense. Patients are told to practice relaxation between sessions in order to achieve it more rapidly. When proficiency is gained the patient merely thinks of his word or tells himself to relax.

In concluding this section on techniques and terminology several words of caution are needed. It should be obvious to the reader that we have merely scratched the surface of techniques and procedures about which many volumes have been written and into which many years of research and development have gone. Readers should have some knowledge of the existence of these techniques from the foregoing section, but they are urged to consult both the references listed and other practitioners who have some experience using the techniques. No technique is effective if used incorrectly.

PRE-GROUP PREPARATIONS
Selection

There are many opinions as to whom to select for a group and whom to exclude. Almost all writers agree that, at the very least, members should be able to listen to each other and be able to talk to each other. Aside from this basic and obvious starting point, group leaders differ markedly. Some prefer only highly motivated and highly verbal members having a great deal of similarity in problem areas. Others prefer the most heterogeneous group possible. In dealing with alcoholism the author's preference is for a heterogeneous group in regard to age, sex, educational level, length of alcoholism and related problems, marital status, and verbal ability. On the other hand, extremes in socioeconomic and educational areas are probably best avoided.

Usually the author will form a homogeneous group when, as mentioned earlier, several individuals are found to share a very specific problem such as assertion or relaxation. The homogeneity centers around the problem area itself rather than around personality characteristics of the members.

When in doubt about the composition of a group and the selection of members, it may be useful to run a larger trial group first (Stone, Parloff, and Frank, 1954). Members for smaller groups can then be drawn based on the performance of individuals in the trial group and the leader's criteria for membership.

Size

The author has found that a group of from six to eight members is optimal. Other writers would tend to agree (e.g. Goldstein, Heller, and Sechrest, 1966).

Assessment

Closely related to the selection problem is the problem of assessing individual difficulties which might be effectively dealt with within a group setting. We have already discussed several important aspects of assessment, a functional analysis of behavior, and objective data on the frequency, duration, or magnitude of appropriate and inappropriate responses. The goal is to identify behavioral assets as well as deficits of excesses and to get some indication of functioning in these areas prior to treatment.

Several other instruments and procedures are used in addition to the Intake Record. First, there is probably no substitute for a thorough interview. The author uses an intake interview which asks for four collateral sources of information for reliability and validity checks, demographic information in terms of number of days worked, highest monthly income, number of days spent in jail or in a hospital for alcohol-related problems, how serious a problem alcohol is, and family history and living conditions, for the six months prior to entering treatment. This information is later compared to what is occurring six months after treatment. This information also tells a great deal about the individual both factually and the way in which he answers the questions.

Frequently the Fear Survey Schedule (Wolpe and Lang, 1964; see Tasto and Hickson, 1970 for an updated version with norms) is administered. The Schedule is a checklist of 122 items which sometimes arouse fear or discomfort. Patients are asked to indicate how much discomfort they would feel to each item on a five point scale ranging from "Not at All" to "Very Much." Often the Schedule provides information regarding fear-arousing cues or situations which lead to heavy drinking. Areas covered include social situations, medical procedures, and small animals and insects.

Another paper and pencil technique which is sometimes used is the Reinforcer Survey Schedule (Cautela and Kastenbaum, 1967). The Schedule, which by no means exhausts all possibilities, attempts to identify activities (other than drinking) which patients might enjoy. Group discussion can often focus on these other possibilities.

On occasion, particularly when there is question of thought disorder, some traditional diagnostic tests such as the MMPI, Memory-for-Designs, and Proverbs might be used. However, if thought disorder failed to appear in the hour-long intake interview, it is doubtful that there is enough present to prevent an individual's participation in a group. Kanfer and Saslow (1969) provide a more detailed discussion of behavioral assessment techniques used in conjunction with more traditional methods.

Time Limits

Depending on the context in which the group occurs, there are probably advantages to both time-limited and time-unlimited groups. Time-limited groups are often useful when maximum gains are sought in the least amount of time, when progress and goals are explicit, waiting lists long, when treatment needs to be standardized (as for example, in process and outcome research), and problems are not so severe as to be expected to take more than two to six months to resolve. Time limits may also bring pressure to bear on individuals "to start shaping up" as the end of therapy approaches and slower members see tangible gains made by other members in the group.

An alternative approach, which combines an ongoing group format with time-limited therapy, is one in which individuals enter and leave the ongoing group when they have reached their criterion levels of performance or the goals they set for themselves with the help of the leader and the rest of the group. Thus, in the pre-group assessment and specification of problems, a timetable of expected progress and termination can also be tentatively formulated. This does not mean that goals and time-tables cannot be revised as new problem behaviors become apparent in the group. Nor does it mean that other group members cannot assist in revising goals, problem solving strategies, and timetables, once the group has begun. On the contrary both are desirable and should be prompted and reinforced.

GROUP MEETINGS

Initial sessions are usually spent establishing ground rules or, reiterating those discussed in pre-group meetings with the leader, refining assessment techniques and problems to be worked on, and restating the implied or written treatment contract.

Common ground rules include such matters as promptness, the expectation that members will try to help each other, that what goes on in the group is confidential,* that relationships among members outside the group should be discussed in the group, that assignments outside the group will be completed and reported on in the group, and that private meetings with the leader can be requested at any time but that what is discussed should be brought up in group either by the patient when he feels he is ready, or by the leader when he feels the patient is ready. Another ground rule is often that members cannot attend group if they have been drinking, but that urges to drink are appropriate to discuss in the group.† This is a more frequently needed rule with outpatients rather than inpatients.

Additions, deletions, and modifications to these rules are often the topic of the first meetings. They can be used as vehicles to get

---

* Confidentiality can be a problem in regard to other staff within an institution who are responsible for the patient but who may not be members of a particular group. Sometimes patients will not discuss material which they are afraid will be entered in charts for others who are less familiar to them to read. Often these fears can be allayed by assuring patients that other staff are professionals who are there to help, or that the information will be charted in very general terms or not at all until the patient feels he is ready to share it with those staff.

† While problems which result in urges to drink are discussed, "drink talk" *per se* is discouraged at least in later sessions. Examples of "drink talk" would be humorous descriptions of events which happened while drunk, favorite beverages, or boasts of how much liquor one can hold. This type of material contributes nothing constructive except, perhaps, to remind us that the individual needs to develop social skills in other areas.

members "warmed up" to talking in the group. By reinforcing
and prompting this somewhat impersonal but interesting and
constructive material, the leader begins making the group itself
more attractive. As the attractiveness of the group increases, so
does its potential for helping through reinforcement of appropriate within- and extra-group activity. During these initial meetings the leader also prompts and models much verbal behavior
which emphasizes the commonalities among the members and
avoids or discourages interaction which might be aversive (see
earlier section on warm-up).

Unless members begin discussing problems spontaneously, the
leader begins prompting the group. He may ask someone to begin
who seemed quite willing to share his problems with the group
in pre-group meetings. The individual may be asked to recount
some of the problems he and the leader discussed, perhaps Intake
Record data or perhaps a contract he is thinking of negotiating
with his wife. This, in turn, leads to discussions of whether or
not others in the group have similar problems, how they are
typically handled, how they can be handled differently, and how
group members can help. The leader, meanwhile, should be
prompting and modeling problem-solving strategies and reinforcing the group for generating solutions to problems. Potential solutions are role-played with the group providing feedback as to
how adequate and comfortable the characters appeared. As the
leader prompts and reinforces the group for appropriate behavior, the group imitates him, especially if this process is made explicit and the group is encouraged to do so. As the group imitates
the leader's behavior, the leader can begin fading his prompts
and reinforcements and allow the group more and more autono-
my. Sessions can be closed with a review of progress and assignments to try some of the rehearsed behavior outside the group
and to record the results.

Later meetings can begin with a summary by a member of
what happened at the last meeting. This in itself may create
fruitful discussion since other members may have different perceptions and remembrances of what occurred. Next, a presentation of what occurred outside the group since the last meeting
usually ensues with questions directed at those who had assign-

ments to carry out in the interim. Throughout the leader must keep the group on its course, the generation and maintenance of new behavior.

It is not uncommon for individuals to begin manifesting behavior within the group which serves the purpose of allowing the individuals to avoid certain subject areas. Fidgeting, extreme nervousness, pacing, lateness, very much or very little talking, monopolizing the group, competing for the leader's attention, long discussions of personal history, complaints of mistreatment, are some of the typical group behaviors which may cause the group to drift off course. Usually bringing these episodes to the group's attention brings censure to the individuals responsible. The inappropriate behaviors may then decrease or they may be denied. In either case, the wishes of the group can be made explicit, and the guilty parties can then be asked by the group for a commitment to decrease those distracting behaviors while increasing other appropriate behaviors. These within-group behaviors also provide additional information for problem areas to be worked on. Cases of extreme nervousness or too little talking, for example, might indicate the need for relaxation training or assertion training.

As the group progresses, new goals might be substituted for those originally discussed. As the new behaviors are learned and practiced outside the group it becomes obvious that the group becomes less and less necessary for certain individuals. The fact that someone is getting ready to terminate should be explicit. This gives the group a chance to provide feedback to the individual as to the progress they have seen him make and to reinforce the individual's self-confidence. The individual, in turn, can give the group feedback on how they have helped him. Rather than terminating abruptly, it is probably better for most individuals to gradually phase out by attending less and less frequently, using the group to support and reinforce the new behaviors being carried out outside the group, and by functioning as a model for other patients to imitate.

CONCLUSION

Many techniques have been presented within a behavioral context. These techniques can be used regardless of the reader's theoretical orientation simply by translating the terminology into language with which the reader is most familiar and using those techniques that seem to make the most sense in a given group situation. It would probably be most effective for the novice group leader to choose a few techniques at first and become thoroughly proficient with them before trying to master a large number. Otherwise, the resulting groups will be a hodge-podge of technique, while common sense and just plain listening will be minimal.

REFERENCES

Cautela, J. R., and Kastenbaum, R. A.: A reinforcement survey schedule for use in therapy, training and research. *Psychol Rep, 20:*1115-1130, 1967.

Goldstein, A. P., Heller, K., and Sechrest, L. B.: *Psychotherapy and the Psychology of Behavior Change.* New York, Wiley, 1966.

Jackson, D., and Della-Piana, G.: Establishing a behavioral observation system: A self-instruction program. Unpublished manuscript, Bureau of Educational Research, University of Utah, 1971.

Kanfer, F. H., and Saslow, G.: Behavioral diagnosis. In Franks, C. M. (Ed.) : *Behavior Therapy: Appraisal & Status.* New York, McGraw, 1969, pp. 417-444.

Lazarus, A. A.: Group therapy of phobic disorders by systematic desensitization. *J Abnorm Soc Psychol, 63:*504-510, 1961.

Lazarus, A. A.: Behavior therapy in groups. In Gazda, G. M. (Ed.) : *Basic Approaches to Group Psychotherapy and Counseling.* Springfield, Thomas, 1968, pp. 149-175.

Moreno, Z. T.: Psychodramatic rules, techniques and adjunctive methods. *Psychodrama and Group Psychotherapy.* New York, Beacon, 1966.

Stone, A. R., Parloff, M. B., and Frank, J. D.: The use of "diagnostic groups" in a group therapy program. *Int J Group Psychother, 4:*274, 1954.

Sturm, I. E.: The behavioristic aspect of psychodrama. *Group Psychotherapy, 18:*50-64, 1965.

Sturm, I. E.: A behavioral outline of psychodrama. *Psychotherapy: Theory, Research and Practice, 7(4):*245-247, 1970.

Suinn, R. M., and Richardson, F.: Anxiety management training: A nonspecific behavior therapy program for anxiety control. *Behavior Therapy, 2(4):*498-510, 1971.

Tasto, D. L., and Hickson, R.: Standardization and scaling of the 122-item fear survey schedule. *Behavior Therapy, 1(4):*473-484, 1970.

Wolpe, J.: *Psychotherapy by Reciprocal Inhibition.* Stanford, Stanford U Pr, 1958.

CHAPTER XI

SELF MODELING AS A BEHAVIOR MODIFICATION TECHNIQUE

DONALD R. MIKLICH and THOMAS L. CREER

ALTHOUGH BEHAVIOR THERAPIES have been for the most part a phenomenon of the 1960's, one of the first formal reports of a successful behavior therapy case was published by Mary Cover Jones almost fifty years ago (Jones, 1924). This study demonstrated how a child's fear of small furry animals could be reduced by "unconditioning." The case of Peter is a classic in the behavior modification literature. Therefore, it is interesting to note that, although Jones described the effective variables in her therapy technique as conditioning, the primary therapeutic technique employed was, in fact, modeling. The failure to explicitly identify modeling was probably a reflection of the fact that in 1924 there existed no experimentally based theory of imitation or modeling. Today, there is a sizable body of experimental literature on imitation and modeling (e.g. see Flanders, 1968). Much of this literature comes from the pioneering work of Miller and Dollard (1941), who attempted to demonstrate in a series of studies that imitation was simply a special case of conditioning. Their work, however, appears to have little direct influence on contemporary theories of imitation, perhaps because they based their work on the Hullian learning model which is no longer in vogue. In the main, though, it reflects the impact of later work by Albert Bandura and his associates (e.g. Bandura and Walters, 1963). The use of modeling as a behavior modification technique has grown directly out of this work (see Bandura, 1969, Chapter 3) and has grown with remarkable vigor. Rachman's (1972) recent review cites seventeen empirical studies which used modeling to modify behavior. These studies show modeling to be not only an effective behavior modification technique, but to have produced even greater behavioral change than systematic desensitization!

Considering the power claimed for modeling, it is remarkable that it is apparently so little used in therapeutic (as opposed to research) situations. Possibly, this is due to the normal delay between the development of a technique and its widespread application. Those who have attempted to use modeling therapy in a clinical environment, however, are aware of another reason: modeling therapy makes excessive demands upon the clinician's organizational resources. It is not only necessary to find models with the appropriate behaviors or models who can be trained to exhibit these behaviors, but the therapist must arrange either to have the models at the clinic at the same time the patient is there or to make films or video recordings featuring the model. If it were possible to make a few films of behaviors that occur at high frequencies and use these with several subjects (patients, clients, etc.) these organizational problems could be managed. Unfortunately, usually the films made for use with one subject are not suitable for use with another, even though there is similarity in the general nature of their problem behaviors.

To overcome these problems, Creer and Miklich (1970) developed the technique of self modeling. With this procedure, videotape recordings are made of the subject *himself* as he performs as an actor might the appropriate behaviors which he needs to increase or inhibits inappropriate behaviors which should be decreased. He then observes these video recordings a number of times. No instructions are explicitly given to the patient to imitate the behaviors he sees himself performing on the video recording, though it seems reasonable to assume that subjects would presume such instructions to be implicit. It can be seen that many of the administrative problems associated with the use of others as models are solved in self modeling. The problem of finding a model is immediately solved, as are many of the problems of synchronous scheduling. While some training of a person is necessary for him to serve as his own model, it is very much less than would be required to train another. Although not unique to self modeling, the technique does have the great advantage of requiring little of the time of the psychologist or other professional in charge of the case. A professional is needed only to organize and supervise the self modeling. All other aspects can be done by paraprofessionals or volunteers with a modicum of training.

Behavior modification by self modeling appears to many persons to be intuitively implausible. Why should a person change his behaviors simply because of watching films or recordings of himself, when he knows very well that what he sees was a totally contrived situation in which he and the others in the scene were only acting? To a considerable extent, these kinds of doubts reflect the deeply ingrained tendency of all of us to think in terms of motives rather than in terms of those variables which have been shown to be functionally related to behaviors. Rather than concerning ourselves with questions of this kind, however, it would be better to consider the evidence favoring self modeling. After all, modeling itself is implausible to many; yet the evidence (Rachman, 1972) indicates it to be remarkably effective. Therefore, we will briefly describe three cases in which self modeling has been employed. These cases have been presented from a more technical perspective and in more detail elsewhere (Miklich, Creer, Alexander and Nichols, 1972). So far as we are aware, these three cases are the only self modeling cases that have been discussed anywhere in the technical literature and constitute the totality of our experience with the self modeling method. While we agree that this sample is limited, we are pleased that we have had no failures. In every case on which we have tried self modeling there has been a favorable outcome.

All of these cases concern residents of the Children's Asthma Research Institute and Hospital (CARIH), a residential rehabilitation center for asthmatic children. Although CARIH includes a hospital for the treatment of acute episodes of asthma, the residents do not live in hospital wards. Rather, children live in cottage dormitories with approximately twenty-four other children of the same sex and age. Except that children at CARIH attend public schools, the CARIH environment is more like that of a boarding school than a hospital. Also, except for their manifest asthma, the youngsters at CARIH are a fairly representative sample of American children. The immediate day-to-day care of residents is in the hands of dormitory counselors, most of whom are college graduates. A full staff of psychologists is available to these counselors to handle behavioral and psychological problems which require professional assistance. The three cases described here were referred in this manner and may be considered as representative of the kind and severity of behavioral problems for which parents and teachers seek professional help and guidance. In each case, the subjects are identified by pseudonyms.

The first case concerned a twelve-year-old boy, whom we will call Howard. His dormitory counselors and peers complained that his table manners were so "piggish" that they made everyone nauseous. On the basis of observation of Howard's eating behaviors, which supported this impression, fourteen different inappropriate eating behaviors were identified and objectively defined. For the next eight weekdays, Howard was observed at sixteen different meals, six breakfasts, four lunches, and six dinners. To simplify the observation of so many behaviors, each observation period was divided into one minute intervals. For each interval, the observer recorded only which of the behaviors had occurred. No effort was made to determine how long or how often any behavior occurred. These eight days' observations served as a measure of the base rate of Howard's undesirable eating behaviors. In other words, they showed the frequency of these behaviors before any attempt was made at intervention. Following the collection of the base rate data, videotapes were made of Howard eating without any of his undesirable eating behaviors. Then for a period of about one month Howard was shown this video recording as many weekdays as possible. At the end of this time, the observer again observed Howard for three meals, one breakfast and two lunches. The average number of undesirable eating behaviors per minute Howard showed during the base rate observations was 1.75. After self modeling, the average number of undesirable behaviors per minute was only 0.07. An appropriate statistical test showed this difference to be significant ($p=.01$).

On two of the three observations after self modeling, Howard showed no undesirable eating behaviors at all, something which never occurred in the base rate period.

The results of the case of Howard certainly give reason to be optimistic about the utility of self modeling. The change in behavior was so great, however, that one is apt to overlook some aspects of the manner in which the case was conducted which should caution against too hastily concluding that self modeling *must* have been effective. First, there was only one observer. It is possible another observer would not have reported the same changes. Second, observing only three meals after the self modeling raises the question of whether some fleeting, momentary fluctuation in behavior was seen rather than behavior changes. Third, there is no evidence that something else, which just happened to occur in the month of self modeling, did not cause the apparently changed behavior. The next case, however, was conducted in a manner to avoid these ambiguities.

Joe was a twelve-year-old boy with inappropriate peer relationships. He was the frequent acquiescent object of his peers' aggressions. He also had the age-inappropriate behavior of sucking his thumb and fingers. Joe was observed for approximately three months. On the basis of these observations, three classes of behaviors which were to be changed were defined. These were thumb sucking, which was to be decreased, and physical interactions (especially self-defense) and verbal interactions with others, which were to be increased. After these three classes of behaviors were identified and objectively defined, three persons were trained in the methods of observation and in the precise definitions of each behavior class. Over the course of this case, two of these three observers (the exact pairs varied from time to time) simultaneously and *independently* observed Joe a total of nine times. Observations were done in ten-second periods. If any of the three classes of behaviors occurred during a ten-second interval, a check was made for that interval, but no effort was made to keep track of exactly how many times during the ten-second interval the behavior occurred. On the nine times that two observers simultaneously observed, they were in agreement 96.7 percent concerning thumb sucking, 94.6 percent concerning verbal interactions and 95.3 percent concerning physical interactions. In this case there is no question of the objectivity and reliability of the behavioral observations as there was in Howard's case.

Thirteen observation periods over a calendar period of nineteen days were used to determine the base rate frequencies of these three behaviors. Then video tape recordings were made of Joe behaving in an appropriate manner for each behavior. Since thumb sucking occurred with great regularity while Joe was watching TV, the first scene showed him watching TV without any kind of thumb or finger sucking behaviors. The verbal interactions film showed Joe sitting with a group of four peers engaging in a social conversation. The physical interaction scene showed Joe physically defending himself against unprovoked aggression from the same group of peers. After a one week pause, Joe was shown these scenes once every weekday for two weeks. During this self modeling, the frequencies of each of the behaviors changed dramatically in the intended direction. Thumb sucking declined from 15.1 percent of the ten-second observation periods during the base rate period to 3.0 percent. Verbal interactions increased from 49.1 percent during the base rate period to 89.2 percent, and physical interactions increased from 2.5 percent to 15.5 percent. These changes, statistically highly significant ($p<.001$), were observed in each of twelve different observation periods over a calendar period of two weeks. Therefore, the second ambiguity of Howard's case does not apply to this one; there was clearly a change in behavior, not a momentary fluctuation.

Only the question of whether some unknown variable, rather than self modeling, caused the behavior changes remains. A thoroughly rigorous demonstration that self modeling was indeed the causal variable can be provided by what is called a reversal design (Risley and Wolf, 1972). This involves reversing the supposed causal variable and seeing if the direction of the behavioral change also reverses. With self modeling, this can be accomplished by showing the patient a video recording of himself performing his customary *inappropriate* behaviors. If such modeling is the effective variable, the frequency of appropriate behaviors should reverse. In order to attempt a reversal with Joe, a videotape recording of his inappropriate behaviors was also made at the time the first (appropriate) videotape was made. This recording also had three scenes with Joe sucking his thumb while watching TV, sitting by four peers having a social conversation which he made no effort to enter, and not defending himself when physically attacked. After the two weeks of watching the appropriate self modeling videotape, Joe watched the inappropriate behaviors for two weeks. No significant change in his behavior occurred. Instead, the improvements seen in the period of self-modeling appropriate behaviors continued. Therefore, some ambiguity remains as to whether self-modeling was the variable which caused the behavioral improvement. It is relevant to note that the probable cause of this failure to achieve reversal was the powerful reinforcement which Joe's improved behaviors received. In an effort to avoid contamination from experimenter effects, all these cases were conducted without the knowledge of the subjects' dormitory counselors, physicians, or other attending adults. Immediately after the conclusion of the self modeling of appropriate behaviors, without our knowledge, these people held a special meeting with Joe for the purpose of praising him for his improved behavior. Since this occurred at the time of the inappropriate behaviors self modeling, it appears that this kind of reinforcement frustrated the attempted behavioral reversal.

At this time the school year recommenced. Because of the reduction in CARIH's summer staff and the change to the school year routine, some confusion in the conduct of the case occurred. Normally, the inappropriate behaviors self modeling would continue until a behavioral reversal occurred or until it was determined that one was unlikely to occur. However, after two weeks of inappropriate behaviors self modeling, the procedures were again reversed, with the appropriate self modeling being repeated. Even this was not done systematically; rather the appropriate video recording was shown only three times, as personnel happened to be available. Behavioral observations, however, did continue for two and a half months. These follow-up observations showed that two of the behaviors, thumbsucking and verbal interactions, had reverted to their base rate frequencies. Only physical interactions, with a follow-up frequency of 7 percent showed a statistically significant (p=.01) continuation of the gains achieved in the first period of self modeling.

Excepting only the failure of the behaviors to reverse during the self modeling of inappropriate behaviors, the case of Joe is free from the ambiguities of the case of Howard. It should be born in mind that the failure of the behavior to reverse does not mean that self modeling did not cause the initial behavioral improvement. The next case, that of Chuck, however, yielded results which are secure from all of the objections raised against the case of Howard.

Chuck was a ten-year-old boy whose immaturity and unwillingness to defend himself had made him the scapegoat for his peers' aggressions. He also showed extremely childish behavior in the presence of adults, frequently jumping in the lap of any seated adult. Two approaches to changing Chuck's inappropriate behaviors were tried before self modeling was attempted. First, he was seen periodically for traditional supportive-type psychotherapy. After approximately one year with this method, no discernible improvement was noted. Operant behavioral modification techniques were then used in an effort to shape more appropriate behaviors. The basic plan here was to positively reinforce Chuck with pennies for making appropriate responses. Remaining seated in a chair while talking to an adult was selected as the specific behavior to be shaped because it is incompatible with jumping in the adult's lap. The results showed that Chuck's behavior could be modified in this manner. However, it was clear that the magnitude and complexity of Chuck's behavioral problems precluded this approach as a practical possibility. Therefore, self modeling was attempted. Preliminary observations determined four specific inappropriate behaviors or classes of inappropriate behaviors to be modified. They were 1) remaining in bed in the morning and not making his bed, 2) not defending himself when physically attacked by his peers, 3) not being able to initiate social interactions with his peers, and 4) interacting in a babyish manner with adults.

Observations were conducted for periods of one hour every weekday evening after school. One observer was present at each of these periods. A second also observed from time to time on a random basis. There were no disagreements in the observers' records, an extremely high degree of reliability which was undoubtedly due to the saliency of the responses being recorded. Getting up and bed making could not be observed in the afternoons, of course, nor was it possible to have an observer on hand every morning to get data on this behavior. Therefore, one of the authors regularly checked Chuck's room every morning after the children had gone to school. If the bed were made and the room picked up, it was safe to infer that Chuck had gotten up reasonably on time, since he would otherwise not have had time to make his bed and pick up his room. The converse inference is somewhat more uncertain, since it is conceivable that Chuck could have gotten up but not have done his chores. The preliminary observations, however, indicated that the sequence of behaviors, "get up, get dressed, make bed, pick up room," constituted a behavioral chain (Skinner, 1935). A behavioral chain may be defined as a sequence of behaviors all of which always occur whenever the first behavior in the sequence occurs. Therefore, it is reasonable to consider assessment of bed making and room tidying as the terminal link of the behavioral chain.

Base rate observations were obtained for two weeks (ten weekdays). On the first Monday following the base rate period, Chuck and two of his peers made two video recordings. One showed Chuck behaving appropriately, and one showed him behaving in his accustomed inappropriate manner. The appropriate recording showed Chuck 1) getting out of bed promptly when called, dressing, and making his bed, 2) physically defending himself against an attack by two peers, 3) appropriately and effectively inviting himself into a game being played by two peers, and 4) entering an office, sitting down, and remaining seated while talking with an adult. The recording of inappropriate behaviors showed Chuck 1) remaining in bed when called in the morning, 2) throwing a temper tantrum instead of defending himself when attacked by two peers, 3) accepting the rejection by two peers when asking to join their game, and 4) entering an office and jumping into the lap of an adult.

Observations were continued for two weeks after making the recordings to determine if the acting for the recordings would itself have any effect on the behavior. The frequencies of none of the behaviors changed by more than one in this period. The following two weeks, Chuck observed the videotape of appropriate behaviors every afternoon after school. The change in his behavior was immediate and sizable. During these two weeks, his bed was made nine out of the ten observation times whereas in the four preceding weeks it was never made. Instances of appropriate aggression increased from one in the base rate period to ten, while "sissy" behavior declined from two to one. Appropriate interactions with others (adult or peers) increased from zero to five while inappropriate interactions decreased from two to zero. Something certainly had a considerable impact on Chuck's behaviors, but was it the self modeling? Obviously, the inappropriate video recordings had been made to test this by attempting behavioral reversal. The next two weeks Chuck was shown the recording of his inappropriate behaviors every afternoon. All the behaviors changed toward their base rate frequencies. Chuck made his bed only once in ten days. He showed no instances of aggressive behavior but six of "sissy" behaviors, and inappropriate interactions with others increased while appropriate interactions decreased. After viewing the inappropriate recordings for two weeks, the last two weeks of the case he again watched his appropriate behaviors. Again, appropriate behaviors increased and the inappropriate ones decreased. The most dramatic change was bed making which was done on ten of ten observation periods. Appropriate statistical tests of the changes in behaviors were significant.

Formal observations of Chuck had to be discontinued after the second two-week period of appropriate behaviors self modeling, and Chuck was discharged shortly thereafter. Informal observations while he remained at CARIH indicated that the improved behavior continued for at least that period. Therefore, while we do not know how enduring the improvement in Chuck's behavior was, the magnitude of the behavioral changes seen, the reliability of the observations, and the fact that behaviors could

be reversed and rereversed indicates convincingly that it was self
modeling which changed Chuck's behaviors.

Major improvements in behavior occurred in each of these
cases. In the last one, these changes were clearly due to self modeling, and it seems reasonable to suppose that it was probably the
causal variable in the first two. Therefore, self modeling may
well be a remarkably effective behavior modification technique.
This may appear paradoxical in view of the already mentioned
intuitive implausibility of the procedure, but it is not the greatest paradox associated with these findings. Consider the cases of
Chuck and Joe. Before self modeling, both boys were frequently bullied. Afterwards, they showed a ready willingness to defend
themselves. The paradox in this is that, every time Joe or Chuck
had been picked on, he had by that very fact been exposed to an
aggressive model. Why had they not imitated that model? Much
time could be spent in speculating upon this interesting point,
but that would not be appropriate here. What is relevant to note
is that self modeling appears to have been effective when modeling of others has not been. While it does not necessarily follow
that a form of modeling therapy, in which the subjects watched
a boy *defend himself,* would not have been effective, it certainly
raises the possibility that self modeling might be more effective
than the modeling of others.

Some support for this interesting possibility may be found in
the research of Rosekrans (1967) who found that children imitate a model similar to themselves more than they imitate a dis-
similar model. Since no model could be more similar to a person
than himself, self modeling may elicit more imitation. Though
only conjecture, there are other reasons why self modeling might
be superior. One is that the stimulus in self modeling is inherent-
ly of more interest to a subject than pictures of others would be.
It seems fairly obvious that any kind of modeling will be effective only to the extent that the subject attends to the model.
Granted that people usually find pictures of themselves to be
more interesting than pictures of others, subjects in self modeling should better attend to the model. Another possibility is that
the manner in which a person acts out a particular behavior will
seem more natural and genuine to that person than will another's

acting. Still another possibility is that, while watching the self modeling scenes, the subject undoubtedly projects himself into the part he played and identifies with his "actor self" much more than he would or could do with another model. Thus, whenever the "acting self" is observed performing socially desirable behaviors (i.e. behaviors which are approved of by others and therefore apt to elicit positive reinforcements), or whenever the behavioral outcome in the acted scene is positively reinforcing to the subject, intrinsic positive reinforcement to the subject for that behavior may be presumed to have occurred. Finally, the very process of acting for the making of the self modeling scenes may have some benefit. Rehearsal has long been a part of many behavior modification techniques (e.g. as in assertiveness training, Wolpe and Lazarus, 1966), and techniques of behavior modification specifically based on rehearsal have been developed (Gittelman, 1965; Sarason, 1968). These rehearsal techniques employ repeated rehearsals and should therefore generate more behavioral change than the few rehearsals necessary for the making of a self modeling scene. Nevertheless, there is probably some benefit from even a single rehearsal which should enhance the effectiveness of self modeling.

In addition to the advantages which are unique to self modeling, there are some it shares with other modeling therapies which are sufficiently important to warrant mentioning. Most significant is the fact that modeling can be employed to modify behaviors which either could not be treated or could not as easily be treated with direct reinforcement. Behaviors which normally occur in private, in a complex social environment, or infrequently and aperiodically are difficult to reinforce. These behaviors can easily be modeled, however. Also, as Bandura (1969, pp. 148-151) has pointed out, modeling effects appear to generalize quite readily, thus simplifying the process of behavior modification considerably. As in the case of Chuck, reinforcements may be quite effective, but the behavior to be changed can be so varied and extensive that reinforcement procedures simply are not practical.

Before discussing the specifics of the use of self modeling we would like to make a plea that users of self modeling (or any other behavior modification or psychotherapy procedures) attempt to conduct every case as if it were an experiment with a single subject. The goal of this is not to generate a large research literature on self modeling, though it is true that there is need for much more research on the technique. Rather, the purpose is to enable the therapist to 1) determine unambiguously the nature and limits of improvement, 2) refine and improve the use of the technique on the basis of the data mentioned in point 1, and 3) provide unambiguous and convincing evidence to whomever is paying the bills that the therapy is indeed effective. The first point would seem to be axiomatic. If one is endeavoring to change behavior, is it not absolutely requisite to be able to determine whether the behavior does change? Nevertheless, and very unfortunately, the custom of not carefully obtaining outcome data has developed in psychotherapy and appears in some quarters to be carrying over into behavior modification. Such blind intervention like blind automobile driving must be inefficient and possibly dangerous. The second point is ignored more frequently and with less justification. Surely any skill as complex and difficult as changing human behavior will always have room for improvement. One of the basic facts of psychology is that without feedback, improvement does not occur (Thorndike, 1927). One cannot learn to do a better, more efficient job of modifying behavior if one does not carefully attend to how, when, and why subjects' behaviors change. The most important reason for conducting each case like an experiment is the last one. It is our firm belief that the day of outcome accountability has dawned in the applied behavioral sciences. Perhaps the strongest evidence of this is that considerable pressure has come out of Washington for Mental Health Center funding grants to include sufficient research support to demonstrate that what is being funded is having the intended effect. As cost squeezes continue, it is only reasonable to suppose that those who have the task of stretching limited resources to fulfill what at times must appear to be unlimited desires will look more and more for objective evidences of effectiveness before making monetary commitments. We feel this problem will be especially acute for techniques such as self-modeling, which, as we have already mentioned, have an intuitive implausibility about them. It is all too likely that any genuine behavior changes caused by self modeling will be ascribed by skeptics to some other adventitious, but seemingly more plausible, factor. It seems somewhat out of place to discuss this problem in a work of this nature. Nevertheless, it is obvious that no matter how much good applied behavioral scientists might be able to accomplish, we will accomplish nothing if we are not able to find and keep financial support for our efforts. This is equally true whether that support is in the form of public budgets for mental health centers, schools, etc., or in the form of private payments for professional services rendered.

In conducting a therapy case in the manner of an N=1 experiment, the first, most important, and often most difficult task is to get objective, valid, and reliable behavioral observations. It will usually be impossible for all observations to be done by the therapist, but it is highly desirable to do at least a few in order to have a better feel for the behaviors at issue. An efficient way to do this is for the therapist to simultaneously and independently observe on a few random occasions for the purpose of determining inter-observer reliability. Even though it requires retraining observers for each new case, it is usually easiest to use the referring person (parent, teacher, etc.) as observer. This person is most likely to be where the undesirable behaviors occur. Highly successful use of this method has been made by Patterson, Cobb and Ray (1972). If it is not possible for the referring person to do the observations, the task is more difficult. If funds permit, one can hire an observer. No special prior educational requirements are needed. In fact, we have had excellent results using adults with less than high school educations if they did not themselves have major psychological or behavioral problems. We have also used volunteers. College students and members of clubs or organizations such as the PTA are possible sources.

Before observations can begin, preliminary observations are needed to define the behaviors to be modified. It is best if the therapist himself or some other well-trained third party observer does these. We have discovered that referring agents are often totally incorrect about the behaviors which they report. The most amusing of numerous examples concerned a chronic problem of CARIH's children missing appointments, which our observer discovered was due to the different ways different departments defined lateness. This misunderstanding could never have been discovered if a third party had not been used to make preliminary observations of the "tardy" children. A related phenomenon is that some behaviors simply disappear while being observed. Creer (1972) has called this phenomenon the "fadeaway baseline," which suggests that the behavior is already undergoing extinction when reported. A third reason for using someone other than the referring person for preliminary observations is that, without behavioral training, even well-educated people often find it difficult to specify precisely and *objectively* an undesirable behavior without referring to the motivational or dispositional construct within which they construe the behavior. Obviously, self modeling or any other behavioral methodology requires that the problem be stated in behavioral terms. Once such a statement has been made, it is usually quite easy to obtain good inter-observer reliability; poor reliability usually indicates inadequate definitions of the problem. Behavioral specification of the problem also specifies the converse of what the self modeling scenes should show. In fact, we suggest it as a rule of thumb that whenever there is some difficulty in specifying just how the self modeling scene will be played, the problem will usually lie with the inadequate behavioral specifications of the problem.

In observing and in defining problems behaviorally, it is well to keep in mind procedures other than the direct observation of behavior which might simplify the task. First, one should look for unobtrusive measures (Webb, Campbell, Schwartz and Sechrest, 1966). Chuck's bed-making behavior illustrates this technique. It was not possible to observe him making his bed, but it was obvious whether it had been made or not. A large number of behaviors leave some more or less ambiguous evidence of their having been done or not. Observing these can greatly ease the task of some behavioral observations which otherwise would be difficult or impossible. Second, look for behavioral chains in the preliminary observations. Again, the bed making behavior with Chuck can serve as an illustration. Since getting dressed, making the bed, and picking up the room were all behaviors which were chained to the behavior of getting up in the morning, it was possible to use one (bed-making) to indicate if the whole chain was done or not. In this case, bed-making happened itself to be of interest, but this will not always be the case. Sometimes the observable behavior is unimportant except as an indicator of another behavior to which it is chained.

When behaviors do not have definite starting and stopping points, one should divide the observing period into many short intervals of equal length. If any behavior occurs during one of these intervals, a count is made for that behavior. Only one count per interval is made for each behavior regardless of the number of times or length of time that behavior occurs in the interval. Attempting to measure the total amount of time spent on a behavior is impossibly difficult. This technique was illustrated in the cases of Howard and Joe. A variation of this method, which is easier for someone like a teacher or parent, is to observe the subject once at the beginning of every interval. If the behavior is occurring, a check is recorded. The advantage here, of course, is that the attention of the observer need be directed toward the subject only once during each interval.

After observers have been found and trained, it is necessary to decide how the case will be conducted. The simplest procedure is simply to make the self modeling scenes, show them to the subject, and observe any behavioral changes. As noted in the case of Howard, only limited conclusions can be confidently drawn from a case conducted in this manner. Though methodologically elegant, the reversal design used in the cases of Joe and Chuck is difficult to use. It requires making twice as many scenes and increased time in which to reverse and then rereverse the behaviors (to end with desirable behaviors). Also, parents, teachers, or other referring persons are usually distressed to have an undesirable behavior reinstated once it is overcome. The alternative to behavioral reversal which we would recommend is called the multiple base rate procedure (Baer, Wolf and Risley, 1968). In this procedure, one does not attempt to reverse a behavior after it has improved. Rather, each separate behavior sequentially is exposed to self modeling. As soon as the first behavior improves, the second behavior is added to self modeling, and so on until all the behaviors have been included. If each behavior improves only as self modeling of that behavior is introduced, it can confidently be concluded that self modeling changed the behavior.

There are two ways to record the self modeling scenes: motion pictures and videotape recording. Motion pictures require less capital as a camera, projector, screen and film can be purchased for less than $200. Purchasing secondhand equipment, borrowing, or renting can further lower this cost. An advantage of home movie equipment is that color scenes can be obtained at little cost, though we feel color is of trivial utility in most cases. There are now available home movie cameras and projectors with audio capabilities. While they cost more than video only equipment, we strongly feel the extra expense to be justified, and in some cases requisite. Videotape recorders have been decreasing in cost. Nevertheless, a minimum configuration still costs $1,000 to $1,500. Video recorders can do many things. Monitoring of behavior or therapy, for example, or even as an aid in ordinary psychotherapy (e.g. Martin, 1971). One may reduce the cost of the equipment chargeable to self modeling if these other activities can share the expense of purchase. Professional movie or recording equipment can be rented and the services of professionals hired to make the scenes. We feel this expense is not justified.

After base rates of the behaviors to be modified are found, one can make the self modeling recordings or films. It is convenient to make all scenes at one time, even if the multiple baseline or reversal procedure is going to be used. It facilitates the self modeling procedure proper if the multiple baseline behaviors are on the tape or film in the order in which the subject is to see them. Self modeling seems to be more effective the more frequently the subject observes a scene. Therefore, arrange the scenes so the most difficult behavior or the one most important to be changed is self modeled first and, therefore, can be seen for the longest period. The scenes do not have to be long. Ours were seldom as long as one minute for any particular behavior or class of behaviors. Also, we have never used more than one scene for each behavior or class of behaviors. In modeling the absence of an inappropriate behavior, choose an environment in which the inappropriate behavior most frequently occurred. The object here is to choose a situation for the scene in which the absence of the subject's customary inappropriate behavior will be maximally salient and apparent to him. In the case of Joe, for example, not sucking his thumb was shown while he acted that he was watching TV because that was where he was most apt ordinarily to suck his thumb.

In the making of self modeling scenes, do not attempt to get "arty." Unusual camera angles, dramatic lighting, scenes of only parts of the body such as facial closeups or shots of subjects' hands (unless the hands are the sole actors in the behavior) are more likely to be distracting than helpful. There is no evidence that art is at all useful in self modeling, and it greatly complicates the scene making procedure. Our scenes have all been made without any special effects, by a single camera shooting the entire scene from a single camera angle and setting. This can be done by placing the camera on a tripod, focusing and adjusting it, then having the scene played within the area covered by the camera. All that is needed thereafter is to turn the camera (or recorder) on and off. Therefore, only the therapist, subject, and other actors are needed for scene making. Whenever possible, we have made the scenes in the environment in which the subject usually resides. However, we had made no attempt to make scenes of naturally occurring behavior. Our primary reason was that this would have been difficult and time-consuming. Another reason is that the acting of the scene may, as has already been noted, help achieve the desired change in behavior. When peers or others are required for a scene, we have always used those persons who already exist in the subject's environment. We have never used scripts for the self modeling scenes and feel them to be neither necessary nor useful. Instead, the therapist describes to the subject (and other actors, if any) in general terms what should be done in the scene and allows them to act the scene in their own way. Frequent rehearsals and retakes are used to get the maximum possible of verisimilitude.

We have not used self modeling with avoidance behaviors. In general it would appear much easier to use modeling of others or procedures such as systematic desensitization in such cases. However, self modeling can be used in these cases, notwithstanding the unwillingness of the subject to act out the feared behaviors. For such a case, the subject would be filmed while attempting to perform the feared behavior. Every attempt could be recorded, with the unsuccessful (or least successful) ones and expressions of fear or displeasure omitted before the scene is shown to the subject. After this scene has been self modeled several times, it would be possible to make a second set of recordings in which the subject attempted to perform even more of the fearful behavior. The subject's behavior at this time serves as a measure of the success of the first period of self modeling. After suitable editing of the second recordings, the self modeling would be repeated with the new scene. This procedure would be repeated until the desired fearless behavior was achieved. The same procedure can be used to shape up responses which the subject in fact cannot perform. For example, in helping a person conquer a fear of the water while learning to swim, the successive self modeling scenes could show the person in successively more effective swimming scenes. It is conceivable that the self modeling might also help in learning the skill as well as overcoming the fear.

The number of times that a subject watches a self modeling scene appears to be an important variable. If we accept all the behavioral changes in the three cases above as due to self modeling, it would appear safe to conclude that the more frequently a subject watches a self modeling scene, the more change there will be in the behavior. In absolute terms, the maximum amount of behavioral change in these cases was found with Howard who showed an almost perfect cessation of all inappropriate behaviors. Howard watched the self modeling scenes for about a month. In the cases of Chuck and Joe, good changes were achieved with two weeks of self modeling. However, in the second self modeling of appropriate behaviors, watching the appropriate behaviors only three times was not enough to maintain the improvement in two of Joe's behaviors.

It is obviously necessary that the subject does in fact watch the self modeling scenes when they are shown to him. We used assistants to observe our subjects to insure that they have watched the scenes, which we recommend. Since no training is necessary the same persons who serve as observers can act to insure that subjects watch the scenes. Our subjects did get bored with repeatedly watching the scenes, due more to the interruption of the subject's activities almost every day for self modeling than to the procedure itself, which only took a few minutes. Nevertheless, on the basis of the well-known differences between massed and distributed practice, we feel it much better for a subject to watch a scene once on several different days than to see it twice as many times at one sitting. In the case of Chuck, his motivation was maintained by allowing him to set up and operate the video recorder. Other such incentives should be used where possible. It might be worthwhile in cases of extreme reluctance to provide rewards as incentive for watching the self modeling scenes. The fact that new scenes are periodically added in the multiple base rate procedure may help keep up subjects' motivation.

Finally, we add a few words concerning methods which might be attempted to enhance the effectiveness of self modeling. If a behavior does not change at all, one might incorporate vicarious reinforcement in the self modeling scenes. As we have mentioned, there is undoubtedly some reinforcing value to the subject merely in seeing himself behaving appropriately and effectively. This could be enhanced, however, by having the subject receive a positive reinforcer in the scene after successfully completing an appropriate behavior or after inhibiting an inappropriate one. If the behavior still does not change, one could attempt to reinforce the subject at the time he watches the appropriate behavior self modeling scene, making it clear to him that the reinforcement is for the desirable behavior displayed in the scene. One should be careful to observe if the behavior is changing in *any* situation. The problem might be due to lack of generalization rather than lack of behavioral change. In this case, more scenes in the situations to which the behavior has not generalized should be made and used. One should keep in mind that neither self modeling nor any other behavior modification or psychotherapy intervention occurs in a vacuum. As in the case of inappropriate self modeling with Joe, reinforcers and other circumstances in the subject's environment which are not controlled by the therapist may be completely obviating any good achieved by self modeling. One manner in which these circumstances might be brought under control would be to include them in the self modeling. Thus, a parent who reinforces undesirable behavior in a child might be included in the self modeling with the child, and the very scenes that show the child behaving appropriately could also show the parent eliciting appropriate behavior and reinforcing its occurrence. Many other procedures which have not occurred to us, will occur to practitioners and everything reasonable should be tried to achieve the necessary behavioral changes.

REFERENCES

Bandura, A.: *Principles of Behavior Modification.* New York, HR&W, 1969.

Bandura, A. and Walters, R. H.: *Social Learning and Personality.* New York, HR&W, 1963.

Baer, D. M., Wolf, M. M., and Risley, T. R.: Some current dimensions of applied behavior analysis. *Journal of Applied Behavior Analysis, 1*:91-97, 1968.

Creer, T. L.: Management of chronically ill children. *CARIH Research Bulletin,* 2, No. 7, 1972.

Creer, T. L. and Miklich, D. R.: The application of a self-modeling procedure to modify inappropriate behavior: A preliminary report. *Behav Res Ther, 8*:91-92, 1970.

Flanders, J. P.: A review of research on imitative behavior. *Psychol Bull, 69*:316-337, 1968.

Gittelman, M.: Behavior rehearsal as a technique in child treatment. *J Child Psychol Psychiatry, 6*:251-255, 1965.

Jones, M. C.: A laboratory study of fear: The case of Peter. *The Pedagogical Seminary and Journal of Genetic Psychology, 31*:308-315, 1924.

Martin, R. D.: Videotape self-confrontation in human relations training. *Journal of Counseling Psychology, 18*:341-347, 1971.

Miller, N. E., and Dollard, J.: *Social Learning and Imitation.* New Haven. Yale U Pr, 1941.

Miklich, D. R., Creer, T. L., Alexander, A. B., and Nichols, L.: Three case histories in the use of self-modeling as a behavior therapy technique. *CARIH Research Bulletin,* 2, No. 4, 1972.

Patterson, G. R., Cobb, J. A., and Ray, R. S.: A social engineering technology for retraining the families of aggressive boys. In Adams, H. and Unikel, L. (Eds.) *Issues and Trends in Behavior Therapy.* Springfield, Thomas, 1972.

Rachman, S.: Clinical applications of observational learning, imitation and modeling. *Behavior Therapy, 3:*379-397, 1972.

Risley, T. R., and Wolf, M. M.: Strategies for analyzing behavioral change over time. In Nesselroade, J. and Reese, H. (Eds.) : *Life-Span Developmental Psychology: Methodological Issues.* New York, Acad Pr, 1972.

Rosenkrans, M. A.: Imitation in children as a function of perceived similarity to a social model and vicarious reinforcement. *J Pers Social Psychol,* 7:307-315, 1967.

Sarason, I. G.: Verbal learning, modeling, and juvenile delinquency. *American Psychologist, 23:*254-266, 1968.

Skinner, B. F.: The generic nature of the concepts of stimulus and response. *J Gen Psychol, 12:*40-65, 1935.

Thornkike, E. L.: The law of effect. *Am J Psychol, 39:*212-222, 1927.

Webb, E. J., Campbell, D. T., Schwartz, R. D., and Sechrest, L.: *Unobtrusive Measures.* Chicago, Rand, 1966.

Wolpe, J. and Lazarus, A. A.: *Behavior Therapy Techniques.* New York, Pergamon, 1966.

INDEX